wind
from a
distant
summit

This book is dedicated to the memory of Karen McNeill

wind
from a
distant
summit

PAT DEAVOLL

craig potton publishing

Written with the support of the

Mental Health Foundation of New Zealand

NEW ZEALAND
ALPINE CLUB

First published in 2011 by Craig Potton Publishing
98 Vickerman Street, PO Box 555, Nelson, New Zealand
www.craigpotton.co.nz

© Patricia Deavoll

ISBN 978 1 877517 46 4

Printed by Astra Print Ltd, Wellington, New Zealand

Contents

Acknowledgements

First and foremost I want to thank Norman Hardie for getting me into this climbing game and for continuing to be an inspiration.

Many thanks to the Mental Health Foundation of New Zealand (in association with the Ministry of Health's 'Like Minds, Like Mine' programme) for awarding me a NZ Mental Health media grant for the writing of this book. Thanks also to the New Zealand Alpine Club for providing funding through the DOW Hall Publication Fund.

Thanks to author Paul Hersey for kick-starting me into action and to Barry Blanchard for agreeing to write the foreword. Thank you to Graham Slow for his patience, encouragement and endless proofreading and to my cat Spot, for the many hours she has kept vigil at my keyboard.

A special thanks to all the climbing partners I've had over the years, in particular Malcolm Bass, Marty Beare, Brian Deavoll and (posthumously) Karen McNeill.

Aroha-ki-te-tangata

Foreword

'Ah mate, Pat is one of the strongest climbers in the country,' Guy Cotter let two beats pass, locked his eyes onto mine in emphasis, then continued, 'male or female.' His eyebrows arched up, eyes wide with the suggestion of astonishment. I stared back to the colour photo on Pat's résumé – Pat looking over-the-shoulder to the lens, a loaded backpack on her back, an intensity in her locked gaze. It was June of 1999 and I was in Queenstown for my first time. I'd been hired to set up a training and safety programme for the actors in the Hollywood film, *Vertical Limit*. The movie would be shot on the South Island over the next year. Pat was one of a pool of talented Kiwi climbers that Guy had assembled to perform as climbing doubles to the actors. The vast number of difficult high-level rock ascents that Pat had accomplished grabbed my attention, and there were many of them sited across Australia, Asia, Europe and North America. Further she had dedicated a full two years to climbing and exploring the Himalaya and Karakoram in the mid-1980s. I was impressed, and Pat got my vote.

One month later I met the dozen chosen climbing doubles, on location, just outside of Queenstown. Pat was wearing a short-sleeved shirt and the telltale braid of veins in her forearms stated that she had put in many miles pulling hard on the overhanging holds of modern rock climbing.

'Pat Deavoll, I could start an IV on you from here!' I blurted, mimicking a dart throw across the two metres that separated us. So North American. She flushed red, glancing to the good friends stood to either side of her, then chuckled an embarrassed and nervous and dismissive laugh. I felt like a dork. High above, the serrated ridge of the Remarkables cut into the pale winter sky like God's own sawblade. Such was the awkward beginning of a fine friendship.

I got to know Pat on the film. Got to climb on the grey rock of Wanaka with her. I began to appreciate the drive and undaunted passion that fires her climbing; the priority it holds in her life. Pat Deavoll is remarkable.

March 2001, minus twenty-five degrees of Celsius had the streets of my town, Canmore, Alberta, locked solid in frost. The parking lot crunched underfoot as I shuffled into the pub to meet Pat. The Arctic cold so common in my home and native land – Canada – but unheard of on the South Island of New Zealand. Pat was at the tail-end of her second winter trip to the Canadian Rockies in as many years. The list of ice climbs that she had accomplished impressed me every bit as much as her rock-climbing résumé had two years before. In a cumulative six months her tally of ice routes equalled what many local 'hard men' could only achieve in a decade. I was surprised to hear that she'd climbed Polar Circus, one of the longest steep ice routes in the range, by herself, solo. I couldn't recall of any other women doing that. Pat was simply a harder woman, yet she told me the only reason that she had climbed it alone was that her full-time climbing partner had left for home a couple of days earlier and that she still wanted to climb, badly, but couldn't come up with anyone else who she was comfortable sharing the rope with. She was a reluctant soloist. She would call upon this trait several years down the road, in the Karakoram, when her partner decided to throw in the towel on Karim Sar. It was interesting to me, at the time, to consider the difference between Pat's solo of Polar Circus and my own in 1988 when I was a 29-year-old firebrand alpinist looking to push my envelope, fully infatuated with the paramount risks involved in climbing alone. Male and female, action and emotion, initiation and receptiveness, Pat examines the themes of partnership, and female mountain climbers, in chapters two and three, respectively. *Wind from a Distant Summit* is so much more than a climbing narrative.

I ordered another Guinness and Pat got a second glass of red wine. We compared the challenges of our spousal relationships as minute glass shards of ice sifted from the cold, clear air outside the window, one in a thousand glittering with the oblique glint of the winter's blue setting sun. It is not easy to be a passionate climber and maintain a committed relationship, another of the aspects of life that Pat digs into in this book. I hope her bringing it into the light helps some of us.

'Oh, I just can't be bothered with the hauling,' Pat concluded. Coincidence saw us both camped at the 7100 foot airstrip on the Kahiltna Glacier in the heart of the Alaska Range in April 2003. Me and a couple of buddies had our eyes set on a direct line up the South Face of Mt McKinley, or Denali as it's also known, (didn't happen), while Pat was there with Marty Beare, a long-time climbing partner on his way to becoming her new life-partner. They'd just made the first ascent of the North Face of Peak 11,520 in the Ruth Gorge before hopping a flight over to the Kahiltna. The peak and its malevolent weather, had tested them mightily, and they were obviously licking their wounds, yet still keen to climb. Tiers of golden granite and azure ice on the magnificent North Buttress of Mt Hunter towered over us as I related my stories of hauling the pack during our attempt on the Moonflower Buttress two years previously. The Moonflower is one of the most hallowed alpine routes in North America, but my stories convinced Pat that a more recent route to its right, Deprivation, would be a place where she and Marty could climb fast and light. And they did, capping off an incredibly successful trip by anyone's yardstick – a new route climbed in harrowing conditions, and a lightning strike ascent of a modern test-piece. Top drawer! Doubly so when Pat's trip into the Alaska Range from the year before is considered – in 2002 she'd climbed two routes on Mt Huntington, the second being the iconic Colton/Leach, a route that she succeeded on with fellow Kiwi, Karen McNeill. Two women up a major Alaskan route in impeccable style – top class! World class!

Nine months later I was on the South Island again, this time to guide three different groups of clients in the Southern Alps over a two month period. But my time was not all work and one fine night Pat and I sat out on the porch of the house that she shared with Marty and sipped red wine. It had been another fine day on the grey rock of Wanaka and I was happy and said as much. Our talk entered into the realm of mood and how mood could affect climbing. Pat began to parcel out the battles she'd endured with depression. I came to hear more over the next five years. I am so proud of her for including her examination of that black place in this book, which took more than just physical courage.

And it was absolutely amazing to run into Pat on the very summit ridge of Mt Cook not one week later. My client, Paul, and I had climbed the beautiful East Ridge of Mt Cook the day before, bivouacking in a famous crevasse at the top called 'The Middle Peak Hotel'. Pat and her two partners had climbed through the dark and the day making a non-stop push up Mt Cook's greatest face – the massive, glacially stacked Caroline Face.

'Pat! Where in the wide world of sports did you come from?'

'The Caroline. We've just climbed the Caroline.'

'Oh my God! You must be happy.'

'Yes, I'm very happy with it.'

The corners of her bright auburn eyes crinkled into smile lines and a huge heartfelt smile lit up her sun-bronzed face. It was a proud smile. She cramponed past me and I could see the soreness in her one ankle. It compromised her gait. In addition to the challenges of the mind Pat has also had to deal with the physical challenges presented by a now fifty-year-old body that has been used incredibly hard, a body that has also been, on occasion, broken. With a faint limp she continued along the ice-glazed edge of Mt Cook employing her crampons and ice axes with consummate mastery. Behind her the Alps stepped down in rows and humps like massive shark's teeth; further out the broken ice of the Fox Glacier churned into the verdant hills, and then the perfect parallel arcs of the waves breaking against the West Coast. Such a beautiful and powerful land. Pat is a daughter of the South Island of New Zealand. I clicked a mental snapshot of her there, in that landscape, and it has helped me to understand how she has climbed out from under some overwhelming challenges. Her spirit knows one direction, and knows it doggedly – up.

When I mentioned this encounter to my fellow guide, David Langrish, a British ex-pat married to a Kiwi, there was no hesitation, 'Pat Deavoll, she's as hard as nails.' And then he smiled.

Over the last decade I've written a number of letters of support for Pat's expedition grants. This has always been a pleasure and it has been so satisfying to see Pat's Himalayan dreams come to fruition. Climbing in the high mountains of Asia is a risky business on a number of fronts, not all of them to do with the mountain, yet the threats of Himalayan mountains have often been managed by affixing tens of thousands of feet of rope to the mountain to ensure a connection to the ground when conditions and weather get challenging. It is called siege climbing and it borrows more than just the name from its military model. Alpine style is the more traditional approach to mountain climbing. A team of two, three or four climbers start at the bottom of the mountain with 'a rope, a rack, and the pack on their back'. In a continuous effort drawn out over hours, or days, they get to the top, or not, and descend. Alpine style is rich and has always been the true test of the mountaineer, exceedingly so on steep and technical peaks. Only the very best succeed. Since 2004 Pat has mounted one, and occasionally two, alpine style expeditions a year to the high mountains of Asia:

2004 attempts on Cholatse, in Nepal; and Janahut, in India.
2005 the first ascent of Xiashe in Tibet.
2006 the first ascent of Haizi Shan in China.
2007 an attempt on Beka Brakai Chhok, and the first of ascent of Wahine, both in Pakistan; and the first ascent of Miandi Peak, in India.
2008 a second attempt on Beka Brakai Chhok in Pakistan.
2009 the first ascent of Karim Sar in Pakistan, climbed solo.
2010 an attempt on the West Face of Vasuki Parbat in India.

The mountains that Pat chooses are inevitably steep and compelling, with the exception of Vasuki Parbat which is as broad, blunt and challenging as a battle hammer. Climbing these mountains in alpine style is a complex and high risk game. It takes thousands of days of experience, and the skills developed therein, just to be able to play. Half the time you make the top, the other half you succeed in surviving. It is a theatre of the real. Pat is performing here with the very best, and she is performing well, uniquely so for a woman. It all comes across. Enjoy this fine book.

Barry Blanchard
Canmore, Canada
May 28, 2011

Introduction

Sunlight tinged with the shadows of the oncoming autumn lingers on the hills above Christchurch. A brisk nor'easterly whisks in from the sea, driving before it small clouds that skip gleefully overhead and across the city. The pine trees at the top of the hill bow and creak. The wind tames the waves at the coast, stretching them evenly and far out to sea. Out to the west, the Southern Alps show off their first inconsequential coating of snow; a further indication of the changing season. They sparkle, as do the waves, as does the air.

It's February 2010, and I'm climbing with friends above the city. It could be any February day of the past twenty years – a bunch of my friends carrying packs and ropes, chatting loudly as they traverse the hillside. Someone has brought their dog and it trots in the lead. The air temperature is pleasant, as the heat of midsummer has passed, but it's left the hills brown and the grass brittle. In the park below, people in white play cricket and their calls carry on the wind. Very different sports, I think, as I put on my harness and squeeze into my rockclimbing shoes.

A few metres away Eric also prepares to climb, and Tony stands beside him sorting the rope. All three of us, plus my belayer, Nick, chat animatedly about something; we've been climbing together for many years now. Eric and I begin to scamper up the overhanging rock wall; the conversation continues, and we just talk louder, turning occasionally to look down to make a particular point. Fifty metres away, Dave is drinking from a thermos of coffee and I can smell it. Nice. Eric and I reach the top together, and as we can't hear the others above the wind, continue our own conversation as we thread our ropes through the steel ring anchors. 'Take me,' I shout to Nick.

'Got ya,' he replies, in mid-sentence.

I lean back, expecting Nick to take my weight on the rope. This is something I've done a thousand times – we've all done it a thousand times – and it requires little thought. I move quickly down the first couple of metres, but there's no alarm; there must be a bit of slack rope in the system, I assume. But then I start to fall … fast. Why is this happening, I think, and alarm bells ring. I make a reflexive grab at the rope, but by now I'm plummeting, far too quickly, free-falling. My head, and then my hip, hit the ground. *Thump-thump.* All is quiet …

It's dark, but I'm aware of two things. First, a deep, cloying pain in my back, and second, voices in the distance saying, 'Fuck, fuck, fuck'. Then, closer, a 'Lie still.' I recognise Eric's voice and open my eyes.

Six inches from my face my hand is in tatters – flaps of skin dangle from the fingers and the palm – and I wince in horror. 'Please put something on that, it looks awful,' I manage to say. Tony wraps his T-shirt around my hand. Then the background conversation becomes clearer and I make out the word 'helicopter'. It dawns on me that they're calling the Westpac Rescue Helicopter.

Oh no, oh no. *I don't want the helicopter.* Get up; stand up, make them stop. I stagger to my feet – multiple arms reach out to help. The pain in my back has me gasping and tears well in my eyes. 'You forgot to tie into the rope,' I hear Tony say. I forgot to tie into the rope? Thirty-five years a climber and *I forgot to tie into the rope*? I've made a mistake *that basic*? I couldn't have! But I have.

Later in the afternoon I lie in the accident and emergency department with an orthopaedic collar around my neck. The pain is bad despite the morphine drip in my arm, and I've just started to think I've been forgotten when a doctor walks up flapping an X-ray in his hand. 'You've broken your back,' he says, as if I've caught a cold. 'See here?' (I recognise a spine) 'These vertebrae should be square, not triangular. You've compressed your L2 and L3. I'm going to admit you to Ward 19.'

I stare at him disbelieving. 'You're going to put me in hospital? For how long? Surely it can't be that bad?'

'Yes, we need to ascertain there's no spinal cord damage,' he says, sauntering off towards another hapless patient.

Tears fill my eyes again; I can't help them overflowing, and soon I'm sobbing. What about my plans for the year? There's so much at stake here; my new job with the Alpine Club, my new boyfriend, my plans to climb Vasuki Parbat in India in the spring. The mountaineering expedition will be my tenth overseas in as many years and I've come to see the planning, the fundraising, the travel and, ultimately, the climb as part of my identity. I can't imagine not having an expedition to look forward to. I have to go to India – I can't let a broken back stop me!

I think back to my last stay in hospital, eighteen months before, when I resorted to an artificial knee replacement in order to keep climbing. For years I'd suffered knee pain but never bothered to consult a doctor, thinking it was just something that happens to middle-aged climbers. But on an expedition to Pakistan in 2007 the pain had become so bad that I couldn't function without multiple doses of strong painkillers, and I arrived home barely able to walk. I agreed to an MRI scan of both knees and my GP reported the findings a week later. 'You have advanced osteoarthritis in both,' he said. 'No cartilage, no meniscus, bone resting on bone.' I remember being flabbergasted. How had my knees reached such a state? What had I done? 'Climbed mountains for decades,' my GP said with a shrug. 'You've been doing it hard. You need to visit a surgeon – see if anything can be done.'

So I went in search of a remedy. The first surgeon I spoke to was in his early sixties and displayed all the trappings associated with a long career in orthopaedics. I took an instant dislike to his pinstripe suit, starched white shirt and ostentatious brogues. Mum was with me for moral support.

'What you need is a bilateral [read double] knee replacement,' the surgeon said pompously. 'And then you can forget climbing – take up swimming. I swim every morning and I find it's a great way to be in the outdoors.'

Back outside, Mum and I were equally despondent. Did I really have to take up swimming? I hadn't swum since high school – could I even remember how to swim? No. I would continue climbing, no matter what it took. I knew the risks if I didn't – I'd lose the most important thing in my life. First and foremost I was a climber. I decided to look for another surgeon – maybe there was one out there who could better meet my requirements.

The first time I visited James Burn was at his holiday home in Wanaka. He was a small man in his fifties who fizzed with a vitality that belied his age. 'I think what we'll do is a hemi Oxford partial knee replacement on your right and give the left a good clean-up, see how it goes,' he enthused, bouncing backward and forward, heel to toe. 'I've had some very good results with the hemi Oxford. We'll have you back climbing in no time. When can we book you in?'

I was speechless. Did I hear 'back climbing in no time'? 'I need it as soon as possible,' I said. 'I'm off to climb in Pakistan next June.'

James looked a little taken aback at that, but rallied. 'OK the earliest would be end of October. I can't promise anything, but if you work really hard you should be ready to climb by June. And by the way, I'm sure you'll be the first person to climb a Karakoram peak with a titanium knee joint,' he said, flashing me a grin.

Six weeks later I woke in the recovery room of the hospital. I sat up and looked at my right knee. There was nothing to see – it was covered in a swathe of crêpe. Hurray, I'm on my way to Pakistan, I thought, but three days later I was less optimistic. The pain was crippling, and what made it worse was the sight of half a dozen seventy-year-olds with brand-new knee replacements like mine walking briskly up and down the corridor.

'Don't worry,' James said, 'your nerve endings are still healthy, that's why you're feeling the pain and they're not.'

A few days later I was out of hospital; after a week I'd ditched the crutches; two weeks after that I was back at the gym. 'Pakistan, Pakistan, Pakistan' was my mantra as I tried to do a leg press. 'Pakistan, Pakistan, Pakistan' pounded through my head as, grimacing, I sat on the floor forcing my knee to straighten. 'Pakistan, Pakistan, Pakistan,' I sang to the cadence of the exercise bike as I pedalled along, lopsided.

At eight weeks I went back to James for a check-up, feeling quite nervous. He flexed my knee this way and that, knocked and prodded, then sat back quietly. 'Congratulations, you are doing fine,' he said. 'I have no doubt you're going to get to Pakistan.'

Leaving the room, I remember feeling so happy. I'd beaten the odds; I could still climb. Five months later, I flew out for Pakistan.

But a broken back! Isn't this a more serious imposition, especially with the expedition only six months away? I leave hospital after a few days with instructions to take six weeks off work. I am also in a back brace. 'Don't take it off till we tell you to,' says someone. 'Come back in eight weeks.'

Eight weeks in a brace? The prospect of eight weeks of not knowing seems interminable. How will I manage? How will I stay focused on the positive?

For the first week I just sleep. Friends visit, bringing little gifts and voicing commiseration. I do my best to appear bright and make jokes of the accident, but inside I'm in turmoil over the thought of having to give up my trip to India. I just can't, I think.

Eight weeks later I'm given the option of going without the brace 'for part of the day'. I take this as permission to start back at the gym, but am appalled at how weak I've become. A sit-up is impossible and I can lift only the tiniest dumb-bell. I visit a recommended physiotherapist, who suggests Pilates, but one session is enough to prove I haven't the patience for such gentle measures. I go back to weight training, but progress is slow.

June 2010 arrives. The departure for India is just eight weeks away. I am morose and anxious, very unsure of how I'll perform – even so, it never occurs to me to pull out of the trip. 'I'm going to be fine,' I say to the other expedition members, my friends in the UK. 'I'm improving fast.' But I'm not so sure; I haven't regained my strength and my back throbs with a constant, deep ache. I tell no one, try to act normally and hope my accident will be forgotten, that I'll forget it. Come September, I leave for India with a huge question mark hovering over my ability to climb.

But I do climb. Not as well as I hope, but I come home secure in the knowledge I've done the best I could under the circumstances. More importantly, the trip reaffirms for me that, after thirty-five years of climbing, the mountains have lost none of their challenge, none of their allure. They enthralled me back at the start, and nothing has changed.

So what is it that motivates a climber? Where does the desire to climb mountains come from? After all, mountaineering is about hard physical work and serious deprivation, and the rewards are intangible and specious at best. Are climbers oddballs? Are they egotists, adrenalin junkies and dreamers? Are they searching for something more than everyday life can offer?

In this book I try to answer these questions through my own story. I was a shy, overweight teenager with a depressive disorder who became a climber and discovered in the mountains a panacea to sustain me into middle age. This is the story of a lifelong passion for the mountains and climbing that's endured the test of time and loss. It's also a book about travel and exploration, and an attempt to explain to the layman what it is that makes a mountaineer tick. I'd like to think of it as a climbing book for both climbers and non-climbers alike.

CHAPTER ONE
Learning the Ropes

Climbing may be hard, but it's easier than growing up – Ed Sklar

When I was fifteen I met the man who set me on the path I'd follow for the next thirty-five years. His name is Norman Hardie and he is one of the greatest mountaineers New Zealand has ever known. Norman is in his eighties now, but in 1955, just two years after Edmund Hillary climbed Everest, he was part of the first ascent of Kanchenjunga (8586m), the third highest mountain in the world. He paid his way through university by culling deer, and made many early first ascents of mountains in the Southern Alps. He was also the leader of New Zealand's Scott Base in Antarctica. His autobiography, *On My Own Two Feet*, was published in 2006. Norman introduced me to the mountains.

Our sheep farm in coastal North Canterbury has been in the family since 1905. My father was born there and took over the farm from his mother in the early 1950s. His father was killed in a tractor accident in 1929, leaving my grandmother to run the farm and raise four children through the Depression years. She had one child crippled with polio and was on the verge of losing the farm to the bank numerous times, but clung on through determination and a desire to provide for her family. She was a remarkable woman. Dad, now eighty-seven, belongs to that rare breed of farmers who have maintained a lifetime passion for the land irrespective of drought or interest rates or the plummeting price of wool. My brother is the farmer now – as the only son he got the farm, while my two sisters and I got a private education. As kids we all worked hard on the farm during our school holidays, driving the tractor, stacking hay bales, crutching lambs and feeding out to stock. We were never paid, but we loved the work and it instilled in all of us an invaluable physical toughness.

I'm not sure where my desire to climb mountains came from. Granted, we were an outdoorsy family, but tramping the Heaphy Track was as intrepid as we got in the mountains. Our adventures were more from the farm – scrambling around the hills and sea cliffs, galloping along the beach on our horses, and mustering in the early morning with Dad. But I knew from the age of twelve that I was going to be mountaineer. Maybe it was the winter view of the snow-capped Puketeraki Range from the top of the farm that inspired this, or maybe it was our infrequent family visits to Mt Cook and the West Coast, touring the South Island in our turquoise Holden station wagon, Dad at the wheel. I remember looking up at the steep, scrubby hills around Lake Sumner and asking him, 'How do I get to the top?'

'Follow a ridge,' he said.

Then again, my desire to climb might have come from something I saw on our black and white TV, bought in 1969 expressly for the family to watch Neil Armstrong take those first bounding steps on the moon. Or could it have come from a book I'd read? I was a big reader. As a ten-year-old my favourite was *With Dersu the Hunter*, the real-life turn-of-the-century adventures of Russian military captain Vladimir Arsenyev and his local guide Dersu in the Siberian taiga. I reordered the book again and again from the country library service, much to the bewilderment of my teacher. He wondered why such a book would interest me. 'Where's the taiga?' I'd ask him.

He had to look in the encyclopaedia. 'What's it like there? Who lives there?' Again, he would turn to the encyclopaedia …

As there were no secondary schools in our area, we were sent to boarding school at age twelve. Around the end of my second year in the hostel I became aware that the school had a tramping club. This was available to girls in their final two years and was based around the school's lodge close to Arthur's Pass. I began to watch, and then envy, the older boarders as they packed and set off for weekends at the lodge, dressed in long johns and chequered bush shirts. They'd leave for the railway station on a Friday evening, an excited rabble lugging canvas packs full of scroggin and oilskin parkas, and return late on Sunday night, exhausted, dirty and sunburnt. Rumours filtered down of river crossings, shingle screes and campfires, and I hung on these stories. I couldn't wait! My sixth-form year finally arrived and I joined the club.

One Sunday in late February 1975, I woke in a tent outside the school lodge, a modest affair with two small bunk rooms and a kitchen with a wood stove. I was on my tramping club introductory weekend. The day before, we'd learnt how to make river crossing; it had been fabulous, and what's more, I was good at it, strong enough to take the upstream end of the long willow pole hitching me and my mates together as we waded into the current of the braided Waimakariri River. Today, we were due to tramp with mountaineer Norman Hardie, who had taken an interest in the tramping club. At 8 a.m., after breakfast, he arrived as promised, a dark, wiry man with large spectacles. Norman told us we would be making an ascent of Mt Binser. 'It's that mountain over there with three peaks,' he said, pointing east.

I was astounded. To begin with, the base of Mt Binser was at least 8km away across a big grassy flat. Then there was the mountain itself. It was huge, and steep, with a dark green carpet covering its lower flanks and a grey-brown expanse above. How we were going to get to the top was beyond my comprehension. But I was ready, my water bottle filled and my lunch and parka packed in my little canvas rucksack, long before anyone else. I sat on the step of the lodge, fidgeting with anticipation, willing the other girls to hurry up.

A noisy bunch of thirty of us headed off across the flats to Andrews Stream, with Norman (or Mr Hardie, as we were instructed to call him) spearheading the assault, his loping stride and relaxed manner speaking of someone at ease in hills. He had on gaiters – making him stand out from the rest of us – and a large H-frame pack full of … what? Some of the girls chatted comfortably with him, but I hung just off his left shoulder, too shy to approach but needing to be up with the action.

After an hour we reached the start of the track to Binser Saddle. By now the group was well spread out, and the slower girls were starting to complain. I hopped from one foot to the other with irritation as we waited for them to catch up. 'We're heading up into the bush,' Norman announced. 'I want us to keep together. We're going to travel at a pace that suits the slowest person. Who wants to go first?' He turned and smiled at me. 'What about you, Pat?' I turned bright red and nodded mutely. 'Don't forget, slow and steady now, you're in charge,' he said.

Acutely self-conscious, I started up the track. In charge! What does he mean 'in charge'? I turned and looked at the line of heads behind me.

'Don't go too fast,' said Sally.

'Those fat ones at the back will never keep up,' said Penny.

Five minutes later, plaintive cries of 'Stop! We need a rest!' echoed through the beech forest.

'You need to pace the group better,' Norman said and, mortified, I nodded in agreement.

After some time, Norman called a halt. 'OK girls, this is where we leave the track and head for the ridge,' he commanded, and led off uphill between the beech trees. The trunks were sooty black and the ground underfoot dry and crunchy with twigs and brown leaves. How does he know where to go, I wondered? There are only trees, how can he see? I quickly manoeuvred myself into a position directly behind Norman, hoping to pluck up the courage to ask him his navigational secret.

Suddenly, we broke out above the tree-line. We were standing among large silvery-orange tussocks, which above us were interspersed with long streaks of greying rock. I looked behind and down with delight – there was the lodge, far below, its iron roof blinking in the sun. Over to the east, the homestead buildings of Grassmere and Coralyn stations stood out like small brown buttons, while to the south, the silver Waimakariri River meandered away and mountains topped with snow scribbled across the horizon. Unable to contain myself, I turned and grinned at Norman. He grinned back. Then the others began to arrive.

After what seemed like for ever, the last of the group reached the tree-line. Norman split us in two, some to go on to the summit, the rest to turn back for the lodge. Good, we can get rid of the slow ones, I thought uncharitably, and as Norman headed for the ridge line I skipped, bounced and sprang along in his wake. Hitting the ridge an hour later, he pointed up and said, 'Look, there's the summit. Why don't you go on ahead while I wait for the others?'

'Really! I can go on?' I hesitated, wary.

'Go on,' he said, waving his arm.

I turned towards the top. Wow! Was I actually going to climb this mountain? I began to move, hesitantly at first, then my feet took flight. I flew upward to the stony summit, arriving alone. A slight wind tousled my hair, tugged at my homespun jersey and shifted the tussocks. Blue-green mountains, shimmering in the midday heat, rolled away as far as the eye could see to the mysterious main divide, the Southern Alps. As I watched Sally and Penny and Norman working their way towards me, I knew something profound had happened. I was soaring, far above the summit of Mt Binser, up among the clouds. It was the happiest day of my life.

In midsummer 1976, I was sitting at the green wooden door of the Alpine Guides office at Mount Cook village. A steady stream of long-haired, bearded men in red monogrammed jerseys went in and out of the door, ignoring me. They had knotted bandanas around their foreheads and wore dark reflective glasses. Their faces were tanned, they strode around the place confidently, and they talked loudly and familiarly to each other. By comparison, I was alone and quite scared, and couldn't think of a word to say to any of them. I was there as part of an eight-day introductory mountaineering course that was costing me $230.

My first year with my school tramping club had ended on a high – I was voted club captain for the following year. That season I planned trips the club had never tackled – long ridge traverses linking passes and cols – and put my ideas to Norman. He always backed me. Saying goodbye to him at our end-of-year club lunch, I'd asked, 'What should I do now?'

'Be a mountaineer, of course,' he'd said. 'Go to Mt Cook.'

On the second day at Mount Cook, a motley selection of would-be mountaineers met in the dining room at Unwin Hut, the New Zealand Alpine Club base. It soon became apparent that I was the only female on the course, and the youngest of the ten participants by a few years. Our two guides, Geoff and Shaun, both in the red company jerseys, introduced themselves. Shaun was a jovial Englishman, who'd not been long out from Britain, and Geoff was a giant of an Australian. I recognised both men from the office the day before.

'Let's do a round and introduce ourselves,' Geoff said. 'I'm Geoff and I work as a mountain guide in the summer and a possum trapper on the West Coast in the winter.' A hardcore mountain man, I thought. The introductions went smoothly: Derek, an engineer on the Mackenzie hydro scheme; John, a traveller from England; Brett, a farmer from Geraldine; another farmer from Canterbury; a builder from Invercargill; a businessman from Auckland ... and so on, until it was my turn.

'I've just left school. I was in the tramping club,' I said with effort.

After an exotic outfitting of ice axes and crampons, karabiners and slings, we loaded up our packs and began the walk to the Alpine Guides tepee, erected as a base for the 'intro' courses in the Twin Stream area. That night we all slept in a circle in the tepee on a bed of tussock grass, but while the men chatted convivially amongst themselves I couldn't say a word. Why am I such a klutz, I badgered myself, feeling very young and socially out of my depth.

Despite my worries, the eight days passed in a blur of satisfaction and I loved every minute. We climbed the peaks around the head of the valley and the slabs on a huge west-facing rock buttress. We spent two nights sleeping in igloos built from blocks of snow on the top of the range, with wonderful views of Mt Cook and Mt Sefton. My social skills grew with my confidence, as I discovered that I could easily keep up with the men and had a better head than most on the steep ground. I developed an enormous crush on Geoff, the towering Australian guide, and blushed whenever he talked to me.

At the end of the course I found myself back in Mount Cook village, glum and at a loose end. What should I do now? All I wanted to do was climb mountains. Then Geoff announced, 'I'm taking another group up to the head of the Tasman Glacier. Why don't you sign up?' I was the first one ready the next morning when he arrived at Unwin to pick up his next lot of charges.

John from England and Derek from Twizel were also on this expedition, which was to be a more serious proposition than our Twin Stream week. Laden down with eight days of food, we took the rattle-trap bus up the gravel road that snakes along the southern edge of the Tasman Glacier, past flowering Mt Cook buttercups and blue ducks that fled away whistling as we rumbled past. Piling out at the sad remains of the old Ball Hut, which had once housed a hundred climbers at a time, we were given a stern lecture by Geoff on how not to dislodge rocks on each other as we descended the moraine wall. We nodded in serious acknowledgement, unsure of what a moraine wall was. Again, I was the youngest and the only female.

The wall, which turned out to be a reckless stack of glacial sand and boulders leading down to the bed of the glacier, was successfully negotiated, and we started the long trudge to Malte Brun Hut. It was hot, and it wasn't long before we were wondering why we'd brought so many clothes, why we'd gulped the last of our water, and when Geoff (a speck in the distance) was going to let us stop for lunch. We arrived at Malte Brun Hut in the evening, tired and sunburnt, but pleased with ourselves.

'Tomorrow we are going to climb Mt Rum Doodle,' Geoff said, and gestured at a small mountain, up and behind him. 'Make sure you are ready to go by 4 a.m.' That was as much instruction as we got. He was lengthening the leash, forcing his charges to take responsibility as mountaineers.

We didn't let him down – at four o'clock all eight of us were standing in the dark outside the hut, blinking and yawning, and wondering what we'd forgotten to put in out packs. Two hours later we were negotiating the steep upper slopes of the Malte Brun Glacier. 'No point roping up,' Geoff said, 'you'll just kill yourselves.' He went on to tell us of a previous client who'd slid over an icefall to his death just 100m from where we stood. We continued up the hard, rock-strewn slope, furiously concentrating on where we put our cramponed feet.

Some time later, we arrived at a little col marking the top of both the Malte Brun and Darwin glaciers. It was a beautiful hot day. To our right towered the rocky West Ridge of Malte Brun, and in front of us the Nor'West Rib and a snow couloir. Geoff told us another alarming story, of a climber who'd fallen the length of the couloir, driven his ice axe through his thigh, and managed to walk out to the Tasman Glacier for a ski-plane pick-up with the ice axe still embedded in his leg. We listened with open mouths.

From here we were to rope up and traverse the snow and rock ridge line to the summit of Rum Doodle. I roped up with Derek, and we set off in front, securing each other with ice-axe belays, while the other pairs followed in our wake. Before long we came to a steep rise, an almost vertical piece of soggy snow forming the back wall of a large crevasse. It was Derek's turn to lead – he looked up and frowned, then turned to the pair behind and said to John, 'Hey man, I'm not so happy with this – do you want to lead it?'

I was dumbstruck! Hang on – what about me? As John made a move to pass me, I looked beseechingly at Derek. 'Oh! Sorry, do you want to try it, Pat?' Geoff, in the meantime, was standing back looking amused.

'Yes please,' I said.

Derek buried his snow stake and put me on belay, as I stepped gingerly across the crevasse and buried my ice axe to the hilt in the soft snow. I kicked my feet in to the wall … and immediately dropped into the crevasse with a loud squawk. Just my head was above the surface. Derek looked horrified, but Geoff burst out laughing and said, 'Try again.'

This time I managed to get myself better established and started punching upward. Ice axe, arm, foot, foot, ice axe, arm, foot, foot. Several times the snow fell away from under my feet and I was left hanging on my arms. After 10m I looked down, and felt very scared. My left leg jerked up and down involuntarily. 'Keep going, you're doing fine,' yelled Geoff as the others stared intently up at me.

OK, don't fall, don't fall, I told myself. Ice axe, arm, foot, foot, ice axe, arm, foot, foot … suddenly, I popped out above the ridge and peered over, looking left and then right. 'Hey, I'm on the top!' A round of cheering and applause rose from below. I turned and looked down with a big grin. This was so much fun. Maybe I was good at it?

At the end of our ten-day Tasman expedition we were sun-blistered, beaten and hungry, but well on our way to becoming semi-competent mountaineers. We'd moved on to Tasman Saddle Hut and climbed Hochstetter Dome and Almer, before crossing Tasman Saddle on the way to Murchison Hut. We'd climbed another small peak and then returned to the Tasman to attempt the pièce de résistance, the mighty Elie de Beaumont. 'I think you are ready,' Geoff announced. 'You are fit, efficient with your anchors and seem able to judge the terrain.' It was a long day for us, but Elie went without a hitch.

Back in the village afterwards, I was at a loss again. I hadn't wanted the Tasman trip to end, and made tentative approaches to Derek and John for a climbing partner. But both were heading away for Christmas. 'Hey Pat, I signed up for another trip in early Jan,' said John, 'to the West Coast. Come along.' I ran to the company office. Yes there was a space for me, I was told, but it will cost $250. By now I'd run out of money. I'd have to go home and do some work on the farm, but all I could think about as I hitchhiked across the Mackenzie Country was the next trip.

When I met up with Geoff and John in the New Year of 1977, I was starting to feel like a mountaineer. My parents had given me money for an ice axe and crampons, and I'd invested in a new frameless pack and a pair of leather mountaineering boots to replace my tramping club John Bulls. I had the requisite tanned face and hands, a funky pair of polarised sunglasses with thick white frames, and had tie-dyed a pair of my grandfather's woollen long johns pink. I even had a spotty red bandana around my forehead.

Our group arrived at De La Beche Corner at the end of the first day's walk to find that the old hut had been pulled down, and Alpine Club members were putting the finishing touches on a new hut. 'Sorry, you can't stay here, we've just polyurethaned the floor,' said a stocky man in a bush shirt. Instead, we spent the night under a big rock. We were away by four o'clock the next morning for Graham Saddle, scrambling down the moraine wall by the light of our head torches and trudging up the rubbly Rudolf Glacier as the sky turned pale silver in the east. I felt happy and at ease roping up to John as the sun rose, but it was a tired crew that stumbled into Almer Hut that night, after a long, hot crossing of the main divide. The descent down the Franz Josef névé in the heat of the afternoon did us in as we sank above our knees in the wet snow and vied with each other not to go first. But as I sat on the step of the hut with a cup of tea, gazing down the tumbling icefall and out over the green Waiho plain to the Tasman Sea, I realised how content I was. Behind me, the kerosene cooker hummed on the bench and the smell of cooking mince permeated the air, while the others sprawled on their bunks kidding with Geoff. The sky was clear, promising fine days to come.

By the time we made it to Pioneer Hut two days later, the team had slowed to a crawl. We'd summitted Mildred and Drummond peaks above the Davis snowfield, and then crossed the seemingly interminable West Ho Pass to reach Pioneer Hut, perched on a sharp rib above the Fox névé. The hut was crowded with seasoned climbers, sprawling on their bunks with an ease born of experience, talking the talk. The hut smelt of kerosene and sunscreen, and there were ropes and ice axes piled in every corner. As novices, we were assigned one bunk between the three of us, into which we collapsed, exhausted puddles of fatigue. 'You'd better hope the weather's bad tomorrow,' threatened Geoff, 'otherwise it's a 3 a.m. start for Lendenfeld.' We groaned as one.

At 2 a.m. I woke reluctantly from my sleep. My whole body ached and I did NOT want to get out of my sleeping bag. I listened hopefully for the sound of rain on the corrugated roof of the hut. Nothing. Wind even? Nothing. I sank glumly back into a doze, willing no one else to move. But what was that? Plink, plink, plink on the roof! Plink! Plink! The plinks got faster and faster until they merged into a muted roar.

'No point getting up just yet,' said Geoff's muffled voice.

'Oh, thank Christ,' said John from the other end of the bunk. I snuggled down into my sleeping bag and drifted back to sleep smiling.

It was just as well we'd been afforded a rest, because the following day was one I've never forgotten. Geoff had us away from Pioneer at 2 a.m., intent on climbing both Mt Haast and Mt Lendenfeld from Marcel Col before dropping over Pioneer Pass to the Grand Plateau. 'Big day ahead,' he said, 'but I'm sure you guys can do it.'

The snow slopes of Lendenfeld went smoothly, and the whole team was back at the col by 11 a.m. 'Now here's a challenge for you,' Geoff said, waving his ice axe at what looked to be a knife-edge ridge leading to the summit of Mt Haast.

John and I set off slowly – we were rather scared, truth be known. There was a big drop down the South Face on our left and an even bigger drop down the North Face to the glacier on our right. But after two hours of tentative pitching we reached the high peak of Mt Haast, and turned for the retreat. The others, of course, were heading towards us. 'Be careful passing,' yelled Geoff. 'No pushing and shoving. Ha! Ha!'

By the time we'd regrouped back on Marcel Col it was after 5 p.m., and we were all so thrilled at having negotiated the ridge without mishap that at first we didn't notice Geoff's look of concern. 'This has taken longer than I thought,' he said. 'We still have to make it over Pioneer Pass and down to Plateau Hut. I think we'll go down there instead.'

'Go down where?' someone asked. Geoff pointed directly down the eastern wall of Lendenfeld to the Grand Plateau. Our eyes widened. Thousands upon thousands of vertical feet lay between us and the floor of the plateau. What was he thinking? But Geoff had us bury our snow stakes in the ground and link them into one large anchor. Then we knotted our ropes together, attached one end to the anchor … and launched ourselves over the edge.

'Don't screw this up,' Geoff said, 'or you will die.'

It took most of the night to abseil down to the plateau. We built anchors with our packs, our ice axes, our helmets – anything that would act as a sufficient drag in the snow. At 3 a.m., as we neared the bottom, we regrouped on a ledge; everyone was exhausted and cold, and I felt close to tears with fatigue. Geoff got out a cooker and, standing there in the dark, we had a cup of tea and a biscuit. 'You guys are just the BEST,' he said. John put his arm round my shoulder and gave me a squeeze, and I felt a bond; we were all in this adventure together. We began to chat and laugh again, standing on that ledge, as away in the east the sky began to lighten.

To my delight, Derek asked me if I would do some climbing with him. We'd finished the course on a high, scrambling up the Anzac Peaks on the way out to Mount Cook village – not before time, as we'd eaten all our food. 'See you round over the summer,' Geoff had said to me after I told him I'd scored a job as a housemaid at the Hermitage. Of course I blushed, but I was beginning to feel part of the Mt Cook scene.

After much deliberation, Derek and I decided on the West Ridge of Malte Brun for our first guideless objective; after all, we'd had a good look at it from Rum Doodle. It was a rock route and we didn't know much – anything, in fact – about rock climbing, but we'd learn as we went, we brazenly decided.

Malte Brun Hut felt welcoming and familiar when we walked in the door late on a Friday evening. There was the same lovely view up and down the glacier, the same smell of candles and kerosene, and the same sooty black ceiling. But even in the few weeks since our last visit, the moraine wall had subsided, eroding the terrace on which the hut sat. What we didn't realise was that within the year Malte Brun Hut would become unsafe for visitors and the Mount Cook National Park Board would dismantle it.

We were away by 3 a.m., both of us a mess of nervous jitters. 'No Geoff,' Derek moaned as he hunted in the dark for his sunglasses, his water bottle, his harness. We stomped up the now familiar and nowhere near so daunting Malte Brun Glacier by the light of our head torches to a point where we could access the West Ridge via a series of interlinking slabs. We changed footwear for the rock. Derek had borrowed a pair of high-tech rockclimbing boots off a friend; I'd decided on my Bata Bullets.

'Up we go,' Derek said, 'slow and steady and safe.' I scampered off up the slab. 'What about the rope?' he said.

'I think we're fine without,' I replied.

'OK,' Derek muttered dubiously.

We hit the ridge line just as the sun poked above the eastern foothills, indicating a peerless day to come. 'Now, we need to build a rock anchor,' Derek announced rather pompously, 'and start pitching.'

'Don't you think we'll be OK without the rope for a while longer?' I peered ahead at the terrain. 'It doesn't look so bad.'

Derek frowned and said nothing. Starting up the ridge line, we climbed first one side, then the other, but as the sun rose, so did our confidence, and soon we were well above the summit of Rum Doodle. 'We must be coming close to the Cheval Ridge,' Derek shouted up to me. We knew this infamous feature would be the crux point of the climb. 'I think we should put the rope ON!'

There it was – a rope length of knife-edge rock with a precipitous drop of hundreds of feet on either side. We studiously draped several slings over spikes of rock for an anchor, ripped them off, rearranged them, and then rearranged them again. 'That'll have to do,' muttered Derek. 'Got me on belay?' He straddled the ridge and started shuffling across on his bum. Out in the middle he slowed down and started to wobble, then sped up again until he reached the other side.

I started to follow using the same technique. Ouch, how uncomfortable, I thought, and I'm wearing a hole in my new overtrousers. I swung both legs to the same side and monkeyed along on my arms.

'You looked like you were going to fall off,' Derek scolded. 'You'd have done a huge pendulum.' I felt suitably contrite.

We moved off again, changing back into our mountain boots when we hit the snow on the final stretch of the ridge. 'Wow,' said Derek as we sunned ourselves on the summit. 'Would you have believed six weeks ago we'd be climbing a 10,000ft peak on our own?'

'Not in a million years,' I replied. I thought back to the first few days of the intro course in December. So many wonderful things had happened since then.

It took Derek and me almost twice as long to descend Malte Brun as it had to climb it. We reversed the Cheval Ridge without problem, but things went awry when we missed the spot for abseiling off the West Ridge, climbing past it into frighteningly steep terrain. Derek eventually made the call to retrace our steps. 'We're just going to get ourselves into more trouble if we go on.'

So it was well past dark by the time we arrived at the place we thought the hut should be. Dog-tired, we criss-crossed the tussock shelf above the glacier, but the hut eluded us. To make things worse, an impenetrable mist had risen up off the glacier, reducing visibility to nil. Close to midnight, Derek made a call. 'An enforced bivouac is all part of the learning process of becoming an alpinist,' he said as he lay on the ground. I lay down, too, and we tried to get some sleep.

Sometime in the early hours I woke to find the moon shining through the fog. I was very cold, but sat up and peered around. Through the thinning haze a large shape loomed, not 20m away. 'Derek,' I croaked, shaking his shoulder.

Derek shot bolt upright with fright. 'Hey! It's the back of the hut,' he announced, incredulously. We rushed inside with shouts of glee, dived into our sleeping bags and were asleep in seconds.

Derek and I continued to climb together on weekends through the remains of the summer. Nun's Veil, Footstool, Edgar Thompson, Aiguille Rouge, Mt Burns, Mt Sealy ... the peaks tumbled in succession before our run of good luck and good weather. We became all too used to success and I longed to tell Norman Hardie, but at the same time I didn't want to boast to someone to whom our triumphs might seem paltry.

One afternoon in late February, just as I was finishing my daily housemaid shift at the hotel, Derek rang. 'I reckon we should go for Cook,' he said, 'the weekend after next. Can you get the time off? I think we are up for it. Don't you?'

I could hardly believe it – I was going to climb Mt Cook! This was something I'd longed for, but barely dared contemplate. The next week passed in a heady rush of heightened anticipation and nerves, during which I could concentrate on nothing but the climb. Suddenly I *needed* to climb Mt Cook, to prove to myself I had the makings of a proper alpinist.

The night before we were due to walk into Plateau Hut to start our climb, Derek rang again. 'Weather's not in our favour,' he casually threw into the conversation after we'd been chatting for a few minutes. 'We might have to leave Cook till next summer.'

As I hung up the phone, a disbelieving numbness swamped me. Our plan had turned to dust. During the next few days the numbness grew into a disproportionate and irrational state of despair over which I seemed to have no control. The other climbs of the summer, which had made me so happy, so satisfied, accounted for nothing if I couldn't climb Mt Cook. The part the weather played was irrelevant – the failure was mine. What would my family and friends think? How could I face the people I'd so happily divulged our plan to? I left my job and left the village.

I'd occasionally felt sad and disappointed with life, but the overwhelming sense of failure I experienced at Mt Cook at the end of that summer was different. I felt so bad that I withdrew from doing things and from having contact with other people. Anyone who has a standard case of the blues can generally continue with their daily lives, but what I was experiencing seemed to be having a far greater impact. What I failed to realise then, but am all too aware of now, was that I was suffering from a serious episode of depression.

People with depression often think that they have developed the condition because things have gone wrong in their lives – the death of someone close, being in an unhappy family, or not living up to their own, or someone else's expectations, for example. I'd put enormous pressure on myself to succeed as a mountaineer and for some reason, which seems bizarre to me now, to climb Mt Cook in my first alpine season. That it was the weather that thwarted our plans didn't register. All I knew was that I'd failed in the one aspect of my life that really mattered to me. In the back reaches of my mind I knew my reaction was unwarranted, but I felt powerless to lift myself out of the deep trough of misery I found myself in.

I tried to move forward, starting the Diploma of Parks and Recreation course at Lincoln College in the beginning of March, but I felt trapped in the campus environment and woefully inept at student life, and dropped out in June. All I wanted was to climb and find again the sense of self-worth and happiness the mountains had afforded me. Then to my joy and amazement I was offered a job with the Mount Cook National Park for the following summer. Someone thought I was worth employing, and I'd be back among the mountains. My mood began to lift.

In 1971, iconic Kiwi mountaineers Jill Tremain and Graeme Dingle captured the imagination of the country when they made the first winter traverse of the Southern Alps. After two months of preparation, they set out on the Milford Track on 5 July, and on 8 September reached Lake Rotoroa, in the Nelson Lakes area. Their adventure finished with a two-day canoe run down the Wairau River. Dingle wrote a book on the journey called *Two Against the Alps*, which enthralled me. What a trip, what an achievement! And what an opportunity to spend months and months in the mountains.

Although I worked a five-day week for the National Park Board, I had another good climbing season. I'd set myself a hefty goal of summitting all the 10,000ft (3000m) peaks in the Mount Cook and Westland national parks, and steadily began to tick them off, including my nemesis, Mt Cook, via Zurbriggen Ridge. I couldn't see what all the fuss had been about.

With each success my state of mind improved and my self-confidence regrouped. I began to wonder why I'd been so depressed. I met other climbers and formed new climbing partnerships – people seemed to want to climb with me. When my summer job finished in February, I was offered full-time employment with Mount Cook National Park, but I had other plans. I was going to traverse the Southern Alps. And I had a partner in crime for the journey – my friend Chris Todd.

The Landsborough River is unusual for a river west of the main divide in that it runs north to south. Speculation from geologists is that it was originally a tributary of the Hunter River until it was 'captured' by the Haast River two million years ago. It winds for 50km between dark spurs of beech-forested mountainside, above which are grand peaks capped with ice. With such a huge catchment area, the Landsborough floods on a massive scale.

It was mid-April 1978 and Chris and I were six weeks into our traverse and had made it to the head of the Landsborough. I'd met Chris at high school and, as we shared a love of the mountains, we'd kept in touch. At eighteen, he was a carefree young hippy with a wild mop of dark hair and laughing brown eyes.

We'd started at the southern tip of Fiordland at the end of February, and by the time we reached Milford Sound we'd had enough of rain and sandflies and were glad to be progressing north towards beech forest and more open country. Gifford's Crack, the Dart and Matukituki valleys, Siberia Stream, the Ngatau and the Burke rivers fell beneath our feet as we loped up the divide. By the time we reached the Haast Pass in early April, lean, always hungry, but very fit, we were completely at home in our solitary environment. The traverse was turning into a fantastic vocation and things were going well. I was constantly tired, but so happy, so content in our mission to reach Cook Strait. We left the Haast River for the Landsborough in buoyant spirits, knowing we'd be at Mt Cook in a matter of days.

But a week-long nor'west storm kept us pinned to the valley floor, and by the time we reached the headwaters of the Landsborough everything – including our sleeping bags and morale – was wet through. We were out of food and fuel, and guessed our families would be worried by now as we were days overdue. (Decades later, both sets of parents would smile at each other and say, 'We shared an experience.')

Much to our relief, on the seventh day the wind and rain died, and we left our rock bivvy at the foot of the Spence Glacier to cross the main divide into the head of the Mueller Glacier. We were so excited; Mt Cook was only two days away. Chris strode ahead up the frozen slopes of Mt Spence, occasionally dislodging a rock, which bounced down the snow and over the moraine wall far below. 'Watch out,' he called, his voice the only thing to break the stillness. Above us hung the broken greywacke slopes of the main divide, and slightly to the south rose the beautiful north buttress of Mt Hopkins. As we inched higher, the summit of Mt Sefton slunk into view.

After several hours of steady climbing, we broached the top of the ridge a kilometre south of Barron Saddle. We began fantasising loudly about what we'd eat when we arrived in Mount Cook village. 'Bacon,' said Chris, rolling his eyes and smacking his lips.

'Oh yes, bacon,' I drooled.

But with the ridge came a shocking blast of frigid air. We looked south. A billowing denim-purple wall of cloud was rolling towards us, and as we watched, it engulfed the last yellow-grey vestige of the Mackenzie Country and began to gobble its way along the Ben Ohau Range. As if to announce its imminent arrival, we were bombarded with a blast of icy sleet, carried a good 20km on the wind.

'Shit! Hurry, we might still make Barron Saddle,' Chris bellowed into the wind as he dashed off along the ridge, only to be brought up short by a steep drop. We rigged an abseil, then hurried on.

'We could try abseiling down the Dobson [River] side,' Chris signalled to me, but I wasn't keen. The base of the valley was thousands of feet below, and the thought of being caught out on the wall by the southerly front frightened me. By now the cloud had slammed into Mt Sealy and was pouring over Jamieson Saddle, down to the floor of the valley. The backwash rose up towards us, and before we knew it we were in a blinding whirl of spinning snow. Visibility was reduced to nil and the cold set in. Simultaneously, we realised we were in trouble.

'We have to stop Chris, we need to find shelter,' I tried to shout above the din. He waved his arm in agreement.

Five metres off the ridge we found a small ledge with a cone of snow, bordered on one side by a 300m drop to the glacier and on the other by a wall of ice-encrusted rock. We started to dig, hoping there'd be sufficient depth for a snow cave. There wasn't. Frantic now, we levelled the ground as best we could and battled to pitch our tent. The wind tore at the fabric, threatening to send it spinning into the cloud. We were both fraught with cold and disappointment at the realisation that Mount Cook village could now be days away.

'You go inside,' Chris gesticulated chivalrously. 'I'll try and tie us down to something.'

Inside the tent I dragged out my sodden sleeping bag and burst into tears. I remembered from Dingle's book that Jill Tremain had a similar moment during their traverse, when she apparently cried 'womanly tears'. Chris joined me as I sobbed, and we did our best to get warm and cheer each other up. But in our minds was the knowledge that we had no fuel and no way of melting snow for water. That we were out of food seemed a comparatively insignificant problem.

We spent three days in our frozen tent at 2600m while the southerly storm blew itself out. We remained sleepless from cold, hunger and dehydration, and there were times, in our naivety, when we thought we wouldn't survive. We repeatedly dug the tent out, taking it in turns to venture outside and shovel the snow with Chris's plate.

But we did survive, and on the morning of the fourth day a patch of blue appeared. Then we heard a plane pass overhead and Chris stuck his head out the door. 'Yahoo! We're outa here,' he yelled to no one in particular.

We shoved our sopping sleeping bags into our packs and set off along the snowed-up ridge, abseiling short drops and scrambling over icy pinnacles, weak from days without food or water. After laboriously down-climbing the last slope to the broad flat of Barron Saddle, we slumped in a daze on a rock in the sun. 'This is heaven!' I said.

Chris and I never completed our traverse. We set off from Mt Cook in early May after four days of blissful respite in the village, walking from Blue Lakes to Tasman Saddle Hut in a long day. We then crossed into the head of the Murchison Glacier, only to be confined to Murchison Hut for a week while another storm raged around us. We finished our books, started on the hut supply of old *Playboy* magazines and endlessly debated whether we'd make it to the headwaters of the Rakaia River on the few stores we had remaining. Friends and family were to meet us there with our next food dump, but it was seven days away. What we admitted to each other years later was that our enforced camp on the tops above the Landsborough had eroded our confidence and drive, and with winter around the corner things were getting hard. We hadn't seen another soul on our traverse and were becoming lonely and homesick; we missed our friends and family. Perhaps we were too young for this escapade? We conceded defeat and walked out down the Murchison moraine to the road, a very subdued pair.

Failure. Back in the real world, I couldn't see the positive in what Chris and I had achieved, no matter how many people congratulated us on getting as far as we had. Chris, who is a naturally buoyant character with a charming self-confidence, picked himself up, headed home and made clear plans for the future. He would go to university the following year, he said, and in the meantime he'd get casual work, have a ski season and enjoy his friends.

I stayed in Mount Cook village through the winter, working in the hotel kitchen. It was very quiet and there was little happening, but this suited me. I couldn't face friends and family, couldn't look people in the eye, and couldn't maintain a conversation without being convinced I was being laughed at. A cloud of wretchedness settled on me; in the back of my mind I recognised a familiar pattern, but I had no idea what to do about it.

The Mental Health Foundation of New Zealand estimates that one in six New Zealanders will experience serious depression at some time in their life. What's more, approximately one in seven young people in New Zealand will experience a major depressive disorder before the age of twenty-four. Women have higher rates of depression than men; one in five women, compared with one in eight men, will have depression over their lifetime. Of course, these statistics were barely available in the mid-1970s, so my spiral into what was undoubtedly a second depressive episode went unrecognised.

Today, more is known of depression, including the fact that it may have no apparent cause or may result from a number of factors, by themselves or in combination. These factors include genetics, a stressful event or a mental illness like schizophrenia. The cause may also be biochemical. In people with depression, mood-regulating neurotransmitters fail to function normally in the brain, resulting in a lowered mood. Certain personality types are more at risk of depression than others, including people who tend to be anxious, have low self-esteem, are perfectionists or are shy. Statistically, as a young New Zealand woman the likelihood that I would suffer a depressive episode was one in five. Taking into account the fact that I was constantly anxious about my performance as a mountaineer, had low self-esteem, was terribly shy and was a perfectionist in that I set very high standards for my climbing, this likelihood increased dramatically.

Depression is now in the public eye and is recognised as a condition in itself. It is one of the most common reasons why people are absent from work, or are unable to run a home or look after their children. Public figures such as ex-All Black John Kirwan have come out to talk about their fight with depression in an effort to promote awareness and dispel discrimination. The World Health Organization estimates that by the year 2020, depression will be the second most common cause of ill health and premature death worldwide. If only I'd known this all those years ago.

At the end of 1978 I received a letter from an old friend who was on the Alpine Guides courses two summers before, and it was this that set me on the road to recovery. English John was coming back to New Zealand to do some climbing. Did I want to try a couple of the steeper south face lines with him? He'd spent a season in the French Alps, had upped his game, he said, and wanted to try some grade 4/5 routes. Why would he want to climb with me and not one of the others on the course, I wondered, but I was flattered and wrote back to say yes. As the days grew warmer my excitement grew: here was my chance to climb something hard, and tick off more of my 10,000ft peaks.

John arrived in late November with a load of new climbing equipment from Europe. He had state-of-the-art clothing made from something called fibre-pile, and alongside him I felt shabby in my mustard bush shirt and tie-dyed woollen long johns. We decided on the Right Hand Icefield on the South Face of Mt Hicks, a route put up a few years earlier by Mick Browne and Keith Woodford. I'd always been aware of the presence of Hicks at the head of the Hooker Glacier – a rounded dome whose south face was reserved for the hard men. But John was confident. 'You should see the stuff I was climbing in the Alps,' he said, proudly ticking off a list on his fingers. 'The Dent du Géant, the East Ridge of the Weisshorn, the Hörnli Ridge of the Matterhorn, the Whymper Couloir ...' Of course, these meant nothing to me then, but I was impressed.

We left on a Saturday morning, and made it to Gardiner Hut easily by the middle of the day. Earlier in the year I'd been this way to climb the low peak of Mt Cook, and I was pleased I could at least contribute my knowledge of the Hooker Icefall. Every time we stopped I couldn't help caressing my new North Wall hammer, bought especially and at great expense for the climb. We pushed on to Empress Hut, arriving just as the sun slipped behind the main divide to find the previous party had left the hut door open. Snow had banked up in the corners and the old mattresses were wet and smelly, but this failed to dampen our satisfaction at being there.

'You are so lucky to live here, Pat,' John said to my surprise, as we sat on the doorstep in the twilight drinking tea. 'If this was Europe the hut would be overflowing, and there'd be a party on every one of these routes. But look! We're alone; no one's been here for weeks. We have the valley to ourselves.' We both sat quiet, looking at the next day's route, reflecting on his comment.

'I've never thought of it like that,' I said eventually.

At 2 a.m. I cranked up the stove for porridge, while John methodically went through the equipment: six ice screws, two warthogs, a dozen karabiners, half a dozen slings, a couple of hexes and the rope. Surprisingly, I wasn't nervous, as I knew the onus was on John as the more experienced and technical climber. I'd made no secret that this would be my hardest climb to date, and that I expected him to do the majority of the leading. We crunched across to the bergschrund at the base of the climb in silence, arriving just as the faintest tinge of pale appeared in the east.

'You wanna go first?' asked John.

'What?'

'Why don't you take the first lead?' he said.'

'Why not,' I replied after a pause. I'd never placed an ice screw in anger but there was no time like the present to learn.

John showed me how to arrange the screws and karabiners on my swami-seat harness, how to fit the wrist leashes of my axe and hammer snugly, and how to order the various slings around my shoulders. 'Right, done,' he said. 'Off you go.'

By now it was daylight, and several hundred feet of the face was visible. A cone of snow bridged the gap between the lower and upper rims of the bergschrund and continued up at a fifty-degree angle for half a rope length. Then the ice began – a white and grey shield glinting in the early-morning light. I felt a sudden twinge of fear. Was I up to this? The wall looked so much steeper now we were standing close. I swallowed hard, and planted my picks above my head, kicked two pigeon-holes for my feet, then did it again.

'Hey, this isn't so bad,' I said to John, and I continued to the top of the snow cone.

'OK, now place a screw,' he said, 'while you can still stand easily.' I extracted a screw off my harness and stabbed it into the ice, then stabbed it again. It wouldn't catch. 'Give it a bit of a tap to get it started,' John said.' Carefully, I raised my new hammer and, leaning on my elbows, gave the screw a small knock. It pinged out and down, landing at John's feet. 'I've got it,' he said. I took another one off the harness and repeated the procedure, and this time it went in.

Twenty metres later I was feeling very scared – too scared to stop and place another screw, although I knew I ought to. 'Better place another one,' John kept calling from below, but I just continued climbing. My calves were burning and my arms could hardly swing – the picks kept bouncing off at odd angles.

At 40m John's voice became desperate. 'Place … a … fucking … SCREW!' he bellowed at the top of lungs.

I forced myself to stop and snatch a screw off my harness. On pure adrenalin, I rammed it into the ice and used all the strength I had to turn it in. Shaking with fright, I threaded a sling through the head, clipped in a karabiner, and attached the rope.

'Holy shit!' yelled John. 'Don't scare me like that, woman.'

At that my blood boiled. 'I TOLD YOU I couldn't lead this stuff,' I flashed. 'I SAID you'd have to do the leading.' In fury I completed the pitch, all fear gone. I was still angry when he joined me on the belay, contrite.

'I apologise, you did great,' he said. I sulked in silence.

It took John and me twelve hours to complete the 500m face. John climbed as slowly as I did, but with more control. My harness worked loose and became annoyingly uncomfortable, I was constantly tightening my crampon straps, my calves ached and my arms became so tired I could barely use them, but I led several pitches and was proud of my efforts. When we reached the sloping summit of Hicks, the shadows were lengthening, but we were speechless with appreciation for the view of the West Coast and the Tasman Sea stretching away to the horizon. 'Can't be many places in the world you get a view like this,' John conceded, with a dreamy smile.

But as we rigged the first abseil, we were both aware there was a long way to go before we could rest in our bunks at the hut. 'You go down first,' John said. 'I'll make sure the ropes pull.'

Of course, they didn't and we spent an anxious hour freeing them, by which time it was almost dark. 'Fuck's sake,' John said, 'We'd better bivvy.'

Not another enforced bivvy, I thought, turning my mind back to the hours spent lying in the tussocks 20m from Malte Brun Hut. We kicked a small ledge, sat down with our legs in our packs, and shared our last orange. Before long I was shivering uncontrollably with the cold, but to my amazement the long hours passed and the sun began to rise. We got stiffly to our feet as the view reappeared. John waved his arm towards the sea. 'My God, you are so, so lucky Pat,' he said.

Back in the village we got a mixed response to the news of our ascent. Some people congratulated us; others, the more experienced 'hard men', said we hadn't enough experience to tackle such a route and shouldn't have been there. John took no notice of the comments, laughing them off even, and began plans for our next climb. I took the criticism as a personal slight, however, and made a point of dodging the hard men, whom I was usually too shy to talk to anyway.

One beautiful evening in early December we hiked up to the tiny hut overlooking the lower reaches of the Mueller Glacier. We hoped to climb the East Face of Sefton. To the south stretched Lake Pukaki, teal-blue and lovely, and beyond that the bleached hills of the Mackenzie Country quivered in the heat. The forecast promised a short fine spell – enough for the climb, we thought. Our plan was to traverse underneath Mt Footstool and the East Ridge of Sefton until we reached the high shelf running beneath the summit ridge. Then we'd angle up a short couloir, cross over the ridge to the west and head on to the summit. We'd descend to the West Coast, and then come back over the Copland Pass to the Hooker Glacier and home. John was nonchalant in his confidence, but I was worried about the exposure, the avalanches and the reaction of the local climbers should things go wrong – or whether we should climb Sefton at all, for that matter.

By eleven o'clock the following morning we'd traversed as far as the base of the East Ridge of Sefton. Conditions for cramponing had been superb, the snow hard and squeaky, and we'd easily negotiated the crevasses. My fear of the exposure proved unfounded. Stopping for food, I gazed down at Mount Cook village, almost 2500m beneath us, and was overwhelmed with happiness – I couldn't think of anywhere I'd rather be than in the here and now. If my old school friends could only see me, I thought. But would I ever be able to explain to them in words the joy climbing gave me? I doubted it.

From our rest point it was a matter of dropping slightly to connect with the high shelf that ran beneath Sefton's long summit ridge. If I hadn't felt the exposure before, I did then. It wasn't steep, but the shelf fell away into space, and at 3000m the void beneath me was dizzying. I asked if we could pitch with the rope and I left the leading to John, who remained strong and level-headed, appearing to be in his element. He treated the route like he owned it, and not for the first time I marvelled that he'd been climbing for only two seasons. I wondered if his state-of-the-art equipment from Europe had something to do with it – after all, he was constantly telling me to get new boots and a proper harness.

At 2 p.m. we broached the summit ridge and headed straight into the teeth of a blustery wind. Out to sea, the sky was streaked with grey and, to our surprise, a stewing mass of convective cloud filled the valleys and smothered the coastal flats. 'Wasn't predicted quite this early,' John said with a frown. 'Why don't we drop back down out of the wind and regroup?'

We were very aware of our situation – above 3000m, in deteriorating weather and with no easy way down. We were climbing well, if slowly, but this scenario was one where our lack of experience could well let us down. I felt vulnerable and scared, but John shook off his doubts quickly. 'We're here now,' he said, 'Let's go for the summit; see if we can't beat this westerly.'

Reluctantly, I agreed – the last thing I wanted was to be stuck on the summit ridge of Mt Sefton in a storm. I struggled into my parka, put John on belay and watched him climb over a small rock buttress and up out of sight.

Two hours later we arrived on the summit of Mt Sefton. Despite the increasingly strong gusts, which held our rope suspended in a wide arc and had us crouched over our ice axes for minutes at a time, we were jubilant. We hugged, took silly summit photos, then lay on our stomachs peering straight down the East Face to the Mueller Glacier, 2500m below. I picked out my temporary home of Unwin Hut; the grocery shop; the row of little huts the guides lived in. There was the Wakefield Track, hugging the bank of the Hooker River, and the CMC Lodge. I didn't care about the weather now – we had made it and it was fantastic to be there.

But the reality was it was that five o'clock in the evening, we had been on the go for fourteen hours and we were a long way from shelter. Our plan had been to descend to Welcome Pass and bivvy for the night before continuing down Scotts Creek to Douglas Rock Hut the next day. But by the time we'd staggered down the West Ridge to the pass, the wind had become a gale, blasting snow crystals into our eyes and slowing us to a crawl. What's more, a huge flying saucer of cloud now hung over Mt Cook and the skies to the west were dark with stratus. 'We need to keep going,' John yelled over the din of the wind, loping off down the steep slope of the Tekano Glacier. I tried to follow, but by now I was so, so tired, and I had a small private snivel. But the severity of our situation returned to me in a flash, and I dashed after John, shouting for him to wait.

The Scotts Creek Bivvy is an overhanging boulder among tussocks and scree that, facing down valley, provides enough shelter for a couple of climbers. The floor is covered in ageing tussock grass, collected and added to by generations of residents seeking a little extra comfort. During times of rain, drips land on the visitors as they lie in their sleeping bags, and for most of the summer the bivvy supports a thriving population of mice, which lie in wait for a feed. Keas (mountain parrots) are also a common visitor. By the time John and I made it to the bivvy rock, it was well after dark and in our exhausted stupor we almost walked past it. It was only by chance that I picked out a row of directional cairns with the beam of my head torch. The smell of rain was in the air, but we collapsed into our sleeping bags, too tired and relieved to care what the weather did. We slept like the dead.

It was broad daylight when I next opened my eyes, and raining hard. I lay listening to the numbing patter of the drops as they hit the ground and the roar of the rising creek. Still half asleep, I stared vacantly at the blurred landscape across the valley, and after a minute became aware of a piece of orange tinfoil, mere inches from my face. A little further away was another piece, and a scrap of paper and then ... a piece of bacon? I sat up. All around the entrance to the bivvy were the decimated and sodden remains of our precious food supply – spaghetti stalks, bacon pieces, gingernuts, orange Tang, chocolate, cabin bread ... I shook John awake in horror. There was an electric pause, during which he stared open-mouthed at the aftermath, then he roared 'Fuckin' keas!' at the top of his lungs.

The local kea population had snuck up in the dead of night, pilfered our stocks and snuck off again before we woke. I collapsed with laughter, all the tension of the previous day exiting in one long guffaw, but it took John longer to see the funny side.

Devoid of breakfast, we left for Douglas Rock Hut in the downpour, hoping against hope that there would be some abandoned food waiting for us.

Two days later, we arrived back at Mount Cook village. We were very hungry. The only food in the hut had been a bag of ancient porridge, stale and weevil-ridden. But we'd carried it with us, and periodically stopped for a cook-up as we crossed the Copland Pass, eating together out of the same pot. Near the summit we met a kind elderly couple walking in the opposite direction who gave us a bag of textured vegetable protein. It tasted like ambrosia. Arriving at the village we expected another lambasting from the Mount Cook 'committee', but the only comment came from an eighteen-year-old climbing protégé who said, 'You shouldn't have done all that traversing. You should've climbed the face direct.'

I'd been avoiding my family for months, worried they'd be critical of my self-enforced hermit's existence at Mount Cook and my menial job of washing pots, but decided to brave it and head back to the farm for Christmas. John and I planned to meet again in the New Year for one last route: the South Face of Mt Cook.

My family glanced at my climbing photographs and left me to myself, and it wasn't until I was readying to return to Mount Cook that my father asked what I intended to do that year. 'I don't know,' I responded truthfully. I was too wary of destroying my fragile equilibrium to make plans, too frightened of falling back into that pit of misery, not knowing if I had the wherewithal to climb back out. The only thing I was certain of was my need to go climbing.

Today, more than a dozen routes grace the South Face of Mt Cook, but back in the late 1970s there were only two to choose from. A year on there would be three, as Colin Brodey and Nigel Perry climbed the iconic White Dreams in December 1980, the beautiful line of interlinking ice floes leading to the top of the Nor'West Couloir. John and I settled on the Direct Route, first climbed solo by Bill Denz several years earlier. Bill was everybody's hero, and I'd seen him around the village numerous times, but I doubted he'd ever noticed an overweight teenager with no social skills. In the end, however, John and I reneged – the Direct Route was dangerous, overhung by ice cliffs, and the hard men told us it was beyond our capabilities. Instead we reverted to the original 1963 route of the first ascensionists, and climbed the mountain in mid-January in our usual methodical, but painstakingly slow style. Again, John did more than his share of the leading. Reaching the low peak late in the evening, after a long finishing haul up the South Ridge, we decided it was too late to descend back to Gardiner Hut and so shared another unplanned bivvy. I felt responsible – was it was my fault we were so slow?

'No way,' John said, as we levelled out a sitting platform at the top of the Nor'West Couloir. 'Sure we're slow, but we're being careful. We should be proud of ourselves – we've only been climbing two years and look at what we've achieved this summer.' He sounded frustrated. 'What's the matter with you? Why can't you see how good you are? You spend more time in the hills than anyone else I know. And how many other girls do you see out here climbing what you're climbing.'

I didn't know, as it wasn't something I paid much attention to. I just assumed the other girls were out there, somewhere.

'And for God's sake, don't worry what other people think, or if you fail sometimes,' he continued. He seemed quite angry now. 'Just do your thing, and find some happiness in it.'

I was stunned at his outburst, and we sat in silence, watching the sunset. I looked across at Sefton, at our route of a few weeks ago. Wow, I thought, was I there? The sky turned pale silver, then deep blue, and a slight wind picked up. The cold set in. I didn't mind, the night would pass. John was right. Climbing was going to be part of my life for a long time to come. I needed to find my peace.

CHAPTER TWO

Trusting Partnerships

Climbing partnerships are the stuff of legend: Messner/Habeler, Boardman/Tasker, Mallory/Irvine, even Simpson/Yates. But how many legends do you know that include a woman in the partnership?

– Leigh McGuigan

Anyone who has climbed mountains knows how important it is to have the 'right' partner, something I learnt very early on in my career. I was lucky to have found a similar focus in Dennis, Chris and John, and without them I wouldn't have accomplished as much as I did in my first few seasons at Mt Cook. Over the years, through trial and error I've whittled the people I climb with down to a small handful, and these few have woven themselves in and out of my alpine climbing for decades. Obviously, climbing with the right partner leads to a higher degree of success, but a good climbing relationship also ups the chance of survival if things go wrong.

In most productive and long-lasting climbing partnerships, the psychological supersedes the practical in importance. In roping up together on a potentially dangerous mountain, each climber is literally putting his or her life in someone else's hands. A mistake by one can bring about the death of both, and a trust born of respect for each other's climbing skill, and an ability to perform together under duress, are all important.

The best climbing partnerships are those where the climbers are willing to put up with equal amounts of hardship and adversity. It's as fundamental as that. A good partnership endures bad weather on a mountain and shares the chores – cooking, melting water, and shovelling the tent free of snow – all of which can be taxing at altitude or in extreme cold. A good partnership also waits out bad weather without demanding entertainment of each other. A good partnership can abseil forty pitches through the night without speaking, because each partner trusts the other to do what's needed. When two equally competent climbers are compatible in adversity, the rest falls into place. This is when the most dynamic and successful partnerships are formed. Unfortunately, finding the ideal partner isn't always easy.

The quintessential mountaineering partnership has to be that of Englishmen Eric Shipton and Bill Tilman, and their story is as relevant today as it was when they first headed to East Africa together in the 1930s. Over eighteen years, the pair climbed and explored in some of the most spectacular and least known mountainous areas of the world: the Nanda Devi and Badrinath ranges in the Indian Himalaya, the Tibetan side of Everest, the Karakoram Range in Pakistan and the high mountains of western China. On many of the journeys they were travelling in areas that had not been mapped or visited by previous explorers, and were undoubtedly under considerable mental stress. They set out up gorges with no known exit, or headed for high glaciated cols with no known descent. The physical deprivations were just as severe. Yet in all those years there was only one reported serious disagreement, which broke out when Shipton wanted to take two shirts instead of one on a four-month expedition. Tilman thought it an unnecessary extravagance.

Another pair of Englishmen who had exceptional success as a climbing partnership was Jo Tasker and Pete Boardman. When they got together for their first Himalayan trip – to Changabang in 1976 – Boardman was much better established than Tasker as a high-altitude climber. Nevertheless, Tasker sensed Boardman was the right person for the trip. He is quoted in Boardman's 1976 book, *The Shining Mountain*:

> But it was not [his climbing record] which made Pete in my eyes the right person to ask about Changabang. It was not the record of achievements that I saw in him but the attitude of mind that I sensed. With some people it is not necessary to have climbed in their company to know that they are of the same inclination and share the same spirit as oneself.

Tasker's intuitive choice proved to be the right one. Although the pair's plan to climb the West Face of 6864m Changabang was considered outrageous at that time, and despite extreme hardship, they pulled it off. The partnership flourished: they climbed together on British expeditions to K2 in 1978 and 1980, and made first ascents of Kongur, a 7719m peak in western China, and the North Ridge of Kanchenjunga, the world's third-highest mountain. The complementary personalities of the outgoing Boardman and the taciturn Tasker were crucial in getting them through danger and extreme deprivation. Tragically, the partnership ended in 1982 when the pair disappeared on the then unclimbed Northeast Ridge of Everest. They were last seen at a height of more than 8200m on a push for the summit.

Not many partnerships are formed as easily as that of Boardman and Tasker. Most evolve through trial and error, from climbing with, and discarding, partners before latching onto someone with whom a successful connection is formed. Despite our youth, Chris Todd and I found this connection as we wound our way up the Southern Alps. We spent weeks alone with only each other for company, sharing the drudgery of day-to-day life on the move. We developed an unspoken routine of daily tasks and survived the torrid experience of being stranded on a mountain in a storm. We came out of the experience the best of friends. I formed a similar connection with my husband Brian and with mountain guide and remarkably skilled climber Marty Beare. Marty and I began climbing together in the early 1990s in the Mount Cook region and went on to climb successfully and hard in Alaska and India (see chapters 5 and 6). I also found such a connection climbing with my sister Christine, and in Asia with Malcolm Bass and Karen McNeill. But there were other partnerships that ran their course. This was not necessarily because we had a bad time together, but simply because our ambitions and drive were at odds.

In 1980 I met the kind, handsome man I'd eventually marry, and we discovered in each other a love for the inland Canterbury high country. I'd grown tired of the posturing and competition amongst the climbers at Mt Cook, and wanted to see new ground. In the upper reaches of the Godley, Rangitata and Rakaia rivers, I found a rugged, windswept appeal. For several years in the early 1980s, Brian Deavoll and I prowled up and down the Havelock and the Clyde, climbed the peaks of the Garden of Eden, the Ramsay and Lyell glaciers, and the headwaters of the Mathias and Wilberforce. I loved the terrain – the expansive dusty riverbeds with their clusters of matagouri, tussocks and merinos, the steep scree slopes, the barren glaciated peaks and the old musterers' huts. For me, the high country east of the divide appealed much more than the valleys of rainforest and mist on the West Coast. 'I like the big views, the big country,' I tried to explain. 'I like to see where I'm going.'

Brian and I travelled and climbed easily together. We went on to explore the Himalaya and Karakoram ranges in the mid-1980s, living in each other's pockets on a shoestring budget for almost two years. But there's more of that later in the book (see Chapter 6). In late 1986 we decided on a traverse of the eastern side of the main divide from Arthur's Pass to Mt Cook, a trip I'd done several years beforehand but thought Brian might enjoy. At the time, my younger brother, Bill, had made an early exit from school at the age of sixteen and was at a loose end. 'Take him with you,' my parents said, and with Bill's approval it was settled. The three of us left Arthur's Pass on a beautiful spring day in mid-October, heading south.

Bill had never held an ice axe or worn a pair of crampons before, and was very excited when we hit our first snow on day two. 'Wow,' he said, marching on the spot, admiring his new crampons. He took wild swipes at stationary rocks with his ice axe, sending them bounding off down the slope as he chanted staccato, 'I'm - so - glad - I'm - not - at - school - not - at - school - not - at - school …' At the top of Whitehorn Pass he struck a victory pose with his axe in the air. 'Only seven more passes to go,' he crowed, before slithering off down the far side on his backside, Brian and I following sedately in his wake.

By day four we'd crossed from the Wilberforce River into the head of the Mathias Valley in perfect weather. Bill, who'd also never carried a pack before, seemed to be settling easily into our routine of early morning rises and twelve-hour days, but one thing Brian and I hadn't allowed for was the amount of food a sixteen-year-old boy can eat. 'He must still be growing,' Brian said in awe, as one night we watched Bill eat our left-overs, then the burnt offering from the bottom of the billy, then scour the hut for ancient and forgotten food.

We were relieved when we reached the head of the Rakaia on day six and could access our stashed food dump. 'We can supplement his calorific intake with extras,' Brian said to me. We basked in the sun on the grass outside Reischek Hut for a day, while over the fire Bill cooked plate after plate of macaroni cheese, bacon, hash browns, dumplings, instant puddings and jellies for the three of us to eat.

'Surely you must be full by now?' I asked Bill as I lay on my back, incapable of moving.

'Actually I'm just off to that hut on the other side of the river,' he said, pointing to Louper Biv, 'to see what food's there.'

By the time we reached the Clyde River on day ten, after racing a nor'westerly storm over McCoy Col, our three-way partnership was functioning like clockwork. We'd wake at 4 a.m. and I would light the fire and boil the water I'd collected the night before. Brian would collect more water while Bill stirred our porridge. I would pack our sleeping bags, then wash the porridge pot and put on more water for a cup of tea. We would all pack while the billy boiled. Bill would sweep the floor of the hut and wipe the bench, then we'd drink our tea and depart. At the end of the day we slipped back into our routine. Bill collected firewood, Brian did the water, and I started tea. Brian and Bill would do dishes while I collected water for the morning. Groundhog Day. And although Bill became understandably fatigued the closer we got to Mt Cook, he never once shirked his jobs and I was proud of him, a teenager in a foreign environment, for slotting into a routine Brian and I had perfected over the years. By the time we completed our three-week journey we'd become a tight unit, and on reaching Mount Cook village it was hard to stop. 'We could keep on walking – go all the way to Foveaux Strait,' Bill said wistfully.

British climber Andy Cockburn came out from the UK to take up an academic position at Canterbury University in 1993. Andy was the ultimate enthusiast and a natural athlete. These days he is a father and professor, but through the 1990s and 2000s he excelled as a rock climber, annoying his friends by being able to climb very hard grades with a minimum of training. He arrived in New Zealand with boundless enthusiasm, a brand-new PhD and, in view of his success on Scottish ice, the intention of ticking off the hard south faces of the Southern Alps. He persuaded me to accompany him to Pioneer Hut over the Christmas period, to knock off the technical Central Gully on the South Face of Douglas.

I was wary. I'd climbed the South Face of Douglas in the early 1980s in what must have been the slowest time ever, armed with my 75cm wooden-shafted ice axe encased in lashings of fibre glass (as was the fashion at the time) and my precious North Wall hammer. During recent years I'd moved over to the dark side, forgoing the mountains to become a kayaker. But I'd try, I told Andy, if he would lead the hard pitches. We took off from Mount Cook Airport in a Cessna 185 on 24 December, and landed on the upper Fox Glacier. There was no one else around and the weather was superb.

Andy catapulted from the plane like a jack-in-the-box. 'Fantastic,' he yelled, leaping in a circle, flapping his arms in the air. He grabbed his pack and tore off in the direction of Pioneer Hut. 'Crevasses!' I shouted after him. 'Come back.'

I introduced Andy to the technicalities of roping up for crevasse travel, then he towed me down the glacier to the empty hut. We spent a pleasant afternoon sunning ourselves on the deck, looking out over the Tasman Sea and eating a box of chocolates. It was glorious. We were at the base of the climb the next morning at 5.30 a.m. It was Christmas Day.

The climb went well, despite my misgivings. We soloed the bottom section of the gully and then began sharing the lead, Andy bolting up the crux pitch in a matter of minutes. The easier angled top section dragged on in the sun, but we topped out shortly after lunch.

'What a Christmas Day,' said Andy, punching his fists in the air and looking like he could climb the whole thing again. 'Oh that was fantastic! Oh, look at that view. Oh ... now, where's that abseil station?' He peered around.

'No abseil station,' I said, 'we've gotta traverse down there,' pointing at the meandering ridge line.

'But in Scotland and Europe you always abseil off on fixed abseil stations,' he wailed.

I led off down the ridge in deep, wet afternoon snow. 'This is dangerous,' Andy called after a few inward-facing steps, his face clouded with anxiety. 'I don't like this at all.' His face became more and more troubled as we traversed slowly towards Glacier Peak. Descending the wide snow slope to the glacier, a large soggy avalanche trundled down the face 100m to our right. 'Arrrgh!' he yelled in fright. Then we had to jump a big crevasse. I suggested, in the interests of his geological know-how, that he take a look inside. 'Arrgh!' he yelled again, as he made an Olympian leap for the far side.

Back at the hut in the late afternoon we revelled smugly in our success and made plans to climb the North Shoulder of Mt Tasman the next day. 'We're here and we have the whole glacier to ourselves, we should give it a try,' I convinced Andy. But we woke the next morning to rain on the roof. As I snuggled back in my sleeping bag to doze, I became aware of Andy, sitting up and moaning softly. 'What is it?' I said, alarmed.

'My face,' he said forlornly.

I looked at him, concerned. Blisters ballooned on his cheeks and forehead, and his eyes and lips were swollen in a nasty way. 'Didn't you use sunscreen?'

'We don't need sunscreen in Scotland,' was his sad reply.

Andy and I never climbed together again. He went on to climb the difficult Balfour Face of Mt Tasman and the South Face of Mt Aspiring, but then called it quits. 'I don't like the objective danger of the New Zealand mountains,' he told me, 'the avalanche risk and the loose rock. The risk isn't worth it for me. I can't stop being scared, and I'm always worried something awful is going to happen. I'd never cope with being trapped on a mountain in bad weather. I'm going to stick with sport climbing, thank you.'

For me, however, the Christmas Day ascent of Douglas, combined with the hilarity of being in Andy's company and his dubious appreciation for what the New Zealand mountains had to offer, went a long way towards reigniting my desire to be a mountaineer. I'd forgotten just how good it felt to be in the hills; how the satisfaction of making a worthwhile ascent lingers like a slow-release drug, adding piquancy to the days and weeks to come. I was a year or two out of the sport, but I'd climbed something quite hard on my first outing. I'd come home feeling happy, satisfied and worthwhile. Perhaps I should try something else, maybe a rock route with my newly acquired skills. After all, I was rock climbing well – grade 26/27 sport routes – and had been to Australia several times to climb. I asked my friend Karen McNeill if she wanted to try the Strauchon Face of Mt Dilemma, a spectacular and lengthy greywacke slab route in the Mount Cook region, to the west of the main divide. Karen, who was making a name for herself as an up-and-coming young alpinist, said yes.

For some reason Karen and I didn't leave Mount Cook village for Gardiner Hut until 3 p.m., hence we didn't arrive at the hut until almost midnight, hauling our way up the metal cables lacing Pudding Rock by head torch. The next day we had a leisurely start, wandering over Baker Saddle and down to a bivvy under the Strauchon Face on a beautiful hot January day. We set up camp on top of a large, flat rock and squandered the afternoon away, scoping the route and making cups of tea. The approach to the face, which started in earnest from a hanging glacier a few hundred metres up, might be problematic in the dark, we thought. We also looked with interest at the West Face of neighbouring Mt Unicorn, which appeared about ten degrees steeper.

Three o'clock the next morning saw us perched upright in our sleeping bags on top of our rock eating muesli. The sky was packed tight with stars and we were silly with the joy of just being there. It felt good, two women tackling a grade 5 route, I thought as I scrambled across the bergschrund and made the first moves up the gully, Karen right behind me.

But climbing steep, water-worn rock in plastic mountaineering boots in the dark isn't easy, and after 50m I yelled down to Karen that I was going to change into my rock shoes.

'Are you on a ledge?' she shouted back.

'No,' I replied, as I struggled to get my boots off and my rock shoes on without dislodging myself or my pack down on top of her. A few minutes later I was off again. 'I'll just go on a bit, Karen,' I yelled down. It was exhilarating, scrambling up in the dark by the light of my head torch. What fun!

Just as the sun rose, I reached the hanging glacier and sat down to wait for Karen. It was just after 5 a.m. My feet were frozen, so I pulled some socks on over my rock shoes and then took a look around. High above Baker Saddle, Mt La Perouse was catching the first of the light. Cook peered over from the back, the low peak swaddled in a pink glow. The sky was the clearest whitish blue. How could I have given this away for kayaking, I asked myself. Nothing could be better than this.

Shortly, Karen appeared and we scooted across the small hanging glacier to the start of the face proper. The first few hundred feet of climbing looked moderate, and then the face seemed to steepen. 'I suppose we could try it without a rope to start with,' Karen said dubiously. I readily agreed, and padded off up the slab, Karen in pursuit.

After half an hour I paused and looked down. Karen was 50m or so below me, climbing carefully, testing the handholds and scrutinising each foot placement. Above us was a huge rock arch, and to its left the start of a corner system. 'I'll go on a bit,' I decided, and veered towards the corner. An hour later I'd reached its entrance. The angle of the face had cranked up a few degrees.

By now I'd relaxed into the route and knew I was climbing well. Hmm, I could solo this. Why put the rope on? This freedom is great. I'll just go on a bit more. I began to bridge up the corner. Intuitively, my arms and legs seemed to know what to do, and before I knew it, I'd made the last move and was looking up at the easy-angled finishing slopes below the summit. Sitting down on a small platform, I pulled my socks on over my climbing shoes again and peered over the edge, back into the gully. Where was Karen? Annoyed, I shouted her name. Nothing, but the 'phat-phat' of stone fall, somewhere out to the left. I yelled as loudly as I could, 'Kaa-ru-u-n', and this time a distant cry echoed back. 'Are … you … oh … kayee?'

I heard a faint 'Yeees' from far below. Forty minutes later, Karen popped out the top of the gully and sat down beside me. I could tell she was shaken.

'Oh God, I was so scared down there,' she said. 'I couldn't stop thinking I was going to fall. I'm such a hopeless rock climber.'

A wave of guilt washed over me, my face reddened and I felt dreadful. As we ambled to the summit all I could think was that I'd put Karen in danger, left her behind, just to satisfy my own ego. I was so selfish. I'd never dash off and leave anyone like that again. Never. I'd been an appalling climbing partner and I doubted Karen would ever want to climb with me again.

But a few weeks later I had an excited phone call from Karen, who had been climbing up on the Grand Plateau beneath Cook. She'd overheard a conversation in the hut common room, she said, while she was washing the dishes. 'These two guys, they were talking about these two FABULOUS women who soloed the Strauchon Face of Dilemma in three hours. It took me a moment to realise ... but they were talking about US!'

By this stage I was hell-bent on re-establishing myself as an alpinist. I seemed to forget the satisfaction I'd gained from kayaking, from taking on a new and very technical skill and progressing with it to the top. I'd been a very good kayaker, but I didn't care any more. I just wanted to get back into the mountains and, unfairly, regretted the years spent on the river that had kept me away from climbing. Now I need another rock route, I decided, something a bit harder. The West Face of Mt Unicorn sprang to mind – Karen and I had noted it with interest from our bivvy under Dilemma. I asked Marty Beare if he wanted to come with me, and he readily agreed.

Marty decided, ambitiously, that we'd do the climb in a day from Gardiner Hut. I told him that I wasn't climbing fit yet, but he dismissed my comment with a shrug. Oh well, I'll go with his decision, I thought, after all, he's a mountain guide. We arrived at Gardiner Hut late one afternoon in early March, but not before Marty had taken a tumble, accompanied by a large boulder, down the moraine wall and incurred some scrapes and bruises. He was looking a bit glum.

The next morning we were away by 4 a.m., over the now familiar Baker Saddle and down the long descent to the base of Unicorn. I was content to let Marty go first and scampered along behind him, grinning to myself in anticipation of the day to come. I could already taste the satisfaction of success. How good it was going to be to stand on the top later today. How good to lie in my sleeping bag back at the hut tonight, knowing I'd truly earned the rest. How good to be climbing with such an accomplished climber.

But I'd forgotten that the mountains aren't always onside.

To begin with, I couldn't find the access gully Karen and I had used a few weeks earlier. Instead, we climbed a difficult, wet and seemingly vertical stream bed in the dark, and by the time we reached the hanging glacier the sun was up. Marty looked up the huge expanse of Unicorn's slick grey face. 'Hmm, we need to go faster,' he said, matter-of-factly. Changing into rock shoes, we began clambering up the dark gulch separating the two mountains. It was full of shattered rock and dirty snow. 'Ugly place,' Marty said.

Then to my annoyance, my feet began to hurt. 'Hey, my rock shoes have shrunk,' I yelped. 'I'm going to have to change back to my boots.' Boots on again, I tried to catch up with Marty, but found myself floundering and slipping clumsily on the frictionless slab. 'Fuck's sake,' I swore loudly to anyone who could hear. I just wasn't in the groove. What was wrong with me? 'Sorry, but I need to change back,' I yelled.

Several hundred feet above, the gulch steepened and narrowed, and the occasional stone whirred past us. 'Hmm,' Marty said again, 'Perhaps we should get out to the left.' We looked dubiously up at the slope – we weren't high enough in the gulch to access our intended route, but this way might be better than being hit on the head by a rock. We ducked to one side as a boulder the size of a television trundled past. The first half-dozen pitches went without incident and, back in my rock shoes I began to enjoy the climbing, and to feel more together. It was a perfect windless day, but increasingly the sounds of what were now very large boulders bouncing down the gulch disturbed the peace. Out to our left was a beautiful crackline, but it seemed to peter out under a huge overhang about 500m above us. We decided to continue by veering up and slightly right in the hope of getting through the overhang at its lowest point.

By now it was lunchtime and, realising we'd been on the go for eight hours without a rest, we hung on an anchor, snacked and drank, squinting up at the route ahead. 'The rock seems to be deteriorating,' Marty said. 'I wonder if we wouldn't be better even further to the right.'

I set off on a diagonal away from the belay and crossed a rib into a shallow gully. Spanning up, I had to agree with Marty that, yes, the rock quality was poor. I belayed him up, and he continued out and right, mumbling away to himself as he searched for solid protection. The further he got from the belay, the more he had to search and the slower he climbed. Finally, reaching a small overhang, he placed two small camming devices for an anchor. 'Hmm, nasty,' he said when I arrived beside him.

I looked up with some trepidation, and led off rather unenthusiastically. Five metres out, I hadn't managed to place any protection. 'Something will turn up soon,' called Marty encouragingly. Another 5m on, and still no gear.

'I don't like this – I'm getting a bit scared,' I grumbled, half to myself and half to Marty. I shuffled on. At 15m out from the belay, and still with no protection, I reached a blocky pedestal, about head high. 'At least I can get a rest here,' I thought, and stood on the lowest block, shaking my arms. Without warning, there was a loud 'crump', a pause … and then I was flying backwards, in slow motion. 'Bonk' went my helmet against the rock, as I completed the first backward somersault, then 'Bonk-bonk' as I completed two more somersaults. Large, dark shapes were accompanying me on my downward trajectory – falling boulders, I realised fleetingly. Then everything came to a halt, everything was quiet and I was facing downwards, with a view of the gulch far below. My heart was pounding in my ears and I was sucking in huge involuntary gulps of air. Somewhere, someone was shouting.

'Pat, Pat, are you OK?' sounded from a distance.

I swivelled around until I had an upside-down view of Marty, hunched under the overhang like a giant spider and taking my full weight, his helmet jammed crooked over his eyes.

'I think I am,' I said incredulously, patting my arms and legs. I wriggled upright. Goodness! I must have fallen 30m, but I was in one piece! I stood to a wave of nausea, and hauled my way shakily up the rope. 'Oh, oh' was all I could say. Then, 'Shit. I could have killed us both.'

Marty patted my arm. 'Never mind,' he said, 'these things happen. But I think it's time we made a retreat.'

Retreat. I'd never thought at the beginning of the day that we'd have to retreat. But I grudgingly agreed – we'd both had a near miss and there was no evidence the rock quality was going to improve. Plus it was getting on in the day. Where had all the hours gone? What on earth had we been doing? We began the long abseil back down the face. Sometime around 6 p.m., thirsty and disgruntled, we reached the gulch again. Our ropes, like recalcitrant children, had tangled in the most execrable way. And the closer we got to the gulch, the louder the constant pounding of rockfall. Hauling down the ropes for the last time, a boulder the size of a kitchen catapulted past. There was nothing for it but to wait until the sun went down, the temperature dropped and, we hoped, the bombardment ceased. We settled in comfortably behind a pile of moraine with a soothing block of chocolate to watch the boulders flying past.

'Well,' said Marty, 'this is turning into an exciting day. I wonder what will happen next?' I glowered at him, and then held myself in check. Hang on. Had I forgotten that things don't always go right in the mountains? There are days like this one, when accumulating mistakes have the potential to spiral into full-blown disaster. It was up to the climbers to bring the situation back under control – and this was where experienced partnership played a part. Between us, Marty and I had over forty years of mountaineering behind us. We were doing OK – we hadn't let things get the better of us … and yet.

As the sun set, the rockfall faded away. 'Let's make a run for it,' Marty said.

Instead of retreating back down our early-morning ascent gully, however, we decided to save time by bolting straight down the gulch to the point where it petered out into the glacier. Marty shot off like a rocket, determined that no last-minute boulder of the day was going to take him out. Still shaky from my fall, I followed more slowly. I down-climbed a 10m vertical section of friable rock, then breathed a sigh of relief. The next drop loomed.

'I really want to abseil this one,' I called to Marty, but he ignored me in his headlong dash for the glacier. Bastard, I thought. Angry and scared, I pressed on. Just a few hundred feet and I'm down and it's all over, I told my-self. After what seemed like hours, I stumbled out the bottom of the gulch onto the snow. Marty was sitting on his pack, composed and waiting for me. It was nine o'clock at night and getting dark.

'We've got two alternatives,' said Marty. 'We can hunker down here and sit out the night, or we can keep going another few hours to the hut.'

Hunker down with no sleeping bag, I thought? No way, I want to keep walking.

'OK,' said Marty, 'but first we need to get some water.' We'd both been out of water for several hours, and were parched. A tiny trickle dribbled down the nearby rock face. We decanted half a bottle, and were just turning back to our packs, when from somewhere high above, and with no warn-ing, a colossal 'rawrawraaaaw' echoed around the valley. 'RAWRAWRAW'. I stood rooted to the spot, momentarily at a loss as to what to do.

'Run!' roared Marty, gesticulating wildly with one arm. 'Run, this way!'

At that I ran, ran like the wind, as thousands upon thousands of tonnes of ice erupted from the hanging glacier above and cascaded down the rock face. Like a tsunami, the mass hit the valley floor and bolted across the gla-cier, a tumultuous wave of blue and white ice blocks and huge chunks of rock. Clutching each other in astonishment, we stood staring, our mouths agape, as the wave ground to a halt. We were both aware that if we hadn't stopped for water, we'd be somewhere underneath that ice.

'What next?' Marty said when the din had died down.

At 4 a.m. we staggered up the last slope to Gardiner Hut. The moon spilt a sublime silver light over the glacier and peaks above, and the ink-blue sky was smothered in stars. But I was too tired to appreciate the beauty. The climb back over Baker Saddle had been endless, and as we down-climbed to the Hooker Glacier I kept drifting in and out of semi-slumber.

'Will we ever get there?' I whined involuntarily.

'Doesn't seem like it, does it?' Marty replied unhelpfully.

We hooted with delight when we finally walked in the hut door. 'What a day,' said Marty. We'd kept the situation under control, kept it together as a partnership … and we'd survived.

After Unicorn, Marty became a regular climbing partner. We concentrated on the Mount Cook region, and focused on the steep ice routes. Trips to Empress Hut, at the head of the Hooker Glacier, became a midwinter routine. We did a number of routes on the South Face of Mt Hicks, and although I'd climbed one or two of these earlier in my climbing career, my climbing potential upped a notch with Marty on the other end of the rope and, later, with over a hundred Canadian waterfalls under my belt (see Chapter 4).

In 1999, we climbed Logan's Run next to the Right-hand Icefields, a short grade 6+ test piece, in thin condition. I easily led the mixed crux pitch, which involved a steep, broken crackline and overhanging ice. I felt on top of my game and attributed this to two seasons' waterfall ice climbing in Canada – I had gone there because I knew it would have taken a long time, if ever, to get the same mileage in New Zealand. We made quick ascents of the Central Gullies and Curver routes on Hicks, and the Hidden Balfour Face of Mt Tasman over the next couple of winters. But as with Dilemma, not all our climbs went to plan.

Vampire Peak is a feisty little mountain of just over 2750m at the head of the Mueller Glacier. Its East Face is steep and menacing – it often has a mix of rock and avalanche debris strewn at its base and, during the summer months in particular, emits the constant racket of rockfalls. But in the winter it is graced with some fine ice lines and in the late 1990s a couple of these were still unclimbed. Marty and I had our eye on one in particular – a direct line following a gully through an obvious overhang to a point where it joined an existing climb. We flew into the head of the glacier in a Porter fixed wing late one July afternoon and skied to Barron Saddle Hut for the night.

The next morning we made a somewhat leisurely approach to the face, arriving at the bottom at about 8 a.m. The way up the small tributary glacier was heavily crevassed, the slots covered with a thin veneer of powder snow. First Marty, then I, fell into a crevasse. Unperturbed, we pressed on until we were within 50m of the bergschrund barricading our gully. This barrier was about 2m wide and had a 3m-high back wall.

'Let's leave our skis here,' Marty decided. 'Hopefully we can descend from the summit that way,' he said, waving at a steep snow slope to the left of the face, 'and ski triumphant back to the hut.'

But when we stepped out of our skis we plummeted to our waists in the powdery snow. 'Bother,' we exclaimed simultaneously.

'OK, let's get back on our skis and see if we can get right up to the edge of the crevasse before we take them off,' said the mountain guide. Climbing back onto our skis was no easy feat, but we managed. Shuffling to the edge of the crevasse, we took the skis off for the second time, and … whoosh.

'OK,' said the half of Marty I could see, 'How 'bout I get back on my skis, and then you climb onto my shoulders and see if you can climb across the crevasse.'

I agreed with some scepticism, and after a few moments of light-hearted swearing was perched on Marty's shoulder.

'Good view of the bottom of the crevasse from up here,' 'I said.

'Never mind that,' said Marty between gritted teeth. 'Have a go, have a go.'

I leaned forward and punched my axe and hammer shafts into the snow. A large, loose block fell away and disappeared into the schrund. We wobbled precariously. More cautious, I tried again, clawing and shovelling at the snow for purchase, but it continued to collapse. Before long, I had created an overhanging trench.

'It's no good, let me down.' I half jumped and half slithered into the snow. For a moment we both stared forlornly up at our route. So near and yet so far.

'Right, Plan C,' Marty announced. 'Let's ski right around that end of this crevasse and try to get back across the top to the base of the gully. I don't know why we didn't just do that in the first place.'

He headed off to the left while I clambered laboriously back into my skis again. With Marty leading, we skied across the top side. The slope was steep and we were both aware, without speaking, of the potential for an avalanche to deposit us ignominiously into the crevasse and then smother us.

'I hope no other guides can see me doing this,' Marty said, glancing over his shoulder. 'I'd be blacklisted by the Mountain Guides Association.'

Eventually it became too steep to ski any further and we needed to get the skis back across the crevasse, so we could collect them later. 'We'll throw them,' I determined, thinking it was time I came up with a good idea. 'This will be easy.'

At that, I took off a ski and, with a push, slid it across the crevasse, where it came to a neat halt on the slope below. I did the same with my second ski. Marty took a different approach – he threw one ski up in the air like a spear, and it sailed lightly across the crevasse to land nose down in the snow next to mine. The second, however, sailed into the air, then plummeted down, down, into the depths. For a moment we were speechless, then I collapsed in a fit of giggles.

'What are you going to do now, mountain guide?' I spluttered.

Marty looked at me, crestfallen. 'My ski,' he said. 'I'd better abseil in and get it.'

We built an anchor and Marty descended into the crevasse. After much grunting and puffing he reappeared sheepishly, covered in snow but with the ski. By now it was mid-morning.

We pushed on up the gully, with me in the lead. The ice, which had appeared good from a distance, proved shallow and insubstantial, and I struggled to find ice-screw placements. There was no improvement with the next few pitches and doubt began to grow in our minds. How were we going to get through the looming overhang? Marty led out up increasingly steep ground, and as I belayed, I looked around. Across the valley, a threesome of skiers picked their way down a narrow gully to the glacier. To the right, Barron Saddle Hut perched squat on the flats overlooking the Dobson Valley. The original hut here, the Three Johns Hut, had disappeared in a storm in 1977, blown off the saddle with four climbers inside it.

I could see also the ridge leading towards Mt Spence, where a couple of decades earlier Chris Todd and I had spent four days incarcerated in our tent in a storm (see Chapter 1). I began to think of that trip, the satisfaction of a long journey with a good companion, when … whack! Something hit me hard between the eyes. I reeled in pain – what on earth was that? Blood began to run down my chin, along with involuntary tears. I felt the spot tentatively – ouch.

'Marty, I've been hit,' I croaked. No response. I began to climb upwards, snuffling in pain and misery. My nose was broken, I was sure it. Smudges of blood decorated my orange Gore-Tex parka.

'Crikey, what happened to you?' Marty exclaimed, as I snuffled up to him. 'You OK to go on?'

'Yeth.'

Marty took the lead again, while I stood at the belay, wallowing in my misery. The rope played out as he climbed up and around a corner, out of sight. Then it stopped, and stayed stopped for a long time. Finally, I heard a faint cry to follow. I dismantled the belay and headed up, leaving a spattering of red droplets in my wake. The pitch was very steep and the ice veneer thin. Rounding the corner, I caught sight of Marty, strung up under the rocky overhang.

'Shhhh!' he hushed as I approached.

'Why?' I said, wiping my nose.

'Because I'm hanging here on a single no. 2 wire and if you make too much noise it will fall out. See if you can get a V-thread in where you are.'

This is all I need, I thought, a broken nose and now the anchor is going to fail and we are both going to fall to our deaths. 'I take it this is as far as we go, then?' I prodded around in the skin-deep ice for an anchor, to no avail.

'OK, we are just going to have to abseil off this wire,' Marty said. 'Let's get it over with.'

With that, he lowered himself gingerly onto the rope, and disappeared down around the corner. I peered at the wire. It was, as he'd said, a very small wire wedged into the back of a very small crack. Don't look at it, just go down, I told myself as I ever so gently connected my belay device and even more gently slid off down the rope.

'Both your eyes have gone black,' Marty complimented me when we'd reached the safety of the glacier. 'I think we've had enough of Vampire.'

The winter of 1999 saw a huge wedge of rock fall off the base of the South Face of Mt Hicks, taking with it the bottom two pitches of a grade 6 route called Original Gun Barrels. The new start was soon climbed by a posse of young enthusiasts, but Marty and I left it a year or more before attempting it on one of our midwinter Hooker sojourns. As we trudged up the final slope to Empress Hut, Marty was looking over his shoulder at the route. 'Doesn't appear to be much ice,' he speculated. 'Might be quite hard.'

I didn't care. I was just happy to be back at the head of the Hooker. The familiar ice runnels on Hicks, the grand Sheila Face of Cook catching the last of the winter sun, La Perouse and its fortress of ice cliffs, the fabulous view down the glacier to the grassy flats around the village all held me in their thrall – and, of course, the hut, perched primly above the glacier, the prize after two days of winter walking.

But the next morning, as we made a beeline across the glacier for the base of the climb, I had to agree with Marty. There didn't appear to be any ice at all on the first pitch, while the second sported some white blobs of snow. I could tell Marty was less than enthusiastic.

'Let's give it a try, see how we do on the first pitch,' I said. 'You can lead.' He grumbled an affirmative.

Marty racked up above the bergschrund. 'No point in me carrying the ice screws,' he said. 'No ice. I'll leave them for you.' He began to work his way up the steep corner, using the picks of his ice tools to hook tiny friable edges of rock as he balanced on his crampon points. After 10m he paused, wrestled a wire from the cluster of gear on his harness, and wiggled it into a small crack.

'That's not very good,' he said, matter-of-fact, as he clipped the quick-draw.

'Never mind, it will be fine,' I said breezily – the climbing looked fun and I was eagerly anticipating seconding it. Marty inched on and fiddled another small wire into an even smaller crack – by now he was 15m up and directly over my head

'I need something better than that,' he frowned, moving on up a particularly blank piece of wall.

'I'm watching you,' I called, serious now.

Marty came to another halt, with the pick of his left ice tool wedged in a small horizontal recess. I watched intently as he extracted a piton from his harness and, reaching across his left arm, manoeuvred it into a narrow crack. With his right ice tool he reached across the left arm again, and gently tapped the piton home. 'Phew,' he said, as he moved off.

By now I was feeling slightly anxious. Marty was a good 20m up with only three pieces of protection in, none of them any good. I willed him to stop and place another piece, but he kept on moving, looking as if at any second he'd fall off. Experienced climbers can recognise when their climbing partners are about to fall – their movements become erratic and they make anxious panting sounds. Marty stopped and dragged a red sling from his shoulder, hitched it over a slim horn of rock, clipped himself in, and slumped. 'Your turn,' he said, with a malicious grin.

Seconding the first 10m went well for me. I felt in control as I carefully hooked the little edges and torqued my picks in the cracks. But by the time

I reached Marty's second piece of protection my arms were feeling drained and leaden. This is really hard, I thought to myself. A really class lead on Marty's part.

By the time I reached the particularly blank piece of wall, my calves, too, were feeling spent. I made a couple more desperate moves and then sat on the rope.

'Take me,' I said, irritated. 'Fuck, I can't even second this.' Then, more charitably, 'Marty, that was a fantastic lead.'

'Thanks,' he said, looking down at me smugly.

It was my turn to lead. Above us the corner became more pronounced, then rose into an overhanging bulge, full of ice-cream scoops of snow. I felt less than optimistic – what if I climbed so far up, and then got stuck and couldn't find any gear to retreat off? I couldn't ask Marty to lead it, not after I'd bullied him up the first pitch. I set off feeling slightly panicked, and after 5m placed a 'security' screw in a small blob of mushy ice. The screw looked the part, buried to the hilt, but I knew it wouldn't hold a fall. Marty's wrinkled brow looked up at me as I bridged on, my crampon points and picks jabbing erratically at any small irregularity. I placed a camming device beneath a dubious flake of rock.

'You reckon that will hold?' Marty called.

'How the bloody hell would I know?' I snapped back, scowling down at him. He looked away with a shrug as I placed another cam. 'And that one's no better,' I yelled. Take that, I thought. Here I am, up on the sharp end, scared stiff (I jabbed another ice screw into some firm snow and clipped it to the rope), while he hangs in comfort and security on the belay (jab – another ice screw in another mushy clump of ice).

By now I'd reached the bulge, choked with overhanging pillows of snow. There was nothing for it – I had to clear the snow before I could climb any further. I stemmed my crampons onto a pair of small edges, and began to chop above my head with my ice axe, my hammer secured into the underside of the bulge. The snow fell in large clumps and I looked down between my feet to see Marty burying his head in his jacket hood as the shower continued. 'Wuss,' I grumbled, as I shovelled on, 'I need a belayer who's watching me. I could be off at any ...'

Suddenly, I was suspended in mid-air, hovering a metre from the rock, still staring at the snow bulge. 'What on earth ...' Then I was flying down. There was a soft jerk, as the first ice screw ripped free, then another jerk. I flew past Marty's upturned face. Pip, pip, pip went the remainder of my protection as each piece was wrenched out by my weight. Then I came to a remarkably gentle halt.

'My God, where am I?' I looked down to see one of my crampons dangling around my ankle. I looked up at Marty's startled face, 25m above me. I looked down again. The start of the climb – the beginning of Marty's pitch, and the spot where we'd racked up – was about 2m below me.

A thin, shaky voice from above said, 'Um, are you OK?'

'I think so,' I said incredulously. I'd free-fallen almost 30m, ripped out all my protection, flown over Marty's head and miraculously missed hitting the wall, surviving with nothing more that a sore backside. 'Better lower me down,' I said in awe.

'I'm going to rap off this sling,' Marty said, still sounding shaken. 'Perhaps you'd better put me on belay, just in case it rips too.' He slid gingerly down the rope towards me.

Back at the hut we had a subdued cup of tea. 'What do you reckon happened?' Marty asked.

I was quiet. I didn't want to admit my crampon had fallen off, and the reason for this was the much worn state of my plastic mountaineering boots – so worn, in fact, that the crampons no longer fitted them properly. Marty had pointed this out to me several times in the past, but, reluctant to spend on a new pair of boots, I'd ignored him. Now I was paying the price, and for the second time I'd nearly killed my partner.

The following morning we left the hut at 4 a.m., intent on climbing the longest route on the face – the Central Gullies. The first pitch was a very steep slab with only a lick of ice on it, and I left it to Marty to lead. But the remainder of the climb went well – my mojo returned, I took my share of leading the dozen or so pitches, and we were on the summit by early afternoon. I was secretly proud of myself that I'd not let my plummet get the better of me. I needed a new pair of boots, yes, but the fall was in the past. I also knew that had I been climbing with anyone else I wouldn't have recovered from the fall as quickly. I was developing an intrinsic trust in Marty as my climbing partner, but I wondered what on earth he thought of me?

My connection with Marty certainly had none of the intensity of the Shipton/Tilman or Boardman/Tasker partnerships, but it cemented a foundation that would allow us to climb well together overseas in the future. It also helped me to realise the personality type I needed for a climbing partner – someone who was quiet, humble, highly skilled and strongly motivated, but with a very real grasp of his or her limitations. This realisation encouraged me, in 2000, to ask my sister Christine if she would like to attempt the first female team ascent of the South Face of Mt Douglas with me. Christine is quiet, very modest and extremely athletic, but at the time had done very little climbing. She had always been extremely competent at everything she'd turned her hand to, and like Jo Tasker with Pete Boardman, I knew intuitively she would be fine on this grade 5-plus route.

We flew in to Pioneer Hut by helicopter on a beautiful September afternoon, taking skis and a tent with us as the hut was likely to be crowded. We pitched the tent, and then skied around the corner to look at the face.

'Oh golly! Do you really think I can climb that?' Christine said as we looked up at the central gully, which split the face and was white with ice.

'Yes,' I said, 'so long as we have our rope system worked out. We'll practise here on the flat.' I bent down and stabbed two ice screws into the snow. 'OK, here's our first anchor. Now you pretend to clip into it.'

We crawled up and down on our hands and knees, pretending we were on an eighty-degree ice slope, and practised our rope work until Christine thought she could reproduce the system the next day on the climb. A team of skiers slid past. 'What are you doing?' they asked, puzzled. I knew we looked like a scene from a Monty Python film.

'Practising climbing, because we are going to climb that tomorrow,' said Christine, turning and pointing up the face. The skiers looked at each other, and then shuffled off sniggering. 'Those women have no idea what they are getting themselves into.'

Christine gazed after them with a frown. 'Are you sure I can climb it?' she queried again.

'Of course,' I said dismissively.

The following morning we were at the base of the gully with the first glimmer of daylight. We tied into the rope, setting our skis upright in the snow so we could collect them later in the day.

'Up we go,' I said cheerfully. 'Let's move together up this first section. I'll put the ice screws in, you take them out.' Ignoring Christine's look of consternation, I scrambled across the bergschrund and began kicking my way up the initial fifty-degree slope, clipping the rope into the occasional screw. After a few moments the rope came tight. I looked down and saw Christine looking intently at the first screw.

'What do I do with it?' she called.

'Unclip the rope, then the quick-draw, and then screw it out,' I shouted back with unfair exasperation, realising I hadn't actually told her how to remove an ice screw.

After forty minutes the climb steepened and I could feel from the tugs on the rope that Christine was moving more conservatively. 'OK, let's belay from here,' I shouted down as I began to construct an anchor.

'Thank goodness,' I heard her say quietly, as she moved hesitantly toward me. After another pitch we reached the crux, and as I built the anchor I realised the sun was creeping down the face and it was starting to warm up.

'This looks really steep,' Christine said, looking up, as we organised the belay. 'Are you sure I can climb it?'

'Yes, of course,' I said yet again, before shimmying up.

Halfway through the pitch I glanced down to see Christine holding an ice screw in her hand, looking at me questioningly. 'This came out of the anchor,' she said. 'Does it matter?'

'Not at all,' I called down, hiding my anxiety.

Christine moved methodically up the pitch. By now she had the hang of taking out the ice screws and, apart from a small yelp of fright at half height, was climbing with aplomb. She looks like she's been doing this for ever, I thought to myself. I knew she'd be good. Because she doesn't know the sport, she has no preconception of what a beginner should be doing. She's such an athlete, she's just doing what comes naturally.

Christine reached the belay and looked up at the finishing slope. 'Do you think I can climb it?' she asked, yet again.

We reached the ridge at 1 p.m., and Christine and I hugged on the exposed summit in the bright sunlight. The Tasman Sea glinted like a jewel in the west and the white of the névé shone beneath us. I felt an overwhelming sense of pride and tears came to my eyes. Not only had we done the first all-female ascent of the South Face of Douglas, but my sister, with no climbing background, had pulled off quite a remarkable climbing feat. We descended off the back of the peak and slowly plodded to the hut in the afternoon heat.

'You're back early,' said one of the skiers smugly. 'I take it you turned back?'

'Not at all,' I said, brimming with pride and happiness.

After Christine's baptism by fire on Mt Douglas, we went on to climb a number of the region's classics over the next few years. No other beginner was tackling climbs like Christine. But for the very reason I'd first asked her to climb Douglas – that, as my sister, I knew her intimately and what she was capable of – I could see no reason for her to short-change herself when her natural athleticism and toughness would allow her to jump straight onto the harder routes. We climbed ropeless the Zurbriggen and West ridges of Mt Cook. On her fourth climb we soloed the classic Syme/Silberhorn traverse of Mt Tasman, reaching the summit at seven o'clock in the morning. We carefully down-climbed the beautiful snow arête leading off the summit as the sun cleared the horizon, and were at the bottom of the hard climb by 9.30 a.m.

Snacking and drinking in the sun, we watched a helicopter fly down the Linda Glacier with something slung beneath it on a strop. The helicopter landed on the Grand Plateau, then returned to the upper Linda and collected another load. It dawned on us that the loads were the bodies of a group of four Latvian mountaineers who had climbed Mt Cook the day before, but who had not returned to the hut that night. We learnt later that the climbers had died when they'd fallen 500m roped together from close to the summit, to land at the base of a huge ice cliff. For the first time, Christine was exposed to a sobering but very real part of what it meant to be an alpinist – death. But by this time I was convinced she was the most talented woman mountaineer I'd ever climbed with, and our success as a climbing partnership was based on our innate knowledge of each other as siblings and our almost identical no-fuss approach to what we did.

Norwegian climber Veikka Gustafsson and American Ed Viesturs have climbed many of the 8000m peaks together without oxygen. Both climbers see in each other an equal, they say, and between them is an almost eerie affinity and similarity of judgement. Their partnership is 'like a marriage' according to Vestiers. 'You know what the other is thinking and you don't have to use words.'

'We click, we think alike. I'll look at him and literally take the words right out of his mouth. I'll say something, and he'll say, "you know I was just going to say that," or, "I was just going to do that." We defer to each other. If one of us is hesitant about something, and thinks, "what do you say we go this way?" The other guy will just go, "Okay, it's good with me".'

Not all the accounts of famous climbing partnerships are as convivial. American climber Rob Taylor accused Henry Barber of letting him fall and break an ankle and then abandoning him on Mt Kilimanjaro. In his book *The Breach: Kilimanjaro and the Conquest of Self,* Taylor says, 'From the start

Harley (Barber) and I were never friends,' and goes on to accuse Barber of defects ranging from social ambition to atheism to snoring. The reader wonders why they ever bothered to link up in the first place. Taylor concludes 'an avalanche is not malicious unto itself, nor was Harley. He was what he was.'

Even the legendary British partnership of Boardman and Tasker wasn't without its shortcomings. In Boardman's famous account of the West Face of Changabang, *The Shining Mountain*, he doesn't hide the pair's 'non-co-operative hostility toward each other in things which did not matter.' The author described his irritation when, huddled high on an exposed ledge, 'Joe seemed to gain a few inches of the ledge every hour. An irrational, miserable little corner of my life started resenting him. I bet he's really warm. I bet he's fast asleep. Why does he always seem more comfortable than me? Why does he need so much room?' Yet after the arduous ascent, the two Britons were fast enough friends to go to Mt Everest in 1982.

American climber and writer David Roberts claims in his book *Moments of Doubt: and other mountaineering writings* that climbers under physical and emotional stress do not behave much better than more sedentary humans, and that the intricacies of climbing partnerships are the stuff of pop psychology books. In one of his chapters he examines the demise of the famous Reinhold Messner/Peter Habeler partnership. The pair made the first ascent of Mt Everest without oxygen, but their partnership came to an end soon after. After interviewing them both, Roberts claimed that 'the breach is the product not of any quarrels or conflicts that took place in the mountains, but rather of wrangles and jealousies that sprang out of the wilderness of print and film and television'. He says that the climbers' respective books give conflicting accounts of their celebrated oxygen-less climb of Everest, and that the media latched on to these inconsistencies. Habeler wrote in his book, 'Reinhold has set this all out in his books, even if the reader may gain the impression that he was the leader and I was simply a passenger. However, I don't feel bitter about this – the books sell better that way. The applause of the general public is not as important to me. But Reinhold needs their recognition.' Messner in turn complained that '[Habeler] sells my problems but not his own'.

Roberts even goes on to debunk the 'mystical affinity' that top climbers claim towards the mountains they conquer, suggesting their motivation is more likely to be the kind of competitiveness that lures others into a business career. 'Love of nature has little to do with it. "Superclimbers" are, on the whole, uncheerful about hiking, impatient with the weather, insensitive to the subtleties of landscape.'

I can't claim to be a superclimber or that any of my climbing partnerships, either during the period I've just written about or in later years, have the intensity of the Messner/Habeler or Boardman/Tasker duos. But I have had enough negative climbing partnerships to appreciate the ones that work. Marty, Christine and Karen all had plenty of drive and plenty of skill, but also modest personalities and an honest appreciation of where they were at. Later, I found the same qualities in Malcolm Bass. But there have been times when I've gone against my intuition and agreed to climb with someone who hasn't had these qualities, and have paid the cost. These days I'm very selective. I have no qualms about discarding a partnership that doesn't work for me. There is, after all, far too much at stake to get it wrong.

CHAPTER THREE
It's a Man's World

Lady an explorer? a traveller in skirts?
The notion's just a trifle too seraphic:
Let them stay and mind the babies, or hem our ragged shirts;
But they mustn't, can't and shan't be geographic.
— *Punch* magazine, 1893

When I first decided to include a chapter on the status of women climbers, I was clueless where to start. Embarrassingly, I knew little if anything about New Zealand's early women mountaineers, and although being a woman in a largely male-dominated sport hasn't always been easy, it's not something I've focused on. When I started climbing in 1977 I was the only female on my alpine instruction courses at Mt Cook and thought nothing of it. The majority of my climbing partners have been men, and I've never felt the need to join a women-only climbing club or to take part on women-only courses. I've been happy doing my own thing with little thought to the wider climbing community and what its make-up might be. I assumed the women were out there, somewhere, doing the same things I was.

When I began my research into early women mountaineers in New Zealand, I discovered to my complete surprise that these Edwardian ladies had launched themselves into mountaineering with no preconceived ideas of how it should be done, simply because no women had been there before them. Not only that, but they'd risen above the oppressive social restrictions enforced on them by their era. The first heyday for New Zealand women climbers was in the inaugural years of 'high alpinism' in the Southern Alps – from 1910 to 1920. During this period women were regularly making up 50 per cent of the climbers in the Mount Cook region and were also figuring highly in first ascents and test pieces. Granted, the overall number of climbers was very small, but women like Freda du Faur, Katie Gardiner and Jane Thomson were flaunting the social norms and indulging in their passion in a truly remarkable way.

I began to wonder why, as a rule, today's women climbers weren't applying the same philosophy to the sport. Supposedly, we have none of the social restrictions these women had – none of the issues of dress, chaperonage or expectation. These Edwardian ladies had no role models to follow, no female guides to nurture them, no all-women clubs to support them. And yet they climbed as well, if not better than, the men and in numbers regularly made up half the climbers of the day. Compare this to the mere 23 per cent of women climbers making up the New Zealand Alpine Club (NZAC) membership in 2010.

Between 1900 and 1914, climbing was mostly based on tourism, where climbers were led up the mountains by guides, but many of the women who took part in this were skilled athletes in their own right. They were often tourists or travellers, were usually middle-aged or older, belonged to the upper-middle class and were generally economically independent through inherited wealth. Most were unmarried and childless. They took their climbing seriously and spent time getting fit for the mountains.

Even very early on, women were beginning to make ascents of some of the more moderate peaks in the Mount Cook region. Forrestina Elizabeth Ross, who began climbing in 1890, made ascents of Mt Bonpland and Hochstetter Dome, and also got well up Earnslaw. All this activity was achieved in a skirt, and with none of the accoutrements of modern climbing like crampons and mountain huts. Ross was the only female member of the NZAC between 1892 and 1895, and for a while edited the club's journal.

By 1900, small climbs and glacier travel had become more commonplace for women, and by 1908 guides were becoming acceptable companions for them in the mountains. Australian Annette Lindon began high climbing with a guide in 1909 at the age of forty-nine. She ascended Mt Cook in 1912 (by no means the first women to do so), then returned to the region in 1920 at the age of sixty for one final season, climbing nine peaks, one of them unguided.

Another of the earliest and most celebrated women climbers was Jane Thomson, who was born in Kaiapoi, Canterbury, in 1858. From 1893 to 1909 Jane lived in Greymouth with her husband John Thomson, and it was from here she began her mountaineering career. With two other women she was part of the first female party to cross the Copland Pass in 1903. To appease their guide, who was unsure of his female charges, one women wore mens' clothing. Jane was less forthright, although she did concede to wearing a pair of knickerbockers.

In 1915 Jane began a two year climbing partnership with Austrian guide Conrad Kain, making ascents of Mt Edgar Thomson, which she named after her son who had died in a football accident, and Footstool and Lendenfeld. In 1916 the pair made what was only the second traverse of the summit ridge of Mt Cook after three previous attempts. Jane was fifty-seven at the time, and Kain was criticised for taking such an 'elderly women' on the climb, but he countered by praising her fortitude, skill and determination.

Jane continued to climb after the death of her husband in 1927, making the first ascent of the low peak of Mt Rolleston at the age of sixty-eight. At eighty she travelled to India to visit the 8000m peak of Nanga Parbat, and died in 1944 leaving a legacy of high alpine achievements and proving that age need not be a barrier to the sport.

The Edwardian woman who undoubtedly played the most inspirational part in the development of female mountaineering in New Zealand was Australian Freda du Faur. She was the first woman to take up high alpine climbing in 1909 and was also the first to climb Mt Cook. Although her climbing career was brief, Freda assembled a remarkable résumé of thirty successful ascents, confirming her position as not only the leading woman climber of the time, but also the most successful amateur climber, male or female, in New Zealand.

Freda was born in Sydney in 1882 and probably developed her passion for climbing when her family lived near Ku-ring-gai Chase National Park. Here she taught herself to rock climb. She started to train as a nurse but never finished owing to the inhibitions of what is now regarded as bipolar disorder. However, she had an independent income that allowed her to travel and climb, and in 1909 she began her alpine career at Mt Cook under the guidance of the famous pioneer guide Peter Graham. He was immediately impressed with Freda and, well ahead of his Edwardian time in this respect, saw no reason why she shouldn't be a mountaineer.

During her first season, Freda climbed Mt Sealy and Nuns Veil, and made the first ascent of the West Ridge of Malte Brun – all with no previous experience. A fortnight after these achievements she and Graham made an attempt on the West Ridge of Mt Cook (remember, she had only been mountaineering a matter of days) but were defeated by a bergschrund and iced-up rock. Freda then made a return crossing of the Copland Pass to finish her season. And what a first season it was.

Bitten by the bug, Freda returned to New Zealand the following summer. After a few warm-up climbs, she and Graham made a first ascent of Mt Burns near Barron Saddle before setting out on another attempt of the West Ridge of Mt Cook. This time they were successful, and Freda became the first woman to summit New Zealand's highest peak. A week later, she was climbing again, making the second ascent of Mt De la Beche, and then summitting Mt Silberhorn en route to a failed attempt at Mt Tasman. Undeterred, she went on to climb Mt Green and Mt Chudleigh.

A late start to the following season saw Freda succeed on Mt Nazomi, followed by a second, this time successful, attempt on Mt Tasman. Three days later, she climbed Mt Dampier, making her the first person to climb the three highest peaks in the Southern Alps. A day later, she made the second ever ascent of Mt Lendenfeld via the Northeast Ridge. By this time Freda was the leading alpinist in New Zealand.

The 1912/13 season was to be Freda's last. She returned to Mt Cook for the fourth and final series of objectives she had set herself – nothing less than the first east–west traverse of Mt Sefton, and what most guides considered the impossible, a complete traverse of all three peaks of the mile-long ridge of Mt Cook. She accomplished both – on 3 January 1913, Freda, Graham and David Thompson became the first mountaineers to complete what is now referred to as the Grand Traverse of Mt Cook, ascending from the Hooker Valley by the Southwest Ridge to the low peak, traversing to the middle peak, then following the sinuous ice ridge to the high summit and descending the Linda Glacier back to the Tasman Valley. She finished her final season with the first ascent of Mt Cadogan and the second ascent of Mt Aiguille Rouge, which was to be her last climb in the Southern Alps.

Reading about Freda, I was flabbergasted. That she achieved what she did could never have happened had she not been an extremely fit and exceptionally talented climber. She made thirty climbs in four short forays to Mt Cook, with no crampons, no prior knowledge of many of the routes and no mountain huts to shelter in, and with no women-only introduction course or fellow female climbers to support her. And she had to do it while navigating all the stifling social restrictions of the early twentieth century! Freda left New Zealand the most successful amateur climber, man or woman, the country had ever fielded, and was certainly one of the most accomplished amateur climbers of her day anywhere in the world. No other Kiwi woman climber before or after can make such a claim.

Freda never returned to the Southern Alps. In 1913, she moved to England to be with Muriel Cadogan, her long-time friend and lover. After Cadogan experienced something akin to a mental breakdown and died in 1929, Freda returned to Australia. Sadly, this woman who had kicked down the barriers of gender stereotyping, yet disconcerted men with her femininity, who was celebrated for her climbing expertise, perseverance and athleticism, took her own life in 1935 after suffering declining mental health.

The First World War gave women more opportunity to climb – some guides were tied up in the war effort overseas, but there were always one or two available. Even with a decline in climbing between 1914 and 1920, the percentage of women participating in the sport remained high. During the war there were six ascents of Mt Cook by twenty-two people; four of the seven 'client' climbers were women. Women also began going on 'guideless' climbs, often led by Horace Holl, an English mountaineer based in Auckland. One of these was Margaret Lorimer, headmistress of Nelson College for Girls. Even though she was over fifty, Margaret was energetic and driven, and climbed Mt Cook by Earles Route in 1918.

After the war, opportunities for women increased further through changing attitudes, better transport and the opening up of new mountain regions. Women began to roam into more remote areas, especially after they had done some climbing from a 'civilised' base. Many remained single and few were under thirty years of age.

One such post-war pioneer was Englishwoman Katie Gardiner, who started her mountaineering career at an early age by accompanying her father on climbing trips to the European Alps. In 1925, after coming across a photograph of Mt Cook, she headed for New Zealand. She was over forty years of age at the time and did not do well on her first climbs – the guides said she was slow and unfit. But she returned in 1928 to become only the eighth woman to summit Mt Cook. She then travelled to the Canadian Rockies and completed an ascent of Mt Assiniboine and six other peaks with guide Walter Feuz, continuing this pattern of summers in the Southern Alps and the rest of the year climbing in Canada and Switzerland for the next ten years. Over the time she became one of the most prominent women climbers in the world. In the New Zealand summer of 1930/31, Katie climbed twenty-seven peaks, nine of which were first ascents. I doubt any climber today, man or woman, can claim to have had a season like that.

In 1932, Katie tried three times to climb Mt Tasman, but each attempt was foiled by bad weather. On the third attempt she was forced, along with her guides Vic Williams and Jack Pope and Englishman A. M. Binnie, to shelter in a crevasse, where they became stranded for nine days. Her survival proved beyond doubt that women had the strength and endurance for the sport of mountaineering. She returned to New Zealand a year later and finally climbed Mt Tasman (the second woman to do so), then headed south to climb Mt Aspiring and Mt Tutoko.

The Second World War interrupted Katie's climbing career, but she returned in 1948 to climb Mt Egmont and Ruapehu. Two years later, Katie came to live in New Zealand for good, making her last climb, the Minarets, at the age of sixty-six. Are there any Kiwi women today climbing the 3000m peaks at age sixty-six? I doubt it.

Like Freda and Jane, Katie climbed in an era when men and women alike relied heavily on guides, which as a woman of means she could afford. However, she was described as a steady climber with 'great stamina' and was held in highest regard by her guides, who named a hut at Mount Cook in her honour. Katie never married and died in Hastings in 1974.

By 1930, mainstream New Zealand climbing had come adrift of guides and was based on tramping. This made the recreation cheaper and hence open to a wider and younger range of women. Clubs were established, creating a broader body of knowledge and benefiting the less confident and less experienced. But other factors worked against progress for women in climbing, notably that the sport developed into a heavy pack-carrying, fitness-based pursuit. And, of course, women were still encouraged to give up climbing when they got married.

Some independent women climbers were, however, starting to emerge, not just from tramping but as guides. Hilda and Molly Haldane were guiding on Mt Egmont in the 1920s, and Betsy Blunden was employed at the Hermitage as a guide from 1923. Betsy was leader on a number of climbs in 1932–34 and was the first woman to climb as an equal to men, being part of the first ascent of Mt Oates (Arthur's Pass) in 1931. By 1934 she was leading all-women climbs, and in the same year summitted Footstool, Cadogan, Du Faur and Madonna with Rosamund Harper, in what were the first 'man-less' climbs for both.

Two other woman of that era who came to climbing from a tramping background were Greta Stevenson and Lella Davidson. In 1933, at aged twenty and twenty-one respectively, the pair made an ascent of the east peak of Mt Earnslaw, and with Ivy Smith made other ascents of smaller peaks in the area. A milestone for women climbers came in 1934, when Betsy, Lella and Rosamund made an all-woman ascent of Sefton from the west, successfully carrying their own packs and choosing their own route.

Sadly, however, this climb did not become a model for women mountaineers. Although progress had been made, the proportion of climbers who were women was dropping. The Depression probably had a detrimental effect, as did the Second World War, with its travel restrictions. It seemed that the initial heyday of women climbers, with its great characters like Freda, Jane and Katie, who defied the norms of gender, age and propriety, had come to an end.

It was many years before another bunch of Kiwi women began making a noticeable stand in the mountaineering world, this modern resurgence in interest being ignited with a bang when, in 1988, Christchurch climber Lydia Bradey became the first woman in the world to reach the summit of Mt Everest without oxygen. Of course, there were other women climbing in the interim, such as Margaret Clark, Vicki Thompson and Jill Tremain, but it is Lydia who is undoubtedly one of the great success stories in New Zealand's mountaineering history. She truly shook up the climbing scene and proved that women could compete alongside, if not ahead of, their male counterparts.

Lydia has great presence and is now sought after as a motivational speaker. She and I began climbing around the same time, in the mid-1970s, but whereas I was moving through my career oblivious of the rest of the climbing scene, content to stay hidden in the upper reaches of remote Canterbury valleys and heading to the Himalayas with only a husband in tow, Lydia did things in grand and flamboyant style. But her rise to mountaineering fame was not without controversy, as her ascent of Everest was to prove.

By the age of eighteen Lydia had made ascents of Mt Aspiring and three of the tougher routes on Mt Cook. The following summer she made the first female ascent of the Balfour Face of Mt Tasman, an iconic ice route that remains a test piece for climbers today. She climbed in Alaska in 1981, attempting the American Direct on the South Face of Mt Denali, the highest peak in North America, before heading to the Yosemite Valley in California.

Here she scaled ten 'big walls', making seven first female ascents of some of the hardest aid routes in the valley at the time. In 1984 and 1986, she joined British expeditions to attempt first ascents of the South Face of Cho Oyu in Tibet and the highest mountain in Bhutan, respectively. The BBC made documentaries of both trips.

But it wasn't until 1987 that Lydia began what was to become a lifelong love affair with the 8000m peaks. She began with a bold alpine-style ascent of Gasherbrum II in Pakistan as part of a multinational team, becoming the first Australasian woman to summit one of the world's 8000m mountains, and possibly making the first oxygen-free ascent of such a peak by a woman. She was back in Pakistan in 1988 with Rob Hall, Gary Ball and Bill Atkinson to attempt K2, the world's second-highest peak. The team was to follow this with the Southwest Ridge of Everest. Six times they fought their way to the upper slopes of K2, only to be turned back by bad weather. They moved on to Everest, where Lydia had a falling out with the men, who left for home. She went on to reach the summit of Everest alone and without bottled oxygen, becoming the first woman to do so and, to date, the only Kiwi to have climbed Everest oxygen-free.

Lydia returned home to a maelstrom. Her male teammates refuted her ascent, saying it was impossible she could have climbed Everest in the time frame she was claiming. A team of Italian alpinists had seen her on the South Summit crawling on her hands and knees and in no state to go on, they said. Disillusioned, she moved away from mountaineering for more than a decade and trained to be a physiotherapist. In the meantime, British climber Alison Hargreaves made a much publicised climb of Everest without oxygen and claimed the 'first female' title. But as Lydia eased herself back into alpinism in the late 1990s, evidence supporting her ascent was made public and her claim was finally accepted.

These days, Lydia works as a mountain guide and physiotherapist. Her guiding has taken her to Mongolia, Tibet, Argentina and Nepal. In 2004, she guided Cho Oyu, claiming her third 8000m peak, and in 2008 climbed Everest for the second time, guiding for Adventure Consultants, the company originally established by her former teammate Rob Hall, who lost his life on the mountain in 1996. She has done a smattering of climbing for herself since re-entering the mountaineering world, including an attempt on Beka Brakai Chhok (Pakistan) in 2007 (with me) and an attempt on Nyambo Konka (China) with Kiwi climber Penny Goddard in 2009. She has also since climbed on the Antarctic Peninsula.

During the period Lydia was putting her climbing career on hold, two other young Kiwi women were making themselves known, both in New Zealand and on the international scene, with their boldness and enthusiasm for the mountains. One was Erica Beuzenberg, who made her name by climbing all twenty-nine of New Zealand's 3000m peaks in the winter of 1989 with guide Gottlieb Braun-Elwert, in preparation for her first mountain guide examination. She went on to make the first winter ascent of the Balfour Face of Tasman by a woman, and in 1993 climbed the Supercanaleta route of Cerro Fitz Roy in Patagonia with Braun-Elwert – another first female winter ascent. It was in that year that she featured on the cover of the yearbook of the German Alpine Club, the largest mountaineering organisation in the world. Erica was also a superb skier and a qualified guide, who tragically died in a guiding accident in 2005.

The other young woman to shine, especially on steep technical ice routes, was my friend Karen McNeill. Born of central North Island farming stock, she began climbing in earnest when she moved to Christchurch in the early 1990s. However, waterfall ice is a rare commodity in New Zealand, and any climber with a keen desire to excel in the sport has to look further afield, as Karen did. In 1995, she quit New Zealand and headed to the Canadian Rockies, married in order to stay put, and as quickly ditched the husband. She then methodically set about becoming one of the leading female ice-climber alpinists in the world. She'd climbed hard in New Zealand but in Canada she stepped up a notch.

For two seasons Karen concentrated on ticking off the major classic waterfall ice routes in the Rockies, before heading to the Himalayas in 1996 as part of a Canadian all-female team. She missed out on summitting Cho Oyu, turning back at 7600m, but was successful on the more technical Ama Dablam. Back in Canada for the 1997/98 winter, her growing reputation won her an invitation to compete in the ice-climbing competition at the Winter X Games at Crested Butte. She trained hard and placed on the podium, finding herself US$1000 the richer for her efforts. Not only that, but she made valuable contacts amongst the other female competitors. She completed a second competitive season, then, intent on another expedition, headed south to Peru with a popular and diminutive American climber called Sue Nott. With a grant from the Canadian Himalayan Foundation and sponsorship from Mountain Hardwear, the pair made successful ascents of Pisco and the famous Jaeger route on Chacraraju before trench foot forced them home a week early. At the time, neither realised that this partnership, both with each other and with Mountain Hardwear, would become the backbone of their climbing careers.

In 2000, Karen and Sue failed on the famous East Ridge of Shivling (India), which at the time had been ascended only twice. After five days of battling the route they conceded defeat, realising they'd bitten off more than they could chew. They consoled themselves with climbing the standard West Ridge, happy in the knowledge they were the first party to summit the mountain that season.

Karen had been on further successful expeditions to South America and Greenland when I met up with her to climb in Alaska in 2002. We hadn't seen each other in a number of years, but had been friends in New Zealand and in 1993 had had a great day out on the West Face of Dilemma, making the first female team ascent of the peak (see Chapter 2). We knew we could climb well together. By now Karen was quite famous, and I was in awe of her. She was more confident and self-assured in her ability to cope with the really big mountain routes, and calmer. I, on the other hand, hadn't been mountaineering outside of New Zealand in years. I felt out of my depth. We were joined by Kiwi mountain guide Anna Keeling and her lovely husband, Scottie. Anna had also being living in North America, and I felt like a Kiwi hick. Scottie and I were to climb together while Anna and Karen paired up. As it was we had a wonderful trip, first climbing the Nettle–Quirk route on the West Face of Mt Huntington as a foursome. After that, Karen and I went on to make an ascent of the more committing Colton–Leach route, also on the West Face, in a thirty-hour non-stop push. Both were steep technical ice routes.

In 2004 Karen went to Alaska with Sue Nott, and they made the first female team ascent of the famous Cassin Ridge of Denali. While poor weather confined all other climbers to their tents, Karen and Sue battled it out on the route for twelve days, spending the final four without food. At that point I began to wonder about the pair's motivation, as they'd pushed the envelope on Shivling and now on the Cassin. Sue especially was known to be extremely driven.

Another woman climber who quit Antipodean shores early in her climbing career was Julie-Ann Clyma. If there is one person in New Zealand's modern climbing history who has truly put Kiwi women climbers on the map with her technical ability and capacity for footing in with the best, it's Julie-Ann.

Originally from Dunedin and now living and working as a mountain guide in Switzerland, Julie-Ann left New Zealand in 1985 and, probably because of this, has accumulated over the past two and a half decades a mountaineering résumé unsurpassed by any other Kiwi climber, male or female. She is without a doubt one of the best exploratory high-alpine women climbers in the world today, if not the best. And she is New Zealand's best climbing export.

After a brief introduction to mountaineering in New Zealand in the mid-1980s, Julie-Ann left for a climbing trip to Peru and then moved on to the UK, where she met her husband, mountain guide Roger Payne. She has been on an expedition almost every year since – to Peru, Pakistan, India, Alaska, Nepal, Kazakhstan, China and Tibet. These have included several first ascents and/or first New Zealand ascents. On top of this, Julie-Ann completed her International Federation of Mountain Guide Associations (IFMGA) certification and gained a PhD from the University of Manchester.

Julie-Ann claims she originally started climbing 'by accident', as her first love was ballet. But an introduction by a friend to the sport and a climb of Mt Sealy in Mount Cook National Park left an indelible impression on her. For years she juggled a research vocation in public health with training for her guiding qualifications and yearly mountaineering expeditions with Roger.

'There was a constant tension between wanting to do as much climbing as possible and keeping involved in the research world,' she said. 'Luckily, I've been given lots of leeway by my employers to allow me to do both. These days I guide full time.'

Julie-Ann's first foray to the Greater Ranges was in 1987, when she was invited on a British expedition to Pakistan to attempt Gasherbrum VI and Gasherbrum II. Unsuccessful but undeterred, she climbed Mt McKinley, or Denali, in Alaska the following year, then made an ascent of Lobuje East in Nepal. In 1991, she became the first non-Russian woman to climb Khan Tengri and Pobeda in what is now Kazakhstan, for which she was awarded a Winston Churchill Travelling Fellowship. She returned to Pakistan the following year to climb a number of sub-6000m peaks and attempt a new route on the Southwest Face of Broad Peak. An attempt on K2 in 1993 was curtailed by severe weather and accidents to other parties. In 1994, she summitted Nanda Devi East, in India, and said she really fell in love with the mountain:

It's described by Tom Longstaff as the most romantic mountain in the world, surrounded by a legend of inaccessibility. Not only is it remote and physically difficult to get to, but since 1982 the Nanda Devi Sanctuary has been closed for environmental protection. The challenge of trying to get permission to get there was irresistible. The struggle we had to climb it means the ascent was that much more satisfying.

Julie-Ann says the struggle came about because the original route the team intended to climb was out of condition. Nearly two weeks into the four-week trip they had to move to an adjacent valley and start the ascent again – great in theory, but a lack of porters meant triple load carries to get there. Despite this, the new route proved so dangerous the team couldn't justify it. By now they were feeling desperate and the prospect of climbing to 7434m was looking remote. But their liaison officer gave them permission to climb the South Ridge, and after an acclimatisation trip up to 6500m to recce the route, the team managed to get to the top in a last-minute seven-day push just before the weather broke down, to make the first alpine-style ascent of the mountain. They got back to base camp four hours before the porters arrived for the walk out. Julie-Ann remembers, 'We got to the top just as the sun was setting behind storm clouds – the only people on the mountain, the only people for miles around – and the sense of isolation and the beauty of the place was overwhelming.'

However, Julie-Ann's most memorable trips were in 1996 and 1997, to the North Face of Changabang in India. Inspired early on in her career by Peter Boardman's book *Shining Mountain*, which tells the stupendous story of the first ascent of the North Face, Julie-Ann leapt at the chance to give Changabang a go. Although she didn't make it to the top, she says she values the experiences she had on the face: 'The climbing was outrageously good, the best, most sustained and hardest I've done at altitude. We didn't get off lightly though – the weather was terrible the second year and conditions dangerous and one of our friends was killed on the descent. So I think of that trip as being both the best and the worst I've experienced.'

After her Changabang years, Julie-Ann went back to India to try the East Face of Meru, and then made two attempts on Pumari Chhish in Pakistan in 1999 and 2000. In 2003, she was in China with Roger, where the pair made a very tough technical first ascent of Mt Grosvenor in the Daxue Shan range. In 2004, the pair made the third ascent of the South Ridge of Chomolhari, in southern Tibet, then in 2005 went to Sikkim in eastern India.

We were very lucky to meet some young climbers from the Sikkim Amateur Mountaineering Association (SAMA) in 2004, and in 2005 we went back to do a joint expedition with them. Because of the military presence on the border it was not possible to get permits for the higher border summits, but we went to West Sikkim and had great fun making a first ascent of a smaller peak, Lama Lamani (5650m) with them, and then on our own making the first alpine-style ascent of Thinchenkang [Thingchinkhang] (6010m).

In 2006, Julie-Ann and Roger returned to West Sikkim to attempt the first ascents of Koktang (6147m) and Ratong (6679m), but unfortunately summitted neither owing to 'bad weather and horrible snow conditions'. They returned again in 2007, and this time got permission to enter North Sikkim to climb Brumkhangse (5635m) and two other 5500m summits. In 2008 and 2009, they made return trips to North and West Sikkim, respectively, guiding small teams and again being able to make first ascents on 5500m summits.

Julie-Ann has a firm philosophy on her climbing. Although she has attempted three 8000m peaks, she differs from Lydia in that they have not been, and won't be, her main focus. She says, 'There are so many people around you always doing stupid things which can end up putting you at risk. I decided I would rather concentrate on lower peaks and try to make first ascents or do new routes.'

The things that motivate Julie-Ann towards climbing have been fairly constant over the years, she says. She loves the technical interest of climbing – how to make the next move, which line to try – and the physical nature of the sport:

> The pleasure of movement on rock when it's really flowing. Pushing your body really hard on expeditions to see how far you can go. Then there are the aspects of enjoying the environment … And you can't ignore the emotional or spiritual aspects – going climbing helps to put the rest of your life in perspective. It makes you realise how much you have.

These days Julie-Ann says she still feels driven, but in a different direction. After twenty-five years of expedition climbing she wants to focus on her rock climbing. For the first time in many years, 2010 saw Julie-Ann and Roger not in the Greater Ranges, but on a rockclimbing road trip in the US. 'After 2010, who knows,' she says.

The successes of these individuals indicate to me that it has been women rather than men – albeit a small group of them – who have carried the

New Zealand flag in the international mountaineering arena over the past two decades. (The exception to this is Athol Whimp, who won the coveted Piolet d'Or for his ascent of the North Face of Thalay Sagar with Australian Andrew Lindblade in 1996.) No Kiwi male has been as active as Julie-Ann in the exploratory field of high-altitude first ascents. No Kiwi male has climbed as much ice or managed to field as much sponsorship for their efforts as Karen. And no Kiwi male has climbed Everest without oxygen like Lydia. Obviously Kiwi women have the potential to be successful mountaineers, so why aren't there more of them?

In the early 2000s, I was teaching outdoor education. One of my outdoor leadership students was Harriet Walsh, an athletic, motivated and a very talented kayaker. Despite her obvious natural talent for mountaineering, Harriet did not want to continue with the sport beyond what was required of her course. She later told me:

> I've been thinking about why I didn't carry on with the mountaineering. I actually found it really hard to answer as there wasn't any real obvious reason. There's the hard work factor … it is bloody hard work, and you need to be super fit to do it otherwise the consequences can be worse than just not being fit for a netball game. I also find it scary. Too many unknowns for me I guess. Too risky.

Christchurch mountaineer Shelley Graham, who is small in stature but has a strength that belies her size, feels the lack of women in the sport is because they aren't prepared to put in the time to gain the required fitness, strength and skills. Women also tend to underestimate their ability to cope and keep up with men, and don't have the confidence to go solo or take a lead role, she said.

> It's a vicious circle – if there aren't many women climbers around then there is less awareness of women's ability to excel and less chance for women to learn off each other. So often we are our own worst enemies and underrate ourselves. We tend to stick with what we know or follow rather than lead, subconsciously perpetuating society's expectations.

Mountain guide Anna Keeling pared it down further. She said she thinks women are naturally more risk-averse than men and alpine climbing 'can be downright scary'. 'My women friends who are alpinists are all A-types, confident, athletic, fit, strong and driven. Women have to be pretty motivated and tough to stick it out in this sport,' she added.

Lisa Auer, who trained as a mountain guide in New Zealand but now runs a guiding business with her husband in Europe, had no qualms in stating bluntly that the lack of women mountaineers 'relates directly to the fact that mountaineering is a high-risk activity'. She continued, 'I think generally women have a different tolerance of risk-taking to men. Perhaps it is a combination of things (nature and nurture) – a biological connection, perhaps partly influenced by society's expectations, family roles, women's physical size and strength, women's psyche vs men's. Slaying dragons and conquering mountains are, at least mythically, a means of demonstrating manhood.'

So are women innately more risk-averse than men? There are endless studies to suggest that this is the case, not only in the outdoor arena but also in business, finance, sex and vocation. So how and why are women like me, Lydia, Karen and Julie-Ann, who have decided on alpinism as a major focus in our lives, different?

I recently came across a 2009 article by Chris Green and Kevin Rawlinson in the American newspaper *The Independent* titled 'Ruthless women have extra testosterone, scientists show: Tough women bosses break the glass ceiling with help from male hormone'. It states that US scientists have found that women with higher levels of testosterone are more likely to pursue risky careers in business and finance. The authors say this demonstrates just how important the hormone is in defining the differences between the genders. While earlier studies have shown that people with high testosterone levels are typically more competitive and dominant, this is the first time the hormone has been proven to have an impact on career choice. I wondered if this applied to women in mountaineering, or other extreme sports for that matter. Do serious and competitive female mountaineers have a top-up of male hormone? The thought of Lydia – who wears make-up at base camp and hangs beautiful lacy underwear in bushes by her tent – being told she has an extra dose of testosterone was alarming.

But seriously, maybe there was something here I'd been missing? The notion that the women who don't flourish as alpinists are actually scared stiff in the mountains through no fault of their own other than an innate aversion to risk was something I'd never considered. Fear can be a destructive and paralysing emotion. I began to change my expectations of women climbers, more so when my sister Christine – whom I'd always touted as the most naturally talented female climber I knew and an exemplar of what women could do in the alpine arena if they put their mind to it – stopped climbing. When I asked her why, she was vague, but eventually revealed that she found it 'just too scary'.

Another issue that periodically raises its head is the role of motherhood in mountaineering. It's interesting to note that neither Lydia, Karen or Julie-Ann, nor Freda du Faur, Katie Gardiner or Annette Lindon, had or has children. Jane Thomson had a son, but he died as a child. Even Karen McNeill, who had a passion for children, who was drawn to teach socially disadvantaged kids on Native Indian reserves in Canada and who anguished over the lives of the infants she met in developing countries, repeatedly baffled her friends with the anomaly of not wanting to be a mother. 'Oh God no,' she'd say. 'I'm a climber, not a mother, always will be.'

But why can't women be both serious climbers and mothers? In Colorado-based mountaineer Ellen Miller's opinion, the issue of children is something that directly affects the gender imbalance in alpinism. After interviewing about sixty women who had summitted Everest, she found that most of them did not have children at the time they were climbing. 'For me personally, and I think for many women, either you want to climb or you want to have a family. I don't think many women can do both very well,' she concluded. 'And when they do, there can be consequences.'

When British climber Alison Hargreaves died on K2 in 1995, her husband faced a barrage of comment about her fitness as a mother. Alison had two small children. Three months prior to heading to K2, she climbed Everest without oxygen. She was touted as a national heroine to be proud of – and then she was dead. With her death she became the focus of vitriolic media attention, which stripped her of her heroine status and condemned her for the irresponsibility of leaving two small children motherless. A debate on motherhood, ambition and risk raged around both the climbing and non-climbing worlds.

David Rose and Ed Douglas, who wrote Alison's biography, *Regions of the Heart*, claimed that the ferocity with which the media portrayed her was evidence of the unequal treatment given to women who choose to raise a family and also climb, compared to men. Most literature written by male mountaineers rarely, if ever, mentions the subject of fatherhood, families or any concerns regarding their participation in a sport that could potentially leave their children fatherless. Nothing negative is mentioned of the fathers who die climbing. If and when the issues surrounding families and parenting are raised in climbing literature, it's usually by women. Lene Gammelgaard, who survived the 1996 Everest tragedy in which Rob Hall and seven others lost their lives in one day, is one such example, saying in her book *Climbing High*: 'I cannot respect men who have kids and simultaneously participate in this deadly game. I imagine when I have kids I will give up the race to summit the fourteen 8000m peaks'.

The media slammed Alison as a selfish woman who thought only of herself, who was commercially driven and who led a life where climbing came first. But before her climb of K2 she wrote in her diary, 'It eats away at me – wanting the children and wanting K2. I feel like I'm being pulled in two.' She also told Rose and Douglas that her deepest fear 'was getting frostbitten hands and being unable to hold her children'. In a public interview in 1994, Alison said:

> Everybody takes risks in whatever they do and for some people the risks are higher. I certainly wouldn't want to see my children without a mother. Or even worse a seriously incapacitated mother through frostbite or brain damage. But at the end of the day I would not go to Everest because of that. I have weighed the risks and I believe they are worth taking.

This woman loved her children but also felt an overwhelming obligation to the mountains. How much she felt she had to tone down the pain of leaving her children to keep her sponsors happy is unknown. After all, the family's livelihood relied heavily on the money she made from climbing.

Spanish climber Edurne Pasaban, aged thirty-six in 2010 and at the time one of only two women to have climbed all fourteen 8000m peaks, admits she has given up much for her sport – more, perhaps, than her male counterparts. 'The years between thirty and forty are the best ones for a female climber, but they are also the years that our culture dictates that we should spend having a family,' she said. 'A few years ago I faced a lot of family pressure to settle down, and I became quite depressed. But now I am very clear about my goals.' Edurne appears to have forgone children for her mountaineering aspirations, but not without facing a personal crisis that her male counterparts are spared.

Two Kiwi women who have compromised their climbing ambitions for motherhood are Anna Keeling and Laetitia Campe. Anna is one of New Zealand's few fully qualified female mountain guides. Throughout her teens, twenties and thirties she juggled her climbing and guiding aspirations with her talent for endurance racing, competing at a high international level. Anna is a dynamo at everything she sets her mind to, hugely athletic, hugely talented and hugely driven. In her late thirties she became mother to Obie, and her life changed. She said:

I like being in the mountains. I always have and always will. I still want to go alpine climbing but family situations and geography (living in Utah) have conspired against me in the last few years so I make do with rock climbing and backcountry skiing. As a mum I have become more risk-averse. I climbed a classic peak in the Canadian Rockies with my husband about eighteen months ago and it felt like a pile of rubbish. I didn't like us both being there together. I never used to feel like that.

Laetitia, who is also a mountain guide, expressed a similar view:

For a few years after having had children I still managed to make climbing and mountaineering a priority. Soon enough I found it less attractive to leave my kids behind so as to follow my own objectives in the mountains. The exposure to the inherent risk felt wrong. It is so self-absorbing that it is less doable as a mother and probably less enjoyable. My last memorable climb was when I first left my second baby (aged two years) and climbed together with my girlfriend a new ice route on the upper Fox névé. Most memorable for its adventure and fun but also the unease at the risk involved. It felt like I could get away with it then but not repeat it too much.

Anna said she still wants to go climbing and hopes to 'do something with my friend Nancy sometime this year'. She continued, 'We are neighbours in Salt Lake City and both have sons who are fairly close in age. We both still want to alpine climb and plan to do something accessible and not too committing.'

Laetitia, however, is ambivalent:

Maybe women have lives that involve other less self-centred motivations? The risk and intensity of mountaineering only suits certain characters and the sport in itself is very beautiful as it is and can hardly be changed. Maybe there is a time in a woman's life when it is more appealing than another? I seem to have lost the motivation; it's just not so important and interesting any more.

I have no children. There have been times when the issue of motherhood has come up, generally because my age and situation have called for it. Then I've checked myself for maternal sensibilities, found none, checked out the threat to my relationship if I don't have children, found there isn't any, then dug deeper into my psyche for the reason for my maternal reticence. I haven't had to dig far. Quite simply, I don't want to give up climbing, the expeditions, the travel, the mountains. I naturally assume children will see the end of my mountaineering career. Motherhood threatens the one thing holding my existence in its palm, the one thing I feel confident to say I do well. And like Edurne, I'm loath to give this away.

So what's to be learnt from this? That it's morally acceptable for a father to take risks in the mountains that can ultimately lead to his death, but not for a mother? Paul Nunn and Geoff Tier, both fathers and skilled mountaineers, died on a mountain close to K2 a few days before Alison but unlike her weren't criticised in the international press for leaving their children without a parent. It seems that motherhood and a committed career as a mountaineer aren't compatible. Alison Hargreaves tried it, and bore the consequences. But it's vague whether this maternal aversion to climbing is something innate and primal, or rather a factor of the pressures of a patriarchal society. Perhaps it's the former, as when I offered to take my younger sister Ali, mother to three small boys at the time, up Mt Cook for her birthday, an opportunity I thought she would leap at, she declined in the blink of an eye. 'I don't want to be hurt and not be able to look after the boys,' she said.

So what drives those women who do become serious mountaineers? Are their motivations different to those of their male counterparts? I know my personal motivations are many and varied. Of most value to me is the refuge the mountains offer from the anxieties of everyday life – monetary problems, relationship turmoils and vocational hiccups. A long trip in the mountains or a worthy ascent can seem like a wonderful job, encompassing personal satisfaction, a sense of accomplishment and a much needed ego-boost all in one. There have been other times, such as failing to meet a self-set goal, when the job has felt like the toughest imaginable. But these emotions have faded with time, to be replaced with a sense of resignation and an eager anticipation for the next mountain trip. I've suffered from depression for almost as long as I can remember, but the mountains have been an overwhelming comfort, offering me more than any drug or therapist. It's for this reason alone that I'm still climbing after thirty-five years.

On a more cheerful level, I love the physical aspect of climbing, of needing to be fit and strong if the experience is to be anything less than abject physical misery. I love the feeling of being able to move fluidly on rock, or without effort on a long ice climb. I love it when my head is in the zone and I'm able to climb without anxiety.

One of my best days ever was climbing the Caroline Face of Mt Cook with two friends. This required us to front-point on ice for nearly 2000m, but at the time I was really fit and on top of my game, and we reached the summit ridge early in the morning after climbing the steep face ropeless in a really quick time. We were laughing and relaxed, the day was bright and windless, and we scooted along to the summit and down to Plateau Hut, waving gaily to the hapless crowds trudging up the Linda as we left them in our wake. Had any of us been less fit or able, this could have ended up a long, drawn-out and serious climb, but instead it was a joy.

Everest summitter Penny Goddard says the emphasis for her is on the adventure: 'I really enjoy the feeling of exploring. Like I'm on an adventure. I think the drive for adventure is the reason why I climb and choose challenging or remote routes, rather than just "visiting" the mountains in some easier way.'

Shelley Graham climbs mainly with her husband, author Paul Hersey. For her, climbing means the chance to spend time away from the trappings of city life, and to enjoy the scenery. She also likes the physical and mental challenge of 'being in high places'. She doesn't mention reaching the summit as being a priority, but she does admit that her most satisfying day in the mountains was an epic she had on the South Face of Mt Douglas, on a grade 5 ice route:

I hadn't climbed any alpine ice before nor had I done any real winter mountaineering. It was early July and super cold and I climbed with a friend who had done no more than me, so I had to lead more and take on the harder sections. I had never led on ice before. We didn't start early enough that morning so didn't make it to the top before nightfall. I gained a lot of knowledge and confidence in my own decision-making abilities, climbing skills and knowing I could survive an unscheduled night out by just keeping on the go rather than stopping.

In this instance Shelley's satisfaction came from overcoming a physical and mental challenge and making the top.

Anna Keeling also talks of the satisfaction of being able to make decisions in a stressful situation when she climbed a new route in the upper Fox névé. She doesn't mention the summit as such, but infers that the prize for her was making the top against the odds:

> I accidentally did a new route with Laetitia Campe on the South Face of Barnicoat once. It felt really significant because she left her two tiny kids at home to go with me and I was fully on my game and just launched up the face knowing I would deal with whatever I had to climb and knowing that Laetitia had the most amazing head space and would cope as well. It was pretty cool to do that together because we were women and had been friends for a long time and she was a mother of two tinies.

Penny, Shelley and Anna all claim to need the physical and mental challenge of the climb itself – the adventure and the uncertainty – to 'heighten and complete' their mountain experience. It's not enough just to 'be' in the mountains.

I have no problem making it known that bagging a summit is important to me, and neither, it seems, do my male climbing friends. For a male it's acceptable to be summit-focused, but I've found for a female it's often seen as insensitive to the finer points of mountaineering – the sunset, the camaraderie, the satisfaction of just being there. Qualities like drive, self-motivation and single-minded focus are applauded in a man, but are sometimes seen in a woman as unfeminine, arrogant and selfish.

When journalist Jennifer Jordan was researching her book *Savage Summit*, the story of five women who died on K2, she became fascinated by the roles women played in the so-called high-altitude game. She said:

> In my reading of Jon Krakauer's brilliantly told story [*Into Thin Air*, recounting the 1996 Everest disaster] I sensed a certain bias, an agenda, concerning the women on the mountain that year, particularly Sandy Hill Pittman, whose wealth and personality he spent a lot of ink chastising as if being arrogant and rich somehow made her less of a climber. Further, while he seemed to blame Pittman for being a client who survived, he made heroes of the guides who died … Why I wondered, had Krakauer chosen to single out Pittman for vilification and not the men whose choices were, at least questionable, and did that bad air permeate the high-altitude experience for other women climbers?

Jordan goes on to state that just as male soldiers have historically had trouble adjusting to female presence in combat, male climbers have often resisted the inclusion of a woman on their very male expeditions to the high mountains:

Whether it be a biological imperative men feel to protect women or the sexual tension from having a woman present during their three month celibacy on an expedition … most men admit that the problem is not with the women, it's with the men not being able to deal with them, but that doesn't help the women who have to deal with the criticism.

Lydia Bradey is the grand example of this vilification. On summitting Everest alone and without oxygen in 1988, she was ostracised by her male teammates and her claim was doubted by climbers worldwide. She arrived home to a volley of criticism, which forced her to retract her claim. She suffered unspeakable misery at the hands of a primarily male climbing fraternity for a feat that, had she been a man, she would have been applauded. 'I was very, very disappointed, by a few people in particular,' she said. 'But it was over twenty years ago: now I don't worry.'

Karen McNeill also used to say that, if not exactly vilified, she certainly felt put down by men for her climbing, and occasionally by male climbers who were close personal friends. She'd brush it off with an 'Oh, they're just jealous', but I knew it troubled her.

Maria Coffey, in her book *Where the Mountain Casts its Shadow*, said women have to put in more effort than their male counterparts for justification and acceptance in the sport. Taking this to the extreme, she said, 'It seems like all the cutting-edge women climbers eventually do get killed. They are just that much more driven. Where a guy might put in 90 percent a woman would try to put in 110 percent.'

Internationally renowned Canadian psychologist, climber and writer Geoff Powter said that often it's the women bitten by the climbing bug who can become competitive with the men, humming to the beat of 'I can do anything you can do … and better'. He said, 'It's usually these who succumb to the backlash created by women's "oppression" in the outdoors, taking it too far, sometimes forgetting why they are there in the first place and then ridiculed for taking risks. They simply put in more effort than men trying to prove themselves … and this can be fatal.'

Unfortunately, this may be the case. Three of the first five women to climb K2, the world's second-highest mountain, died on the descent, and the other two died a few years later on other 8000m peaks. I know when I decided to climb Karim Sar alone in 2009 after my climbing partner backed out (see Chapter 8) that I was terrified at the prospect, but I was even more terrified of receiving criticism if I returned home from Pakistan unsuccessful for a third year in a row. Karen McNeill and Sue Nott made the first all-female team ascent of the Cassin Ridge of Denali in Alaska in 2004 completing the route over an arduous twelve days, and pushing on in bad weather when all other climbers in the area were content to stay in their tents. In 2006, they forged ahead on the Infinite Spur of Mt Foraker, one of the most difficult mountain routes in the world, in the hope of another first female ascent, despite losing a pack, a sleeping bag, radio and fuel. Did they feel they had to prove something? I suspect their motivations included a need to justify themselves as equal to the other seven male teams who had climbed the route.

I won't say I've felt vilification – this is a powerful and emotive word – but for most of my climbing career I have felt a need to live up to my male counterparts. Not just in mountaineering either, but also in the kayaking arena. When Mick Hopkinson made the first descent of the grade 6 Nevis Bluff rapid on the Kawarau River in 1990, no one repeated the feat for a year, cowed by Mick's superior skills and his reputation as one of the world's great kayakers. When I made the second ascent in 1991 it opened the floodgates for other kayakers to paddle the rapid. 'Crikey, if she can do it, so can we,' said the kayaking fraternity. Which was essentially true, but at the time I saw it as a put-down.

In mountaineering, most of the negative feedback I've had is from younger men. Recently I was in Plateau Hut at Mt Cook and became embroiled in an argument with a young and inexperienced male guide. He lambasted me for winning a Sport and Recreation New Zealand (SPARC) grant for two of my recent expeditions to Pakistan, when he had been unable to get a grant for a ski mountaineering trip in the South Island. The SPARC Hillary Expedition Fund is for 'cutting-edge' expeditions that showcase New Zealanders as being 'world leading in their field'. The guide couldn't understand why my expeditions had more winning potential under those simple criteria than his, or that my thirty-five years of climbing experience made me more capable of a cutting-edge achievement.

These days I try to let the criticism go. More often than not, I get support and encouragement from men – not so much from New Zealanders, but certainly from the international climbing community. And as New Zealand lags well behind in mountaineering standards, this means a lot to me. I get a kick when my climbs feature on a Polish or Italian website, when I'm approached by an American climbing magazine or British journal for a story, or when my gear reviews feature in an international catalogue. After thirty-five years of hard graft, I feel I've earned some respect.

Almost a hundred years ago, Freda du Faur and her compatriots were at the forefront of New Zealand climbing, breaking down the barriers of gender and age to prove that women had the capabilities to be top mountaineers, despite the social restrictions of the Edwardian era. Freda said in her book, *The Conquest of Mt Cook and Other Climbs*:

> I was the first unmarried woman who had wanted to climb in New Zealand, and in consequence received all the hard knocks until one day I awoke more or less famous in the mountaineering world, after which I could and did do exactly as seemed me best …
>
> It is some consolation to have achieved as much as this, and to have blazed one more little path to the ever-growing beacon lighted by the women of this generation to help their fellow-travellers climb out of the dark woods and valleys of conventional tradition and gain the fresh, invigorating air and wider view-point of the mountain-tops.

What was it that made these Edwardian women shine in a field so alien for their time and gender? There must have been more to it than their childless state, endless free time and money to burn. Perhaps they rode on the wave of the suffragette movement? After all, only a decade prior to Freda's conquests New Zealand had been the first nation in the world to give women the vote.

Sadly, the cause of women climbing in New Zealand seems little further forward. There are some, like Lydia, Karen and Julie-Ann, who stand out, and who outshine their male counterparts through sheer talent and hard work. But why, in a nation of mountains and opportunity, aren't their more women willing to forgo the risk and take to the mountains? I think Penny Goddard comes closest to the answer:

> I think a lot [of women] simply don't want to [be alpinists]. Most women seem to think it's a bit mad and is the last thing they would want to do. I think the style of mountaineering that New Zealand offers will probably appeal less and less to young people of both genders as time goes on, as

mountaineering here involves a long time commitment, plenty of physical work, many uncertainties due to changeable weather and no guarantee of success. Current generations tend to want more of a 'quick fix' and want rewards more quickly. They may choose activities which don't demand so much commitment. I believe that mountaineering will probably always only attract a small percentage of the population and an even smaller percentage of women than men. This doesn't strike me as a problem. It's just the way it is.

CHAPTER FOUR

On Thin Ice

Courage is the mastery of fear, not the absence of fear. – Mark Twain

Ice is a rare commodity in New Zealand: our climate is too maritime and too warm, and our mountains aren't high enough. The waterfalls that freeze in winter do so for only a short time before the spring sun peeps over the horizon and the ablation begins. The south faces of some of our highest peaks – Cook, Hicks and Tasman, Douglas and Aspiring – sport long-lasting alpine ice and offer climbers a sublime winter challenge, but by midsummer these routes have largely deteriorated into walls of steep, crumbling greywacke rock. Enthusiasts of the Darran Mountains in southern Fiordland insist the area will come into its own as the ice-climbing Mecca of the future, but I have my doubts; climate change, if there is such a thing, could put an end to that.

Consequently, if a Kiwi mountaineer gets a dozen days climbing on ice per annum, he or she is doing well. In reality, to be really good at climbing this medium, it's necessary to spend some time overseas. Karen McNeill realised this early on in her climbing career and left for North America. She never looked back, and within a short time had become one of the best female ice climbers in the world. Other Kiwis who've headed to Canada to climb ice have come back more proficient and better able to tackle New Zealand's ice routes with speed and competency.

In the late 1970s and early 1980s I made ascents of some of the country's classic south face ice routes, the Central Couloir of Douglas, the South Face and White Dream routes on Cook, and the Right-hand Icefields on Hicks being those of which I was most proud. I repeated them again in the 1990s, but this time in better style. During the original ascents, I'd never felt really comfortable – the routes had taken many hours, two had ended in enforced nights out, and I'd usually left the majority of the leading to my climbing partner. My harness (a swami seat made from inch-wide nylon webbing) invariably worked loose, I was always tightening my crampon straps, and I felt permanently in danger of dropping my 70cm straight-shafted wooden ice axe and my coveted North Wall hammer because there was nowhere on the swami seat to hitch them. Add to that the extended time it took to place the state-of-the-art galvanised ice screws of the day, with their minimal thread and lack of a sharp point, and a day out on a south face would be for me a long, protracted affair.

When Karen left for Canada in 1993 I was on the brink of a serious love affair with rock climbing, which would distract me from the mountains for a while. By the time my partner Andy and I left New Zealand for a nine-month sabbatical in 1998 (he was an academic), I'd rock climbed in Europe and Asia, and had had a dozen trips to Australia. The ensuing five months of the sabbatical, first in Sheffield, the home of UK rock climbing, and then Boulder, Colorado, another world-renowned rockclimbing destination, were everything I'd hoped they'd be. I climbed daily and climbed well. When we drove north to Canada for the last four months of Andy's academic leave, we were excited about our season passes to Lake Louise Ski Resort. Winter had arrived and we settled into a warm house in Canmore, from which Andy would commute to Calgary University, 100km east along the freeway. Two days later we were skiing.

Along the forty-minute drive to Lake Louise, frozen waterfalls flourished either high on the mountain sides or in drainages close to the road. It wasn't long before curiosity got the better of me. I needed to try this odd sport of climbing frozen waterfalls, so rare in New Zealand. I bought the local guidebook *Waterfall Ice: Climbs in the Canadian Rockies*, by Joe Josephson, and poured over it, inspecting the information and photos carefully.

'Winter climbing in the Canadian Rockies can be an intensely rewarding experience,' Josephson wrote, 'a place few can match. Climbing in the Rockies can also be very sobering – the mountains are big, the hazards and challenges are many.' Then 'avalanches are the single greatest hazard to ice climbers in the Canadian Rockies. The majority of the climbs are at least partially threatened by avalanches.' And 'the Rockies are legendary for extended Arctic fronts. Temperatures can plunge within a few hours to -30°C.' And finally 'this guide book covers an area of 30,000 sq km and contains 800 routes, one of the greatest geographic areas of any climbing guide in the world'.

'I need to find myself a climbing partner,' I told Andy, 'and preferably a local, someone who knows what this place is about.'

My first day waterfall ice climbing dawned cloudless; not a puff of wind disturbed the drifts of powder snow lying on the back lawn, not a skerrick of cloud marred the eggshell-blue sky. I was very excited, if not a bit apprehensive – I was going climbing with Trevor, who had been a very active and well-respected ice climber in the 1970s and who was happy to take me out for the day. We were going to climb Silk Tassel, a grade 4 climb that was 55m long. I had my entire kit ready, including my five battered ice screws from home and my Grivel ice tools, one of which had a straight shaft and a home-made wrist leash.

Trevor arrived promptly at 7.30 a.m. in a large RV. He was tall and wide and had a booming voice. 'Let's go,' he said. 'And by the way, I've just clocked -25°C on the thermometer.'

I was learning quickly that the days that looked the coldest in the Rockies (the days when it was snowing) weren't. It was the days that dawned bright and cloudless that sported temperatures well below -20°C; days when a breath was a shallow gasp, cars refused to start and a belayer could freeze solid. As I held Trevor's rope on the first pitch of Silk Tassel, I realised I'd have to invest in three essentials: a balaclava to protect my nose from the cold; a beefier down jacket than the one I was wearing; and the best pair of gloves money could buy. Shivering, I willed Trevor up the short pitch. No wonder this damn place has so much ice, I thought.

'OK, up you come,' bellowed Trevor. 'You can lead the next pitch.'

The ice on the scrabble up to Trevor was as diamond-hard and fragile as a chandelier, and nothing like the sticky, viscous and forgiving substance I was used to in New Zealand. With each thwack of my tool, it splintered and fell in rattling shards to the ground. It took several kicks for the front points of my crampons to get any purchase. Kick, kick, KICK. I struggled to get the screws out and, to my embarrassment, dropped one of Trevor's, which disappeared into a pillow of snow at the bottom of the climb. I then got myself hopelessly tangled in my home-made wrist leash. To my dismay, by the time I reached the belay, I was hot and bothered.

'And that pitch was only grade 3,' Trevor said smugly.

I looked up at the next 40m of ice. It was undeniably steeper than anything I had climbed in New Zealand – steeper than the Central Gully on Douglas, steeper even than the South Face of Hicks. What had I let myself in for? Could I tell Trevor I wasn't up for it? Should I relinquish the lead? I could … but somehow I didn't want to. I'd give it a try – after all, it was only a Canadian grade 4, which was nothing given that the grading system went up to 7 and, according to Trevor, it was an easy grade 4 at that. I racked the ice screws on my harness, arranged my ridiculous leash as best I could, turned to Trevor and said, 'Climbing'.

The first 10m went smoothly. Thwack, thwack, thwack. Kick, kick, kick. I felt a semblance of control. 'Hey maybe this isn't so bad,' I congratulated myself. 'OK! Time to place a screw.' I whacked the pick of my left tool into the ice, then, realising I hadn't released the lock on my wrist loop, wrenched it out again. I used my teeth to undo the lock and whacked the pick back in.

'OK,' I muttered under my breath, 'now get the ice screw off the harness.' I reached down with my right hand … where was the screw? The karabiner attaching it to my harness had flipped upside down. 'OK, stay calm, sort it out,' I told myself. Fumbling, I righted the karabiner and unclipped the screw, then tried to turn it into the ice, but nothing happened. No matter how hard I pushed, the tip wouldn't penetrate.

'Hang in there,' called Trevor, less boom and more concern in his voice now. 'Ye-aah! This ice is like iron; make a little hole for it with your pick.'

I placed the screw back on the harness, reached for my left tool, used the pick to make a small indentation in the ice, whacked the tool back into the ice, and reached for the screw again. OK, this time, this time …

By now I was fighting panic as my right arm, which was bearing my full weight, was beginning to fail. But the screw went in. OK, now the rope.

'Hey, quick-draw first,' yelled Trev from below.

Oh yes, the quick-draw, hold it together, stay calm. Visions of a 20m plummet, as ice picks impaled body parts and snagging crampons broke ankles, were ricocheting through my head. And my right arm was screaming, screaming for relief. Oh, the rope, where's the rope, I wondered. It took all my nerve to lift the rope to shoulder height and clip it through the quick-draw. Then, Oh my God, I'm safe … for the meantime. I shoved my left hand into the wrist loop, extracted my right from the leash and shook it frantically. Oh help, I thought, how am I going to climb the rest of this pitch?

I did climb the rest of the pitch. From somewhere came a steely resolve not to make a complete Kiwi ass of myself in front of Trevor. He's waiting for me to bail, I know he is. Well I'm not going to, I told myself. By the time I'd reached the 30m mark I'd placed another three ice screws with less drama and more assurance that the first. From here the ice steepened to vertical and ended with a rounded, concave lip. I had one remaining ice screw hanging on my harness.

'I reckon you should just go for the top,' called Trev nonchalantly. 'You're going to get really pumped if you stop and try and place a screw on that next steep bit.'

I looked up at the remaining 10m of climbing. Ten metres, that equates to 30ft – that's a long way to fall. But he's the expert, I reasoned. He knows best. I'm … GOING FOR IT!

Up I went, 3m … 6m … 9m. I was balanced just beneath the rounded top, 8m above my last ice screw … and I was absolutely, fundamentally, prehistorically terrified. 'Trevor, I think I'm going to fall, I'm going to fall off,' I yelped.

'C'mon gal, you can do it, relax and see if you can't place that last screw,' said Trevor, changing his tune.

I glanced down at the screw hanging at my waist and saw my right knee was shuddering involuntarily. Oh God, I don't have the strength to place a screw, I worried. At that I made a split-second decision. The only thing to do was to go on to the top – it was that or fall to my ignominious death. Thwack, thwack, THWACK. Kick, kick, KICK. My left tool reached up out of sight, over the lip. Thwack. No purchase. Thwack. Still no purchase.

'C'mon gal, you can do it.'

Thwack. This time I felt the pick bite and wildly kicked both feet up a few inches. Then I reached over the top with my right tool, and wonderfully, magically, the pick took immediate hold. All I needed to do now was take out my right pick and move it up again. And then move my feet. At that I scrambled to a large pine tree and wrapped my arms around its trunk, thinking I'd never been so pleased, so thankful to finish a climb in my entire life. I began to laugh, and below Trevor whooped and hollered.

'That showed real spunk, gal!' From that moment, I was hooked.

On the back of Joe Josephson's guide is a quote by Barry Blanchard, one of the great mountaineering characters of the Canadian Rockies: 'We've got it here; acres of wonderful azure and chrome ice, so many routes to do … a "destination" for ice climbers worldwide. It doesn't matter how desperate the rest of the world is for ice, it's *always* happening here.'

What Barry said is essentially true. There are numerous other waterfall ice-climbing destinations around the world – Colorado, the European Alps, Norway, Korea and Japan, and even certain areas in northern China are beginning to attract ice climbers. But none has the length of season or reliability of the Canadian Rockies. The Rockies is *the* home of waterfall ice climbing.

The sport first took hold in the early 1970s and has progressed from being 'an obscure diversion for a few fanatics', according to Joe, to a popular and common winter pastime. It was the advent of the pterodactyl ice tool, with its drooped pick, the better for penetrating ice, that really got the sport going. These days the range of technical equipment available is staggering. What's more, a decade ago, bored with climbing just ice, the elite members of the sport began linking smears, chandeliers and free-hanging pillars of ice by climbing the rock between them – hence 'mixed climbing' was born.

More so than other climbing medium, the grading of waterfall ice tends to be subjective and often doesn't reflect the difficulty of a route at any given time. Climbs tend to become easier after the first ascent of the season, which will clean off any chandeliered or fragile ice and create 'hooks', or holes formed by the picks, which can be used again by subsequent climbers. These days, grading focuses on the steepness of the climb and not the more subjective mental aspects or technical difficulty of the first ascent, hence the downgrading of several notorious Rockies routes that were in poor condition when they were first climbed.

Grades begin at 2 and go up to WI6+ (water ice 6+), this being 'vertical or overhanging with no rests, and highly technical'. A WI4 climb, such as Silk Tassel, has 'near-vertical steps of up to 10m, with generally sustained climbing requiring placing protection screws from strenuous stances'. To compare, WI5 climbs have 'near-vertical or vertical steps of up to 20m, sustained climbing requiring placing multiple protection screws from strenuous stances with few good rests'. There is a mythical WI7, but apparently there are no test pieces of this grade in the Rockies.

Trevor said he could climb with me again in a couple of days, on Moonlight and Snowline, two other grade 4s in the Kananaskis, an area south of Canmore. It wasn't soon enough for me, and I spent the intervening twenty-four hours purchasing new gloves, three new ice screws and two new state-of-the-art wrist leashes. Trevor arrived at 6.30 a.m. and as we purred along the freeway listening to country and western music he told me stories from his climbing days in the 1970s. We stopped for a breakfast burger at a rather bleak little industrial town aptly named Dead Man's Flats.

Moonlight and Snowline ran vertically up a steep cliffline opposite an impressive peak called Mt Kidd. It took over an hour to ski along a track to the base, but I enjoyed watching the sun come up over the range and stopped to take photos.

'We can't hang round too long,' Trevor said, 'because these climbs are popular and we want to be first in the queue.' But when we arrived there was no one else around.

'OK, we'll try Moonlight,' he said. 'You're up first.'

As I racked ice screws on my harness, I thought of Silk Tassel, of how muddled I'd been placing the ice screws, and how terrified near the top. 'This time I'm going to do better,' I said under my breath. 'I'm going to keep my head, be organised.'

I put my hands into my new wrist leashes and stared up at the first pitch. A thin 50m hose of near-vertical ice stared back at me

But from the moment I stepped onto the ice, I knew the climb was going to go well. For a start, the day was at least 10°C warmer and consequently the ice had a delightful plastic consistency that drew in my picks and crampon front points like a magnet. My new ice screws cut like butter, my new gloves caressed my hands, and my wrist leashes were no longer my enemy. I flew up the pitch like an old hand.

'I can't believe I just climbed that,' I called down to Trev from the belay, incredulous.

'Yeaahh, pretty impressive, good on you gal,' he drawled back, nodding and giving me the thumbs-up.

Trevor climbed casually up to join me and we swapped the ice screws and karabiners onto his harness. The next pitch was a short, vertical, free-hanging curtain of ice that eased off after about 15m. Trev was climbing with a set of his own home-manufactured ice tools, and I glanced at them suspiciously. The shafts were made from fibreglass tent poles, and he had bolted a spectre onto the end – this is a large metal claw that some climbers like to hammer into the ice.

'Are you sure those things are going to stay in one piece?' I said, trying not to sound too incredulous.

'Of course they are. These are going to revolutionise the future of ice climbing,' he said cheerfully as he moved off the belay and smoothly climbed the pillar. I noticed how relaxed he was standing on the front points of his crampons, how methodically he placed his ice screws, and how easily he swung his odd tools. By the time I'd completed the pitch my arms were deadened with the effort and my right leg had begun its involuntary shudder.

'I've still got a long way to go before I climb like you,' I said, a bit despondent.

'You are doing fine,' Trev encouraged. 'Now let's do Snowline.'

By then it was lunchtime and another pair of climbers was waiting nonchalantly at the bottom. They were mountain guides from Seattle it turned out, and as Trevor and I sat at the base of Snowline drinking coffee from his thermos, they systematically soloed the route and abseiled off. I was impressed. I wondered if I'd ever have the skill and head space to solo a grade 4 route.

'You're up,' said Trev, packing away the thermos.

To my relief, the first pitch of Snowline didn't look steep, but rather than a lovely azure-blue, the ice was dark grey. 'That's cos it's only an inch or two thick, you can see the rock through it,' Trev said. 'So you'll need to hunt around for places to put your screws.'

Something different, I thought, as I took a good swing with my left tool to get me started. The pick hit something hard, and the tool bounced back and hit me in the cheek. A smattering of ice fell around my feet.

'Gentle,' said Trev, 'or you'll knock all the ice off.'

I took another swing, this time with more finesse, and another, then brought my feet up under me. The front points scraped on the rock and I pedalled frantically, trying to find purchase.

'Be delicate,' bellowed Trev.

Be delicate, be delicate. I tiptoed up to the 10m mark, too precarious to dare to stop and place a screw.

'Ahhh … how 'bout some protection, gal,' Trev said nervously.

Oh cripes, where am I going to put a screw? Perturbed, I began thwacking my picks here and there, trying to find a secure stick.

Another 'Be delicate' boomed up from below.

I can't be delicate, I'm about to die, was my internal response. Then I saw something out the corner of my eye, on the rock to my right, a familiar shape. It couldn't be. It was … a bolt! An innate reflex took over and within a split second the bolt was clipped and the rope secured. Trevor and I both laughed out loud. As did the two mountain guides, who were lounging on their packs, watching with amusement.

As Trevor and I skied back to the road end in the growing dark I couldn't contain my excitement. I told Trevor how much I loved the climbing and how grateful I was to him for taking me out. I wanted to climb ice all day every day. 'Can we go out again tomorrow?' I said.

'How about the day after?' he replied. 'I need to do some refinements to my tools.'

Trevor and I climbed together frequently over the next two weeks, ticking off a host of the classic grade 4s: Nothing but the Breast, Essendale Right, Pretty Nuts, I Scream, Guinness Gully, Weeping Wall Left, Coal Miner's Daughter … the list went on. With each climb I became more confident and my climbing became less frenetic, less prone to drama. And the more I did, the more I wanted to do. One evening, as Trevor was leaving, he said, 'I'd like to see if I can still do a grade 5. What say we go and try Carlsberg Column tomorrow?'

I knew Carlsberg to be one of the Rockies' WI5 test pieces that formed every year without fail, and I nodded like an excited puppy. That night I tried to explain to Andy how much I was enjoying the ice climbing. 'Uh huh,' he said, turning away.

The next morning, after a short walk through the trees, I stood at the base of Carlsberg and looked up. I was impressed. The climb was steeper and more sustained than the grade 4s: 60m of dead-vertical ice with a small belay cave at two-thirds height. The view to the sides and above was forest, but I knew that far above was Mt Dennis and that this climb, and a number of others nearby, was subject to avalanche after heavy snowfall.

Trevor started climbing, and again I was struck by how controlled and at ease he appeared. He gave no sign of expending energy, but would pause, look up and assess his moves, then make every stick of his picks, every front-point placement of his crampons, with deliberation. I had seen a number of other climbers during the time I'd been out and about with Trevor, athletic young bucks who shouted at their belayer, grunted 'Aw's as they climbed and trumpeted their success. Trevor was pushing fifty, was portly to put it kindly, and hadn't climbed consistently in years. But even I, a rank beginner, could see who the superior climber was. I just wish he wouldn't insist on climbing with those damn home-rigged tools, I mused.

Trevor reached the belay cave, turned and said, 'I think I'll keep going to the top – should make it on rope stretch.' Fifteen minutes later he reached the rounded crest and disappeared. 'Come on up,' came the call.

I'm going to climb this with Trevor's panache, I promised myself. But by the time I reached the top, 60m later, I was so fatigued my arms were only just hanging on and my knees were shaking. All the same, Trevor congratulated me.

'Not bad going for your first grade 5,' he said.

As I was abseiling to the ground, a Scottish voice called out, 'Hey Pat.' I looked down between my legs; someone in a red anorak and white helmet was looking up at me, smiling. 'It's me, Jonathon.'

Jonathon was a young Scottish climber I'd met in New Zealand a few years before. He was out in the Rockies for his second season of ice climbing. 'Wanna do some routes?' he asked me.

A couple of days later I got a call from Trevor. 'I've had an accident,' he said mournfully. He'd been fine-tuning his tools-of-the-future at a small ice crag, when one had inadvertently dismantled and he'd taken a fall. 'The spectre came off,' he said. 'I've got a badly sprained ankle.'

Oh damn. My first thought wasn't for Trevor, but rather for the loss of my climbing partner. But in the same instant I thought of Jonathon; could his offer of a partnership be for real? He was staying at the Canadian Alpine Club Lodge – I rang, hoping he'd be there.

'Sure,' he said. 'I'll pick you up at 6 a.m. tomorrow. I'd like to have a go at Kronenbourg.'

As we drove up the road in the early-morning darkness, chatting casually about New Zealand and mutual friends, I felt a jolt of excitement. Kronenbourg was a thin grade 6 to the right of Carlsberg, very steep and very technical. It would be quite a challenge for me to second it. I'd checked out the guidebook the night before: 'The first pitch is on thin and unprotectable steep ice for a few metres followed by a free-standing pillar of brittle ice. Then a short vertical section leads to the top.' It was given an extra 'run-out' rating.

'I'm a wee bit n'voos about this,' Jonathon said in his Scottish accent, 'but I'll give it m' best shoot.'

Tucked in behind the bottom pillar, out of the way of falling debris, I cautiously belayed Jonathon as he leaned out and got established on the ice. His face was a mask of concentration. 'Wootch me carefla here.'

I gripped the rope tighter as he made a couple of tentative moves upward, then a couple more, and then stopped. By now his feet were a metre above my head. 'Come on Jonathon, you can do it,' I called after a pause, wondering if it was the done thing to encourage someone of his experience.

Jonathon hung straight-armed on his tools, made a step up, then stepped back down. 'I'm not shoor aboot this,' he said, sniffing. 'I'm going to come doon. What say you lead Carlsberg instead?'

What! But I seconded Carlsberg yesterday and only *just* made it to the top! It would be ludicrous for me to try and lead it … wouldn't it? But then again, why not?

Jonathon helped me rack my ice screws. 'You want to save your best ones for the hardest part,' he said, 'when you're the most stressed.'

Weighted down with twelve screws and twelve quick-draws, I looked up at Carlsberg for the second time in twenty-four hours. Can I do this, I asked myself. Yes, yes, I can. Ten metres off the ground I stopped to place my first ice screw, and waited for the all too familiar flutter of fear to arrive ... but it didn't. Five metres later, I placed my next screw, and still I felt in control. I'm not overdriving my tools, I thought. I'm searching for the placements and looking down for my feet. I'm doing OK.

Twenty metres later I'd placed another two screws and was approaching the belay cave. There I could stop and bring Jonathon up to me, doing the climb as two less arduous pitches. Or I could go straight through as Trevor had. Above the cave was the crux of the climb – did I need a rest before tackling that? No, so far I hadn't reached anything like the same level of fatigue I felt the day before; I'd go on.

'You sure?' Jonathon asked dubiously, as I bypassed the cave.

Ten metres later, the first twinge of fatigue crept into my arms. I paused and gave each a shake, one at a time. A flutter of doubt – will I have enough strength to place the next ice screw? Yes, just think how good it will feel to have made the top, to have succeeded. I inched on, slower, an air of randomness in my tool placements now.

Jonathon saw I was getting tired. 'C'mon, I'm watchin' you, not far noo.'

Oh help, it would be so easy just to rest on an ice screw, I thought. I'm getting scared, I'm going to fall. I struggled up another 10m and reached for a screw. 'I don't think I have the strength, Jonathon.'

'Yes you do, yes you do, FIGHT FOR IT!'

Fight for it. I remembered the battles I'd had on rock routes, when I'd used every ounce of strength, and then managed to find more from somewhere. OK, I'll find it. I climbed on, grimacing with the effort. The top came closer; 5m ... 3m ... 1m ... then I was scrabbling over the top, overwhelmed with relief and elation. I looked down at Jonathon, beaming.

'Wow!' he said, beaming back.

That night I couldn't wait to call Trevor. 'Way to go, gal,' he congratulated me.

Jonathon and I continued to climb together for the next two months. We worked our way through the guidebook, ticking off the three-star grade 4s and 5s – O La Tabernac, Weeping Wall Right, Polar Circus, Kitty Hawk, Whiteman Falls, Red Man Soars, The Sorceror, Malignant Mushroom, Super Bok. Sometimes we got up as early as 2 a.m. to drive to out-of-the-way climbs that had been recommended, or stayed at the small youth hostels dotted up and down the Icefields Parkway, the road between Lake Louise and Jasper. Often Andy came with us and we climbed as a threesome, vying to lead the best pitches. By the time Jonathon left for Scotland, I'd climbed on ice for over forty days. I'd be lucky to get forty days in a lifetime back at home, I contemplated.

With Jonathon gone, I thought I'd be at a loss for climbing partners, but it didn't work out that way. I led my first grade 6 with a young Canadian climber called Rob. Iron Curtain lay a forty-minute ski journey up a scenic 'road' and involved 60m of very steep technical ice. I'd started off 'nervously', I heard Rob tell a friend in the pub later. 'Then she was the bomb!'

Was I the bomb? I knew my confidence grew the further I climbed, and the final overhanging groove was pure joy. OK, it must be time to go for Kronenbourg, I thought when I got home that night. Am I up for it? I wondered what Jonathon would think, considering he'd backed off. Andy agreed to come and hold my rope the next day.

There was a party on Carlsberg when we arrived early the next morning. 'I wish they weren't there,' I muttered to Andy. 'I don't want an audience. What if I make a complete dick of myself?'

'You won't,' he said simply. 'And they're probably thinking the same thing.'

I racked up especially carefully – twelve ice screws, twelve quick-draws – counted them again, tied into the rope, and stepped out around the narrow pillar, into space. Immediately the ground seemed to fall away. Peering up, I saw that the climb was, in fact, in two very thin pillars, each pitted with hollows and fragile pipes and chandeliers of ice. 'You don't want to strike too hard,' Jonathon had warned me, 'or you'll bring the whole lot down on your head. You have to "hook" everything you can.'

Following this advice, I began to hook, slotting my picks into the recesses and crannies, knowing intuitively what would hold my weight, what wouldn't. Then I realised I could stem my feet wide between the two pillars and that way take some of the weight off my arms. Time for a screw … but where? The ice was so fragile, so ephemeral, there seemed nowhere for a solid screw placement. I felt an edge of panic.

'Come on, work it out,' muttered Andy from below.

I forced myself to calm down. 'OK, here's a place for a screw,' I told myself. I moved on up. 'Time for another. OK, here.'

Then it dawned on me. This was the most glorious, exhilarating climbing I had ever done. It was grade 6, but it didn't involve strength; it required finesse and precision, gentle handling, a light, gymnastic touch. It was like rock climbing on ice. And I was climbing it really well. I glanced down – the Carlsberg crew was back on the ground and watching me intently. I reached the top of the climb elated. There were cheers from below.

'Way to go Patsy!' yelled Andy. I was so happy; I wanted to climb Kronenbourg again and again.

From then on I had the confidence to tackle other grade 6 climbs. A visiting friend of Andy's followed me on Pilsner Pillar, a totem pole of vertical ice 60m long. We climbed Curtain Call and had a wonderful day out on the Upper Weeping Wall, where again I was struck by the sheer exhilaration of the top (crux) pitch, a 50m overhanging groove of bulges and recesses that required a bold, athletic approach. We drove into the Ghost Valley and climbed Hydrophobia, a magnificent but lonely route high in a cirque surrounded by towering rock walls. By now I was very fit, and could take as much time climbing as I wanted, knowing I had the strength to hang on indefinitely. I'd climbed for almost sixty days. I was completely and utterly engrossed in my new sport.

What is it that makes people want to take on such a high-risk activity like climbing frozen waterfalls? After all, the outcome of a fall is very serious, as is the likelihood of having ice collapse on your head or out from under your feet. There are times when the sport is quite simply terrifying, for even the most skilled climber. But I knew I wasn't alone in wanting to climb waterfall ice day in, day out. There were dozens of people climbing ice in the Rockies at any one time. Why?

In their research paper 'Life Would be Pretty Dull Without Risk: Voluntary risk-taking and its pleasures', Deborah Lupton and John Tulloch said:

Against the dominant discourses on risk that portray it as negative there also exist counter discourses in which risk-taking is represented far more positively. People ... have raised the positive aspects of voluntary risk-taking. Risk does tend to be associated with danger, uncertainty, threat and hazard but these attributes in certain contexts are seen as positive rather than negative.

These days, most risk in western society is portrayed as negative, something to be avoided. The average person is risk-averse, constantly seeking ways of avoiding risk. This is strongly associated with the idea of a civilised way of life, with its increased emphasis on control and regulation. To take unnecessary risk is commonly seen as irresponsible, even deviant evidence of an individual's stupidity.

But studies of skydivers, young male criminals and female boxers have revealed that voluntary risk-taking is often pursued for the sake of facing and conquering fear, displaying courage, seeking excitement or achieving 'self-actualisation'. It may also serve as a means of conforming to gender or, for women, as a way to challenge gender stereotypes.

Risk-taking is also fundamentally associated with emotion. Involuntary risk results in fear, nervousness and discomfort. But to take on a risk deliberately is to experience a heightened degree of emotional intensity that takes us out of the here and now, the mundane of everyday life. Risk-taking is a form of release; it gives a sense of heightened living, or of being closer to nature, and of breaking the rules that society imposes.

High on Mt Rundle, overlooking the tourist township of Banff, is a group of ice climbs collectively known as the Trophy Wall. It is called this for the obvious reason that to ascend any of the three climbs on the wall is seen as an accomplishment beyond par. The right-hand route is called Sea of Vapours and was first climbed in 1993 in very lean condition. The first to achieve it considered it the hardest thing they'd ever done, giving it a grading of WI7. It has since appeared in every conceivable condition, and can form up anywhere from grade 5 to grade 7 depending on the thickness of the ice. In the winter of 1998/99, it had formed in a thin but climbable condition and I wanted it to be for the pièce de résistance of my first season. Nothing else would do. If I could climb Sea of Vapours, I could go back to New Zealand knowing I'd achieved a notable standard; more importantly, I'd also go home feeling good about myself.

But who would climb it with me? Andy shook his head, saying, 'No way.' I tried a few more friends. 'I'm not fit enough,' said Blob; 'Still having trouble with my ankle,' said Trevor; 'Have to work,' said Rob. But word had got out of a Kiwi woman on the constant look-out for a climbing partner, and I was approached by a tall German with orb-shaped spectacles called Gerhardt.

'Ja, I will come if you do the leading. I'll break the trail up the hill as payback,' he said. 'I'll come collect you at 2 a.m. tomorrow morning.'

We parked at the Banff golf course, the blinking eyes of dozens of elk dozing on the greens breaking the darkness. Their soft barks seemed reassuring as I followed Gerhardt's head torch along the base of the mountain, looking for the telltale drainage indicating the start of the trail up the hill.

I remained with my own thoughts, content to follow Gerhardt as he broke the trail in knee-deep snow, up through the forest and out across the sparkling white slopes to the base of the wall. But by the time we'd climbed the last small bluff and were in view of the climbs, my mind had worked itself into a frenzy of anticipation. I'll be so happy if I climb this, so happy – please don't let me fail.

The three climbs were huge and irregular smears of white, slapped roughcast on the black of a limestone wall. The Terminator (the first of the three to have an ascent) was only partially formed, its frightening free-hanging pillar truncated at half-height. In the centre, The Replicant was broken into three vague sections interspersed with a series of overhangs, from which dangled dozens of grey icicles. Sea of Vapours alone looked a contender for an ascent. The cascade descended two-thirds of the way down the wall, but on the left another smear of ice rose from the ground and between the two spanned a 5m section of wet, featureless rock, which would have to be climbed. I stood and stared, eyes wide, while Gerhardt fussed around with the belay and the ropes. 'OK, let's get this show on the road,' he said, looking at me meaningfully.

The first 30m up the left-hand pillar went without incident. I knew I was climbing smoothly and methodically, and occasionally I'd glance down at Gerhardt for affirmation. He would nod and smile, spectacles glinting. 'Good, ja?'

The pitch ended at an overlapping corner of rock, from which the ice seeped. There was a random nest of rusty pitons in the back, and I warily linked several together with a sling to form an anchor. To my right was the horizontal section of rock, water-worn, scraped by the ice, featureless and very steep. On the other side was a splatter of ice, clinging doggedly to the rock. I took a moment to mull over how I was going to tackle this before giving Gerhardt the OK to join me.

'If I was to climb this in the true mixed tradition, I'd hook the rock with my picks,' I said to Gerhardt. 'But I don't know how. I'm going to have to take my gloves off and climb it bare-handed.'

'It looks ver hard, and the ice above ver thin. Help. Rather you than me,' he replied with a silly grin.

I poked him with my ice axe. Help, indeed.

Committing to climbing bare-handed in temperatures of -15°C isn't a decision made lightly. I'd have done it differently if I'd had any mixed climbing ability, but I didn't. By the time I reached the ice on the far side of the traverse, my gloves dangling from my wrists, my hands were waxy white with cold, and I was confronted with the problem of getting the gloves back on.

'I'm going to place a screw and sit on it, to put my gloves on,' I said to Gerhardt in alarm. But there was nowhere for a screw – the ice was less than an inch thick. I jabbed randomly with my picks, panic growing.

'Don't fall off,' Gerhardt exclaimed sharply. 'You will land on top of me with your crampons.'

By now my arms were beginning to pump with fatigue and fright. I couldn't hold on much longer – what should I do? Climb 5m back into the corner and rest? I didn't think my frozen fingers were capable of climbing the traverse a second time. The only other option was to continue up in the hope a screw placement would appear soon. I was close to tears with fright and frustration, and I looked down at Gerhardt pleadingly.

'Climb on,' he urged, 'Climb on.'

Breathing heavily, I reached up with my right tool. There must be something I could hook up there somewhere – there simply must be. I found a tiny slot in the rock, and pulled on it. It held my weight. I reached up with my left pick; it sank into a small globule of ice. I moved my feet, cringing as I weighted the tools.

'Ja,' Gerhardt said.

I reached up again with my left tool, and this time found a sizeable groove to hook, placing my right pick in beside it. Now my feet, don't kick, slide the front points in. Now stand up. And reach up.

'Ja,' came again from below.

Half an hour later I'd run out 25m of rope, but was yet to find ice thick enough for a screw. I was still barehanded and was looking at a 50m fall. Below me, Gerhardt had gone quiet. But I had calmed; amazingly, I had calmed. My breaths were long and regular, my pick and front-point placements acts of utmost precision, my hands were no longer aware of the cold. All was silent other than the chip and tap of metal on rock and ice. I didn't need to look down, didn't need confirmation from my belayer. I was in a dream, completely absorbed in the task at hand, the here and now. Time had stopped. I was in the zone.

Back in New Zealand, I couldn't forget the experience. The impact it had on me was profound, but I discovered with reading that the 'zone' or 'flow' is a widely recognised phenomenon across many sports. Put simply, it characterises a state in which an athlete performs to the best of his or her ability.

In their research paper, *The Zone: Evidence of a universal phenomenon for athletes across sports*, Michelle Pain and Janet Young described the zone as 'a magical and special place where performance is exceptional and consistent, automatic and flowing. An athlete is able to ignore all the pressures and let his or her body deliver the performance that has been learned so well.' Other terms for the zone are 'peak', 'perfect moment', 'mindfulness' and 'peak experience' the authors said, and cited psychologist Mihály Csíkszentmihályi as identifying ten factors contributing to the experience. These include a clear goal, a high degree of concentration, lack of self-consciousness, a distorted sense of time, direct and immediate feedback, a good balance between the level of activity and the challenge, a sense of personal control over the situation, effortless action, a lack of awareness of bodily needs, and a focus of awareness on the activity itself. This couldn't have described my experience on Sea of Vapours better.

According to Csíkszentmihályi, being in the zone means completely focused motivation. Emotions are not just contained and channelled, but 'positive, energised, and aligned with the task at hand'. To be caught up in depression or anxiety is to be barred from the zone; rather, there is a feeling of spontaneous joy while performing a task. In an extreme state of being in the zone, time slows down and, without making the conscious decision to do so, the individual loses awareness of all other things – time, people, distractions and even basic bodily needs (like warm hands, in my case). This happens because all of the attention of the person in the zone is on the task at hand; there is no more attention to be allocated.

History hints that Michelangelo may have painted the ceiling of the Vatican's Sistine Chapel while in the zone. He painted for days at a time, and was so absorbed in his work that he didn't stop for food or sleep until he reached the point of passing out. He would wake up refreshed and start to paint again, re-entering a state of complete absorption. Formula One racing car driver Ayrton Senna explained the feeling after the qualifying round for the 1988 Monaco Grand Prix: 'I was already on pole … and I just kept going. Suddenly I was nearly two seconds faster than anybody else, including my teammate with the same car. And suddenly I realised that I was no longer driving the car consciously. I was driving it by a kind of instinct, only I was in a different dimension. It was like I was in a tunnel.'

Was Senna's tunnel my dream? I know that up on Sea of Vapours all sense of time left me, as did the fear of falling, any doubt about my climbing ability and any sense of lost control. I'd never experienced such focus on the 'here and now' before, such heightened awareness of what I was doing. Sea of Vapours was my universe, nothing else mattered, and the satisfaction on completing the climb late that afternoon was beyond description. Coming back down through the trees as darkness descended, I felt nothing short of euphoric. If only this feeling could last for ever. If only I could sustain this sense of pride in an achievement, this sense of having performed beyond my hopes.

But when I tried to relate my euphoria to Andy, he was disinterested. I couldn't understand why – I wanted to share the moment with my partner.

'Sea of Vapours must have had dozens of ascents by now,' he said dismissively.

'But that's not the point,' I tried to explain. The point was that I'd discovered a perfect moment; I'd climbed the best I'd ever climbed. It was as if all the climbing I'd done up until then had merely been in preparation for that one pitch on Sea of Vapours.

As we flew out of Calgary, bound for home at the end of the winter, I wondered what I would find to fill the huge gap that was waterfall ice climbing. I'd climbed all day every day for almost four months and reached a standard that had earned me the respect of many Canadian climbers. Jonathon had said, 'How 'bout same time, same place, next year?' Could I take him up on the offer of another Canadian ice-climbing season? I secretly hoped so, and set to work to save the money.

The opportunity to work on a Hollywood film being produced in New Zealand helped the funding; I earned good money but was away from home for months. The same year Dad had a dreadful accident on the farm, putting him in intensive care for many weeks and taking him as long again in recovery. From somewhere he found the resilience to survive despite his age and the severity of his injuries. Any of us could die at any moment, I realised. Our hold on life is so insecure. I decided that I didn't want to go without having wrung every ounce of experience out of my lifetime.

In early December 2000 I flew out for Calgary, to meet Jonathon for my second ice-climbing season. But I went without Andy's blessing.

After finishing on such a high the season before, I expected to jump in where I'd left off, confidently leading whatever grade 6 came my way. This wasn't to be, as neither my head nor my fitness would allow it. Instead, Jonathon and I had to make do with warming up, as we generously dubbed it, on grade 4s and 5s. We repeated our favourites, and hunted out interesting new climbs that required long ski approaches up forested drainages, across frozen lakes or over snowed-in firebreaks. One such was Blue Angel, a much recommended grade 5 in the Castle River Basin, down towards the border with the US.

'The position of the route and the surrounding scenery make this a must visit. One of the best routes in the Rockies,' said Josephson's guidebook. It was also on Jo Jo's twenty all-time great climbs list on the back page, and Jonathon had made it his mission to climb each and every one of these.

'Follow the Castle River logging road for 16 miles until the climb comes into view on the left hand side,' the guide said. Simple enough, we thought, as we turned off the highway in our small hire car. But we'd only driven half a mile when there was a soft 'bump' and we came to a halt. Oh no! The tyres had broken through the surface snow crust and we were bellied to the axles. We tried to go forward – nothing. We tried to go back – the wheels just spun. The only thing for it was to get our snow shovels out of the trunk and dig our way back to the highway, a task that took the remainder of the day.

Not to be outdone, we agreed to be back at the turn-off at 4 a.m. the next morning, this time prepared to ski the 25km to Blue Angel. Equipped with all our climbing gear and a big bag of banana sandwiches, we left the road in -20°C chill under a sublime star-studded sky. We were optimistic we'd be back at the car by mid-afternoon, after having ticked off yet another Rockies classic. But what we hadn't figured on was the surface of the road, polished hard by the previous weekend's snowmobile activity. It was impossible to ski. We skidded and shuffled along for the first 16km, then in frustration decided we'd be better off walking. 'Booger this,' Jonathon said, as he threw his skis into a passing tree.

Several hours later we rounded a final corner, and there was the climb, a beautiful white cascade, shimmering against the green-grey of the forest. But our faces fell. The climb was on the left, as the guidebook had said, but what it had omitted to tell us was that Blue Angel was at least 450m up a steep forested hill, perched on a cliff at the edge of the tree-line.

Jonathon rallied first. 'Never mind,' he said, 'there's bound to be climbers' tracks from last weekend.' Feeling less confident, I followed him on along the undulating road until 1 p.m., when we reached a point directly below the climb.

'OK, where are those tracks?' questioned Jonathon, poking his head in the bushes. There was none. Obviously the climb wasn't as popular as we'd hoped. We began to flounder through the trees, up to our thighs in snow. Every few metres we clambered over a fallen log. Undergrowth whipped our faces and snow fell down our necks. Come three o'clock we stopped for a conference.

'Look Jonathon, it'll be dark in an hour and a half, we've still got 500ft to climb, and that will take us at least another hour,' I reasoned. 'Then we've got to climb Blue Angel, get back down the hill, and walk, then ski, 16 miles back to the car. I hate to be a spoilsport but it's not going to happen.'

Jonathon peered longingly up at the climb. 'I suppose you're right,' he said, after a time. With a last forlorn glance over his shoulder, he turned and began to wallow back down the hill. We were in retreat.

Jonathon and I made it back to the car at 1 a.m. the following morning. Our bag of banana sandwiches was long gone, we were tired, dejected and very, very hungry. After sleeping in the car, we drove to the nearest settlement for a large hamburger breakfast. The town was a far cry from the sophistication of Canmore or Banff. We sat on the footpath munching our burgers alongside some locals, who'd never heard of ice climbing. Once we'd eaten we began to see the funny side.

Aussi Beau Que C'en à l'Aire translates as 'As Beautiful as It Looks', and in my now very tatty guidebook was listed as a grade 5+ climb high on Mt Klapperhorn. Beside it was another climb called Harder than it Looks, ranked as a grade 4. Both had three stars of recommendation but despite this we could find no one among our now considerable bevy of Canadian friends who had climbed either. 'Where the hell are those climbs, man?' they'd all reply. So we set off on the long drive north to find out for ourselves.

Eighty kilometres west of Jasper we pulled into a lay-by and got out the binoculars. There they were, prominent and graceful lines glinting in the winter sunlight, high on the north slopes of Mt Klapperhorn.

'Watch for avalanches in the approach drainage,' Jonathon read from the guide. And, 'it's possible to climb both in a day'.

We crossed a set of railway tracks and began the long hike up the steep, snowy creek bed leading to the bottom of Aussi Beau, which we intended to climb first. Halfway up, we stopped for a cup of tea from Jonathon's little thermos. He tossed it to me, I failed to catch it and it bounced end over end down the slope, gathering speed until it disappeared, with a final teasing bound, into the trees. Jonathon looked sadly after it. 'I hope that's not a bad omen,' he said.

But Aussi Beau went well. I led the crux, a beautiful sustained pitch of intricate chandeliers and overhanging curtains of ice that required a gentle touch. I was relaxed and confident, I was getting back into it, and my head space was improving. To the north the cloud had lifted and, as I roped Jonathon towards me, I looked across at the South Face of Mt Robson, the highest peak in the Rockies. It can't get better than this, I thought. This is the real Canada.

Back on the ground, we rued the loss of the thermos as the sun had dipped below the mountains and the temperature plummeted. 'Right, next climb,' Jonathon said, rubbing his hands together.

I looked across at Harder than it Looks, about 500m away, then looked at the time, 3 p.m., then looked at Jonathon. 'We've got an hour and a half of daylight, Jonathon.'

'Noo problem,' he said as he floundered off across the slope waist deep in snow.

I tunnelled after him and we reached the base of the climb an hour later; in time to watch the sky turn a beautiful orange, then a subtle pink ... then a deep purple. 'Shite,' Jonathon said, at the encroaching twilight. 'Oh well, we've got head torches.'

I laughed. Why not? The climb was 180m, four pitches of grade 4, but we were both climbing well – there was no reason why we couldn't do this in the dark.

At 9 p.m. we were back on the ground, having summitted the climb by moonlight. Across the valley, Mt Robson was a benign silver presence hovering far above us in the night sky. The frozen Fraser River snaked away through the dark shadows of an ancient forest ... to where? A tiny zephyr stirred the trees, shifting the sparkling snow crystals.

'If someone was standing right here a century ago,' I said to Jonathon, 'this is exactly what they'd see. This is timeless.'

A few days later we decided we'd go and climb Cold Choice, a 100m grade 5 situated above Emerald Lake. The guide said the area was 'very scenic', which turned out to be true. It also said, 'the Emerald Lake Lodge remains open in winter and tradition has it to stop for a drink of scotch after a good day of climbing', which appealed to Jonathon's Scottish sensibilities. The climbs were also rated as 'high avalanche potential', but this was the last thing we were thinking of as we skied across the frozen lake at dawn. It was -30°C and we both complained bitterly about our skis' lack of grip and the effects of the cold on the tips of our noses. But the sky was a peerless orb of the lightest blue, signalling a lovely day to come.

As we slogged up the large avalanche cone beneath the route we noticed two climbers skiing across the lake behind us. They turned out to be a pair of Germans, Thomas and Hans, who'd been competing with Jonathon and me for the title of visiting climbing team of the season. We'd crossed paths more than once during the past two months and swapped information on what climbs were 'in' and the condition of the approaches.

They arrived as we were gearing up. 'We'll follow you,' they said, 'once you're up a bit.'

I started to climb, and soon finished the first pitch of straightforward grade 5. From the hanging belay, I took in the scenery – it was glorious. I looked across the lake to the west, where Mts Burgess, Field and Wapta dominated the ski line. Down the valley I could see Mt Dennis and was studiously trying to pick out the Carlsberg, Kronenbourg and Pilsner Pillar climbs when Jonathon arrived on the belay.

'Phoof! Aren't you hot? I'm sweating,' he said, mopping his face with his balaclava. He was right. The day had warmed up dramatically; it must have been close to 0°C now – a rise of 30°C in just a couple of hours. Oh well, it was nice not to be shivering for once, I thought.

We swapped the gear over and Jonathon moved off up the next pitch – again, it looked straightforward and I expected him to be on the top within half an hour. He placed one screw, and had only taken a few steps upward when suddenly, without warning, the sky went black – completely black. A sound like a breaking wave built over the next few seconds to a roar, and something heavy drummed furiously on my helmeted head and back. I was pushed off my feet and hung cowering against the ice wall, reflexively wrapping both fists around Jonathon's rope. For a split second I had no idea what was happening, and then it struck me. For the first time in our eighty days of climbing ice together, Jonathon and I were in an avalanche.

The noise faded and the sky reappeared. From somewhere far in the distance I could hear the Germans shouting, 'Are you OK? Are you guys OK?'

I looked up at Jonathon. He had a layer of snow packed hard in the neck of his jacket, over his shoulders and helmet, and even inside his gaiters. He was frenetically building an Abalakov anchor and I could see he was shaking with fright. 'Holy shite, get me down!' he wailed.

'It's OK Jonathon, we have to stay calm.' He looked at me incredulously for a second, then clipped into the rope and in a flash disappeared to the ground.

Well, I'm not going without my ice screws, I thought as I dismantled the anchor. And I'm damn well going to get that one up there, referring to the screw Jonathon had neglected to retrieve 5m above the belay. I clipped my abseil device onto the rope and hauled up to the abandoned screw, rescued it and zipped to the ground. I found the others hectically trying to uncover our skis, which we'd inadvertently placed in the path of the avalanche. I joined them in the hunt; every few seconds one of us would glance agitatedly up at the climb in anticipation of the next deluge, and there was a collective 'Thank God' when the last ski pole was unearthed and we could move out of the danger zone.

We stood in a huddle looking at each other with raised eyebrows, speechless for half a minute. 'Well then,' said Jonathon, a smile twitching his lips. 'I think that calls for that whisky, don't you?'

By the end of February Jonathon and I had spent over fifty days on the ice. Sometimes we'd climb for two weeks without a day off, and primarily on grade 5 and 6 routes. Nemesis, French Maid, Acid Howl, Suffer Machine … the list of climbs grew, but despite our ever-increasing skill, they kept us at a consistent level of physical and mental suspense. On the odd days we didn't climb I would go to the Canmore gymnasium and weight train for several hours at a time, hoping to become stronger and fitter.

When I allowed myself to think about it, I realised I was trying to relive the high I'd achieved on the Sea of Vapours. It would come by climbing hard and often, and by training, I convinced myself. But despite being a better climber and doing well on many of the difficult climbs, I couldn't rediscover that moment of euphoria. I came close on a couple of occasions, one being a new route I did with local mixed-climbing aficionado Rob Owens on the Trophy Wall. We called the route Stuck in the Middle, and it was so physically and emotionally strenuous I was still feeling the effects a week later. The other was a solo climb of Polar Circus, 500m of grade 5 that I doubt I would ever have attempted had Jonathon not left for home a few days before me. On the final crux pitch, high above the road, I expected to find that same fearless joy, but all I felt was scared – not of falling but of being hit from above by an avalanche. Both of these climbs were fine achievements, but the exultation of the Sea of Vapours eluded me.

I arrived home towards the end of March feeling I'd underperformed, even though my climbing statistics said otherwise. I realised that the old nagging feeling of not living up to self-set standards was still there. What's more, my relationship with Andy was foundering. I tried to explain my need to explore the one aspect of my life I thought I was half-good at, but he wouldn't buy it. He thought my climbing was a waste of money. I was dreadfully hurt – I needed Andy's acceptance and approval more than anyone else's. My doctor suggested counselling and anti-depressant medication to lift my mood, but I declined both. What I thought I needed was another climbing trip to look forward to.

CHAPTER FIVE
The Last Frontier

I now walk into the wild. Might be a very long time before I return South …
I now walk into the wild.

– Jon Krakauer, Into the Wild

In the mid-1990s, American writer Jon Krakauer wrote the book that would set him on the road to becoming one of the great investigative journalists of the modern era. Called *Into the Wild*, it is the story of university graduate Christopher McCandless, who left his well-to-do family in Washington DC to become a homeless man on the road. He walked into the Alaskan wilderness and set up home in an abandoned bus, keeping a careful diary of his time, his thoughts and his reasons for shunning society. Eventually, he decided 'nature is only a refuge for a short while' and that 'true happiness can only be shared with others', and attempted to walk to the road, only to be forced back to the bus by a flooded river. He died alone from cold and starvation, and his body was discovered months later by a group of hunters. Krakauer said he was haunted by the particulars of the young man's death and spent more than a year retracing McCandless's journey and gathering material for the book.

I was hooked by Krakauer's narrative from the start, but for a different reason. I wanted to know what it was that made McCandless choose Alaska for his ultimate test. Why not Montana? Why not the Yukon or the Arizona desert or the Arctic wastes of Canada? Alaska obviously had a mystique in which McCandless, as an aesthete, saw the ultimate challenge for living out his dream. 'Alaska has long been a magnet for dreamers and misfits, people who think the unsullied enormity of the Last Frontier will patch all the holes in their lives,' Krakauer wrote.

My chance to visit Alaska came in May 2002. Karen McNeill was going there to climb with Anna Keeling in the Alaska Range, and they invited me to team up with Anna's husband, Scottie, as a climbing partnership. I was very excited at the prospect: Alaska promised boundless ice and long, sustained routes, and I was begging to try out my new-found Canadian ice-climbing skills on a really big mountain. Plus there was the aura and mystery that had so attracted McCandless; I wanted to see what Alaska was all about, even if only for a brief while. To add to the excitement, I was offered sponsorship in the form of climbing equipment by a prominent New Zealand outdoor company called Southern Approach and clothing from Macpac. I tried not to mind Andy's obvious lack of enthusiasm for my trip, and worked laboriously on the details of clothing and gear. After all, the Alaska Range was sub-Arctic, it could be very cold, and we were going to be camping for a month on a glacier 50km from the nearest blade of grass.

Alaska is huge – one-fifth the size of the entire United States and larger than the next four largest states combined. The Alaska Range is a great 800km arc of mountains that sweeps across the southern reaches of the state. The central part of the range in particular offers 'some of the finest climbs on earth', according to the Internet. The highest peak, Denali, is the central focus, and attracts hundreds of climbers every year. For that reason, it's easy to organise a forty-five-minute ski-plane flight into the range from the small town of Talkeetna.

Owing to its close proximity to the coast, the range gets some of the most brutal weather on earth. It's situated at 65°N – that's some 4000km further north than Mt Everest. 'This attributes not only to cold temperatures, but a thinner atmosphere and lower pressures, so that 20,000 feet on Denali feels much higher and colder than the same elevation in the Himalaya,' I read, remembering Karen got frostbite on her first trip into the range. And there was continuous daylight in the middle of summer – how strange. But I could hardly contain my excitement – it was over two years since my last ice-climbing trip to Canada, and apart from an interesting excursion to China where I'd spoken to a number of 'outdoor clubs' in Beijing and Shanghai, I'd been nowhere. I was feeling morose and without focus, tired of my career as an outdoor instructor but unable to get out of it. Andy was still at odds with my desire to climb outside of New Zealand. Regardless, I counted down the days until the four of us would meet in the Alaskan capital.

Arriving in Anchorage at 1 a.m. after an exceptionally cheap long-haul flight via Seoul, I was amazed to be greeted by a dusky grey midnight sky. There was plenty of activity around the airport – it could have been Christchurch on a summer's evening – with people eating in the cafeteria, drinking in the bars and crossing the car park with trolleys piled high with luggage.

I set off to meet the other three at a downtown motel in a boisterous mood, but as befitted the hour, they were asleep. The next morning, Karen, Anna and I noisily planned to shop for supplies while Scottie sat in the background with a calm half-smile on his face. We left for Talkeetna the following day in a minivan driven by a man called Hank. I thought he was the archetypical Alaskan, with a huge beer gut, wild beard and long, stringy hair. He was dressed in baggy jeans, a checked shirt and a baseball cap. 'Born and bred Alaskan, I bet,' I sniggered to Karen. But it turned out Hank had only just moved up from New York to escape a career in futures trading. I began to wonder if his name really was Hank at all.

Talkeetna was a quaint little town. I imagined women in pinafores inside the verandahed houses stitching patchwork and making bread while their menfolk chopped wood in the back yard. The town had a prolific mosquito population that rampaged out of control at night, causing a mass human exodus indoors. And it seemed everyone had a large fluffy dog named Sequoia or Inuit. The main purpose of the town was to cater to the crowds of climbers flocking from around the world to climb Mt Denali or, like us, the outlying mountains. Our objective was the West Face of Mt Huntington, and from the photos Scottie had sent me, it was a steep, elegant peak of 3730m covered in lots of ice.

The following morning we lugged a lifetime of food and equipment across the tarmac and loaded it into a little plane owned by Talkeetna Air Taxis. Paul, the owner of the company, was going to fly us the forty-five minutes into the head of the Tokositna Glacier, but I had doubts we'd get off the ground, so jampacked was every nook and cranny. Lumbering down the runway, I was alarmed to see Scottie and Paul in an animated, hand-flapping conversation in the front seats. Concentrate, I willed the pilot. Karen, Anna and I sat across the back, bags of equipment, ice tools, helmets and boxes of food piled on our laps, craning to see out of the small windows.

I pressed my face to the glass. Below, dark conifer forest blended with broad reaches of snow and small, half-frozen lakes. Occasionally, the intrusive tracks of a snowmobile scoured the snow; very occasionally, a tiny cabin came into view or the rusting hulk of an ancient truck. Then the terminal moraine of a large glacier appeared. We tracked it west, between rocky peaks. As the mountains grew larger, the glacier turned white, and we followed until it entered a large cirque, at the northern end of which was the graceful pyramid of Mt Huntington. The three of us fought for a view as the plane banked and circled, then lined its skis up with faint tracks on the snow. We landed with a heavy bump.

'My God, we're here,' said Anna in her loud voice. The plane throttled to a halt, and we piled out into the glare of a perfect day, surrounded by very white mountains. In unison we pivoted 360 degrees, holding our hands above our eyes. The West Face of Huntington was directly above us. As the pilot cranked up his engine, we tossed our bags and boxes onto the snow, then the little plane roared off across the névé and was last seen disappearing down glacier waggling its wings. 'Whoa, outrageous!' boomed Anna.

Setting up camp for a month on a glacier was not something I was familiar with, but the others were old hands. We dug a pit and pitched Karen's Mountain Hardwear Kiva (read tepee) over the top – this was to be the living/cooking area. We set up our satellite tents around it, and Scottie dug a 'barbeque' area for fine-weather cooking. We even had neighbours, who came over to introduce themselves and get an update on the weather – Malcolm Bass and Paul Figg from the UK, John and Matt from Minnesota and, most surprisingly, a friend of mine called Dick and his buddy Bill, whom I'd met rock climbing in Colorado. Before we knew it, a cocktail hour was in progress and we laughed and drank tequila mixed with Gatorade into the early hours of the morning. 'This trip is going to be fun,' I giggled to myself when I finally collapsed into my tent.

Although it is overshadowed in elevation by Denali, Mt Huntington is a steeper, more spectacular peak. From every direction, faces drop more than 1500m and even the easiest route is significantly more technically challenging than the standard route on Denali. For this reason it's a favourite with ice climbers.

The mountain was first climbed in 1964 by French alpinist Lionel Terray and his party in expedition style via the northwest ridge (now called the French Ridge). This remained the standard route for the next twenty years, despite a second ascent via the West Face/West Rib (Harvard route) being made the following year by some Americans. In the mid-1980s, the West Face Couloir became a major focus, and was finally climbed in 1989 by Dave Nettle and James Quirk. This has since become the most commonly attempted route to the summit, with several parties establishing camp at the head of the Tokositna Glacier each spring in the hope that a suitable weather window will open up and offer them a chance at the climb. We were one of these parties. Along with Dick and Bill and John and Matt, we hoped to climb the Nettle–Quirk route before embarking on whatever else took our fancy. Malcolm and Paul wanted to do the Harvard route.

Anna and Scottie had brought along a spotting scope, a stumpy telescope on a tripod, which we set up in the midst of camp and spent the best part of two days squinting through, investigating our route. The first 450m seemed straightforward – a steep snow slope capped by a rock buttress that could be circumnavigated on the right. From there, towering granite walls rose up to meet the French Ridge. A steep, narrow couloir of glimmering ice, no more than 30m wide, angled right at seventy degrees to hit the Harvard route at 3000m. Then a broad face of mixed ground and ice slopes reared more than 600m to converge with the summit ridge.

'Then a short walk along the ridge will have us on the top,' Scottie said. 'Lotsa parties spent two days on the route, but I reckon we can do it in one. If we can be up and down in twenty-four hours we'll be doing well. Now, let's get a good night's sleep girls – we'll leave at twelve o'clock.'

Even though I'd been in Alaska for several days it still felt strange to have daylight, albeit muted, when I struggled out of my sleeping bag not long before midnight. I tried to eat granola, but soon put my bowl aside, preferring the strong cup of coffee Scottie thrust into my hands. The sky was cloudless, and I wondered if the fabled diabolical Alaskan weather was, in fact, just that. We marched off in silence, two pairs roped together. There was a muffled 'Good luck' from Malcolm's tent.

Three hours later we were in good spirits, having reached to the top of the snow slope without incident. The first rays of sun glinted above the horizon and the great bulk of Denali dominated the western skyline. To its left was Mt Hunter, on whose north side was the Moonflower Buttress, one of the most famous steep ice routes in the world; I secretly hoped that at some stage on the trip I'd get to see it. Maybe the pilot could be persuaded to fly past on the way out, I wondered. Above us the couloir struck up to the right, like a big arrow. Karen and Anna were busily sorting their ice screws – Karen was going to take the first pitch.

'You wanna lead first?' Scottie asked me.

'Sure,' I replied. I would take a steeper line on Karen's right – that way we wouldn't knock ice down on one another.

As I climbed away from the belay, I felt nervous. The ice was brittle and hard, unlike the pleasant viscous medium in New Zealand. Like Canadian ice, I thought. Thirty metres up, the angle increased to eighty degrees and I began to feel the pull on my arms. What's more, the ice was a fragile detached crust, and made a disturbing 'bong' with every strike of my tools. 'Come on, slow and steady,' I lectured myself when I realised I wouldn't be able to place ice screws. It was with secret relief that I reached the end of the pitch and was able to set up a rock anchor. 'Come on up Scottie,' I hollered.

Scottie made quick work of the next pitch, while 30m to his right Anna thumped noisily over a vertical overlap and began to angle towards the start of the couloir proper. 'Hey, that had me worked,' she laughed in American speak.

By the time all four of us had congregated at the bottom of the third pitch I was also feeling 'worked' myself and wondered how I was going to keep up the pace for the best part of twenty-four hours. But the angle relinquished slightly, the next 300m went easily, and we managed to move together on the rope, placing intermediate ice screws as some semblance of protection. Scottie and I reached the top of the couloir first and hung together on an anchor for a rest and a snack. We were still discussing the surrounding mountains when Karen stuck her head over the lip. 'Man, I'm hooped,' she said.

For the next few hours we wound our way up through steep pitches of mixed ground to the bottom of the summit ice cap. By now it was midday and we were all feeling the effects of twelve hours of climbing. I was out of water and on the verge of calling a halt for a rest when Karen piped up. 'Hey, I really am tired,' she said. 'How about we have a cuppa?'

We all nodded and mumbled appreciatively, and on reaching the summit ridge had a short picnic on the first flat ground we'd encountered all day. Then it was on to the summit, guarded by a 20m-high crevasse wall of soft, unconsolidated snow. Scottie shovelled his way to the top and Karen, Anna and I duly followed.

Sitting on the summit of Huntington half an hour later I couldn't believe my luck. Here I was, only a few days out from New Zealand, and already with an Alaskan summit under my belt. What's more, the weather was superb – windless, cloudless, sunlit. Climbers waited years to summit an Alaskan peak like Huntington in these conditions. I knew a Kiwi who'd camped for a month at the base and never stepped foot on the mountain. How lucky was I!

We sat on the top for an hour while Scottie pointed out the various peaks and routes he'd climbed. The Tokositna stretched away to the east, a snaking river of ice, and running parallel to it were the expanses of the Ruth and Kahiltna glaciers. High in the west, the broad summit of Denali glistened aloof in the afternoon sun. But soon it was time to pick up our tired bodies, gather together our stuff, and go down.

By eight o'clock in the evening we'd abseiled over a dozen pitches and were through the rocky mixed ground. It was good to be back at the top of the couloir, knowing it would be a simple matter now of descending on easily constructed V-thread anchors to the top of the snow slope. Halfway down I inadvertently dropped one of my precious new sponsored gloves, and in my depleted state, I shed a few tears.

'Don't worry. It'll be waiting at the bottom,' Scottie commiserated.

We finally reached the snow slope at midnight, in the twilight. I was ahead of the others, methodically kicking my way down, facing in, alone in my own world of fatigue and satisfaction. An hour and I'll be in my sleeping bag, I thought. Tomorrow we'll rest and eat and tell the other teams of our glory, and they will be impressed and envious.

I stopped at the bergschrund and waited for the others – I needed a belay. Anna arrived first, and we tied into the rope. 'I'll go first,' she said, and marched towards the schrund while I stood firm, holding the rope. She lifted her right leg high in a goose-step … and that was the last I saw of her. In an instant I was flying through the air head first, like Superman; something had yanked me off my feet. Landing on my stomach, I was dragged down the slope. All the while, the thought DO SOMETHING! screamed in my head. I took a couple of cursory stabs at the ground with my ice axe, but the edge of the crevasse rushed closer. I plunged the pick into the snow with as much force as I could muster and skidded to a halt, in a shower of snow crystals, just 1.5m from the lip.

'Anna, Anna, are you OK?' I shrieked, imagining her bleeding and broken at the bottom.

'Fuck. Fuck. Fuck,' came a tiny voice from the depths. 'Get me outa here.'

I looked around frantically. 'Oh Christ, Scottie's got my snow stake,' I panicked, realising I had nothing to build an anchor with. Scottie was still a couple of hundred metres above me, descending slowly. I could hear him singing to himself.

I'll bury my pack, I thought, and began furiously shovelling a hole with my hands. All the while, a barrage of expletives continued to rise from the crevasse. I was just about to ram the pack in the hole and cover it with snow when Scottie arrived.

'Where's my wife?' he asked, looking around airily. 'Has she headed for camp?'

'Um, well, actually … she's down there,' I stuttered, pointing.

'Where?' Scottie questioned, still looking vaguely here and there.

'In the crevasse.'

At that point Anna voiced her opinion of her position particularly vocally. Scottie looked horrified. I continued to pile snow on top of the pack, then attached the rope.

'OK Anna, come on up,' I shouted. The rope began to jerk, and increasingly loud huffs and puffs came from the depths. Then a head appeared over the lip, the helmet perched on it skew-whiff and covered in white. I moved forward and grabbed the back of Anna's pack, hauling her onto the flat.

'What the hell?' said Scottie.

'Yes, well, that was rather embarrassing,' Anna said with a sheepish grin, brushing off the snow.

Back at camp we slept, ate, relayed our adventure to the others, then slept and ate some more. Anna told the story of her plummet in the crevasse numerous times, to much amusement. Dick and Bill went off to try the Nettle–Quirk for themselves, with John and Matt following close behind, but neither team made the summit.

'Boy, that ice was brutal,' said Dick on arriving back at base camp. 'My calves just cramped right on up.'

John and Matt, meanwhile, were almost taken out by an avalanche at the top of the snow slope and made a frightened retreat.

After a couple of days, our team was starting to recover. 'OK, what's next?' we asked one another. To the left of the Nettle–Quirk route was a second steep couloir that joined a long, rising traverse running across the top of the West Face, terminating high on the summit ice field. The route was called the Colton–Leach, because, not surprisingly, it was first climbed sometime in the 1990s by a pair of Brits called Nick Colton and Tim Leach. It was a more serious proposition than the Nettle–Quirk and had seen fewer ascents, but we felt comfortable we could climb it. We left camp at 2 a.m. on the same day Malcolm and Paul headed for the Harvard.

But things weren't meant to be that day. Karen and Anna turned back low on the route. Scottie and I reached midway up the couloir before retreating.

To his dismay, Scottie discovered that one of his boots was grinding a raw wound on the side of his foot, and back on the ground said, 'I need to give my foot a few days to recover. Why don't you and Karen give the route a try? Then Anna and I can do it later.'

Karen and I looked at each other enquiringly. 'OK, why not?' I said.

Malcolm and Paul arrived back at camp, suitably chastened after having failed on the Harvard route. 'Too much loose rock,' explained Malcolm.

For the second time in twenty-four hours I was up at midnight, trying unsuccessfully to force down breakfast. Karen and I had discussed tactics the night before: we would do the route in a single push and take no bivvy gear, not even a stove. 'Keep it light and go fast,' Karen said, and I bowed to her greater experience on long climbs. She wasn't even taking a Gore-Tex jacket – this appalled me coming from New Zealand, where you don't go anywhere without a rain parka. But we were away again at 2 a.m., pigeon-holing up the steep runnels of snow leading to the base of the couloir in the semi-daylight.

The couloir was spectacular – a steep, slick wand of grey-blue ice stretched between formidable granite walls. It had the ambience of a cathedral. High in the upper reaches, impressive gargoyles of snow perched, ready to break off and hurl themselves down in leaps and bounds, until crashing out at the bottom they'd give anyone at base camp a big fright. These worried me, but no one else had voiced their concern, so I kept mine quiet. We could see the cornice running like a curtain across the roof of the couloir and wondered vaguely how we would get through it onto the start of the traverse.

'Let's worry about it later,' Karen said, grinning at me.

'Onward and upward then,' I agreed.

The first ten pitches went without incident. We both climbed well and ran out the rope lengths quickly and systematically. Towards the top, the couloir steepened and we began to wonder where the best place would be to break through the cornice. By now it was mid-morning.

'What about we try there?' Karen said, pointing up to a particular spot where a useful rock was embedded in the overhanging snow. She scratched her way up to the overhang, then paused, obviously thinking hard.

'Hmmm, not sure about this,' she said to no one in particular.

'Have a go,' I encouraged, 'it might not be so bad,' although I was coming to realise that the overhang was bigger than we had thought.

'I don't like it,' Karen called down. 'Do you want to have a go?'

Not really, I thought to myself, but to Karen said, 'OK, I'll give it a shot.'

It was my turn to perch under the overhanging curtain, and I made some cursory thwacks above my head with my tools. A bucket load of unconsolidated snow shook loose, so I burrowed some more, and to my surprise found a solid placement with my left tool. Encouraged, I sketched my right crampon up the rock and slammed the front points onto a small edge, then brought my right tool up beside my left. I was now arched uncomfortably backward and very off-balance, and was fast realising there was no way I could reverse the moves I'd just made. 'Watch me Karen, I think I'm stuck,' I bleated.

'Can you place a screw?' she replied with concern.

'No, I can't let go.' I couldn't climb down; I couldn't place an ice screw; I'd have to be bold … I'd have to go up. With an inelegant lunge I punched a hollow in the overhang with my left knee, then just as clumsily rammed in my cramponed foot. I dragged the other crampon up the rock, at the same time headbutting the roof of the cornice with my helmet until a big U-shaped chunk of snow tipped out over my shoulder. It landed on Karen, who swore loudly. More headbutting, then 'Elbows, use your elbows,' I urged myself. I hitched them over the lip and, flailing my legs vigorously, flopped like a penguin onto flat ground. I lay on my back puffing for a minute while Karen rejoiced below. Clever me, I thought as I stood up, shaking off the snow. We'd reached the traverse.

It had taken us the best part of two hours to negotiate the cornice, and the dilemma had so absorbed us we hadn't noticed the large grey clouds that blanked out first Denali and then the mountains fringing the Tokositna cirque. As we sat resting it started to snow lightly. The temperature dropped. I looked to Karen askance – after all, she was the experienced Alaskan climber. We knew there was an abseil further along the traverse that we wouldn't be able to reverse – once we'd passed that we'd be committed to going forward. And up. 'We should decide there,' Karen said. 'Perhaps the weather will improve by then.' We climbed on.

It took us a further twelve hours to work our way along the steadily rising traverse. The position was astounding; above us, granite cliffs soared towards the French Ridge, while below they dropped thousands of feet towards base camp. We passed the abseil without a word and pressed on, pitch after pitch merging in a blur of increasing tiredness as we battled deep, wet snow perched tenuously over a base of ancient metallic ice. Our situation was serious, but we were in tune – we both wanted this route, even if we had to climb it in bad weather. We pressed on until midnight and reached the summit ice fields of the upper Nettle–Quirk route, realising to our fuddled surprise that we hadn't stopped for a rest since the top of the couloir, half a day ago. I glanced at Karen and burst out laughing – she looked a fright. Her eyes were half-closed and her cheeks and jawline were swollen beyond recognition.

'You're the same,' she giggled back. 'We're oedemic – we haven't drunk enough water. At least the weather hasn't got any worse.'

We hung on the anchor and contemplated our situation. We'd been to the summit of Huntington just days ago, and we were at the point where the two routes joined. Did we need to summit again? No! We wanted down.

Below and to the left of the mixed ground the route fell away for several hundred feet to the top of the Nettle–Quirk couloir proper. Directly below us, steep granite slabs led down to a spot in the upper reaches of the couloir. Could we abseil directly down?

'Do you think we'll find anchors?' Karen said, looking worried.

I wasn't sure, but I knew if it did work we'd cut out several hours of descent. We were both ready to be off this mountain, back at base camp where people were cocooned in their warm sleeping bags, oblivious to the trials of two tired and fractious women thousands of feet above them.

'OK, let's do it,' I said.

The first two rope lengths went without incident and deposited us on a small ledge of snow. The next took us to the middle of a very blank wall, and time passed slowly as I hung frightened on the rope trying to fiddle an insubstantial V-thread into a tiny vein of ice. By now the couloir looked very close, but the rope jammed, and our exhausted brains struggled to resolve the problem. We eventually had to cut the rope, making it considerably shorter. The final abseil was a terrifying diagonal traverse into the couloir; our crampons clawed for purchase on the wall and the threat of a big pendulum and a long struggle back up to the anchor was very real. But at 2 a.m. we were, for the second time that week, hanging on ice screws in the top of the Nettle–Quirk couloir. Only 300m of ice to abseil and 450m of snow to down-climb, and we'd be back at base camp. Simple as that.

Unfortunately, it wasn't as simple as that. Because of the shortened rope we couldn't take advantage of the V-thread anchors we'd built a few days ago and had to make new ones. At one point I abseiled over an overlap into space, and had to climb back up the rope using prussick loops – something I was only *just* physically capable of doing. I dropped another glove. Karen dropped a precious bundle of abseil cord. I dropped one of Scottie's camming devices. We knew we couldn't make any more mistakes, and sat on an anchor to regroup.

'Hey, look!' Karen exclaimed, pointing. I looked around. Far below, beside the tents, there was a group of people. They were facing our way and waving. The basecamp crew – although it was 3.30 in the morning, they weren't snuggled in their sleeping bags but were looking out for us. Cheered, we negotiated the final abseil pitches. There was now only the snow slope to go …

An hour later I sat slumped on my pack at the bottom of the slope watching Karen slowly descend. I was totally spent, and could not remember ever having felt so tired. My glove, I thought, and stumbled half-heartedly over to a scattering of avalanche debris. To my delight, there it was. And what's that other black dot over there? It was my other glove! 'Hey Karen, look,' I yelled, waving them both above my head. She gave a whoop as she joined me. We trudged the final few hundred metres back to camp, where the others were waiting with cups of tea and snacks and congratulations.

'You guys look like death, ha, ha,' Anna said, snapping a photo of the two of us. Karen and I hugged each other and grinned widely. The route had taken us thirty hours but I was happy beyond belief.

Scottie and Anna flew home a few days later, but Karen and I stayed on in the Alaska Range for another two weeks. After a seven-day storm that confined us to our tents, we bumped by plane to an area called Little Switzerland and climbed long granite rock routes. The weather was bleak and unsettled, and by the third week in June we were ready to head back to Talkeetna and civilisation. Hiring a car in Anchorage, we spent five days driving to and from the coastal town of Valdez, terminus of the Alaskan pipeline and home to feral fishermen and a legendary sunken oil tanker. There was little to accommodate visitors like ourselves. Along the way was bleak tundra and low forest, punctuated by isolated ramshackle homesteads ringed by the rusting carcasses of abandoned cars. What do these people do here, I wondered? There was little evidence of agriculture – no animals and no crops – and with 80km between each outpost, presumably no visitors. And the winters, how did they survive these? The people we encountered were sullen, distrustful and ugly. But the drive instilled in me a vague sense of what McCandless had been searching for: a paring down of the basics of existence, a life determined by nature. It was all too easy to imagine a derelict bus, 40km beyond the road, housing a strange boy at odds with society. The drive left me thoughtful and somewhat glum. Alaska was a 'magnet for dreamers and misfits' Krakauer had said, and I was beginning to understand why.

The Moonflower Buttress refers to both the entire northern tower of Mt Hunter as well as a route up it. It was the route I began to dream of: 1200m of extraordinarily steep runnels, rock buttress and ice fields that, if you succeeded in climbing it, elevated you to the echelons of the world's best mountaineers. When I found out one of the first to ascend it was Kiwi mountain guide Paul Aubrey, I went home from Alaska in 2002 gagging to return, even if it was to just set eyes on the route.

But once I was back to New Zealand, the idea of just setting my eyes on the Moonflower developed into a real desire to climb one of the routes on the North Buttress. I read in an American climbing magazine, 'Each season there is a lineup of potential climbers wanting to ascend a route on the North Buttress. These so-called Moonies [from the Moonflower name] can be found lurking throughout Base Camp, posturing and waiting for the right weather and conditions.' I wanted to be a Moonie, I decided, but I needed a fellow Moonie, and pounced on Marty Beare as one of the few people I knew with the capacity to attempt the North Buttress with me.

After a ten-month hiatus, I arrived back in Anchorage with Marty in tow. Nothing had changed; I hardly seemed to have left. Also as part of the team were Karen and my sister Christine, who were going climbing in the Ruth Glacier. As our respective planes warmed up on the Talkeetna runway, we said an emotional goodbye. 'See you back here in a month,' I called to the two girls. 'Be careful.' I was a wee bit worried about them.

Marty and I needed to warm up on something before we tackled Hunter, and settled on the first ascent of a mountain in the Tokositna that the four of us had made a brief attempt at the year before. It was a 3511m unclimbed, unnamed peak that was steep, glaciated and avalanche swept, but with some fine ice and what looked like first-class lines. Anna and Karen had climbed high on the mountain, but Scottie and I had turned back early on our route, worried about the soundness of the snow pack. However, it was worth a second go, I told Marty, 'and we might get a first ascent out of it'. Marty agreed, for lack of a better idea. He knew nothing about Alaska.

It was déjà vu – pilot Paul, his little plane, the same campsite under the West Face of Huntington. The only difference a year on was the weather; it was noticeably colder. For the first week it snowed … continuously. We spent our time digging out the tents, cooking in the open (no Kiva this year) and establishing an advanced base camp (ABC) at the bottom of the peak, a two-hour ski trip across the névé. This camp consisted of our small Gore-Tex single-shell tent, and going backwards and forwards provided us with something to do and a means of keeping our ski track open. The first time we returned to ABC after a two-day absence, the tent had disappeared under more than a metre of snow and it was only with the aid of the GPS that we managed to locate it.

Back at the main base camp, renowned climber Erik Weihenmayer arrived with his guides to do the Nettle–Quirk route on Huntingon. Erik became famous after making the first blind ascent of Mt Everest and was friendly, generous and kind, but his two guides exhibited all the worst traits of American egotism. They did come with a good story though, of a pair of climbers, camping alone under Huntington several years back, who had looked across the cirque one day to see a large black something meandering towards them. When it got closer, the something turned out to be a bear, badly lost and 30km up the glacier from its nearest source of food. The bear realised a potential meal was close at hand, and bolted towards the camp, at which the climbers headed for the nearest piece of high ground (Mt Huntington). They sat up on the wall for several days, watching the visitor shred the camp and eat every scrap of food. Eventually it wandered off in search of fresh pickings. How true the story was I've never been sure, but at the time I listened incredulous.

Eight days after our arrival, the clouds rolled back and we were able to move over to ABC for good, in readiness for our ascent. It was a lonely, windy spot, with our nameless mountain standing guard to the south, and another, called Kahiltna Queen, to the north. At the western end of the cirque was the bulk of Mt Hunter. The wind had pushed the snow into large drifts reminiscent of sand dunes. Malcolm Bass and Simon Yearsley had climbed two new steep ice routes on Kahiltna Queen, and we thought that if our peak went well we would attempt one of these afterwards. But first things first. After a day of waiting for the last of the fresh snow to shed from our mountain, we left at midnight under a clear sky. It was very cold.

The route we'd chosen was a fine-looking ice gully running the complete length of the face – about 1200m, we estimated, or twenty pitches. We'd climb it in a single push and descend the same way on V-thread anchors. It would be tiring but straightforward, and if all went well we'd be back the day after next with a first ascent under our belts. As we skied the short distance to the base I was a bit apprehensive, but was still confident I could replicate the successes of 2002.

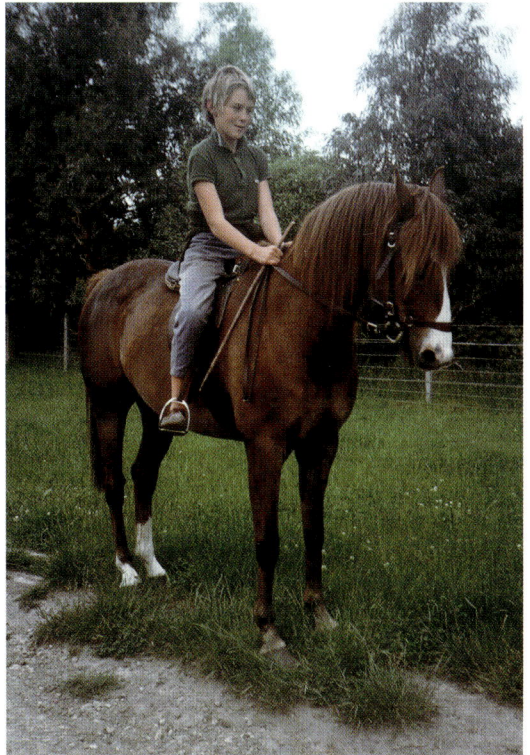

Top left My Grandfather with his sheep dogs. He was killed in a farming accident in 1929.
PHOTO: PAT DEAVOLL COLLECTION

Top right My Grandmother on the farm. She brought up her four children and ran the farm alone after her husband was killed in a farming accident.
PHOTO: PAT DEAVOLL COLLECTION

Right Early days on the farm: with my horse Rangi at age 11.
PHOTO: SUE BYRCH

Top In 1978 Chris Todd and I attempted a traverse of the Southern Alps. Here I am overlooking the Dart Glacier on about week four. PHOTO: CHRIS TODD

Bottom Leading the crux pitch on Logans Run, grade 6+, South Face of Mt Hicks.
PHOTO: MARTY BEARE

Top Jonathon and I climbing Cold Choice on a beautiful Canadian morning, only moments before we were hit by an avalanche (Canada 2000).
PHOTO: PAT DEAVOLL COLLECTION

Left Climbing the traverse of Sea of Vapours, before entering 'the zone' (Canada 1999).
PHOTO: PAT DEAVOLL COLLECTION

Top From the left; Anna Keeling, Karen McNeill and I in the back of the plane on the way into the Tokositna Glacier (Alaska 2002). PHOTO: SCOTTIE SYMPER

Bottom Belaying Scottie Symper on the first attempt at the Colton-Leach route on Mt Huntington (Alaska 2002). PHOTO: SCOTTIE SYMPER

Karen McNeill high in the Colton-Leach couloir, Mt Huntington, just before we climbed through the cornice (Alaska 2002). PHOTO: PAT DEAVOLL

Top The North Buttress of Mt Hunter, the prominent snow and rock line to the left of the picture (Alaska 2003). PHOTO: PAT DEAVOLL

Right Making the final moves on Deprivation, the North Buttress of Mt Hunter; the happiest day of my life (Alaska 2003).
PHOTO: MARTY BEARE

Top Lunch time at Base Camp, Sudenbam Meadow after a snowfall on the Jankuth 2004 expedition (India 2004). PHOTO: ANDY BROWN

Bottom Malcolm Bass (India 2004). PHOTO: ANDY BROWN

Top Marty Beare and I reached this high camp at 6500m on the summit ridge of Jankuth before turning back. I am standing beside the tent. The Gangotri Glacier stretches away beneath (India 2004). PHOTO: MARTY BEARE

Bottom Approaching the summit ridge of Jankuth on the summit bid with Marty Beare. Below is the Miandi Barmak, in the middle of which is the site of our Camp 1 (India 2004). PHOTO: MARTY BEARE

Top The Chaukumba Massif commands the head of the Gangotri Glacier (India 2004).
PHOTO: PAT DEAVOLL

Bottom With a cheerful and diminutive sadhu on the walk into Base Camp on the Kharchakund expedition of 2007 (India 2007). PHOTO: BRUCE NORMAND

Top Bruce Normand at our top acclimatisation camp on Kedar Dome on the Karchakund Expedition. In the background is Shivling (India 2007). PHOTO: PAT DEAVOLL

Bottom Kharchakund: Bruce Normand and I attempted the ridge on the left-hand skyline and reached a point about half way up (India 2007). PHOTO: PAT DEAVOLL

Top Karen McNeill amongst the inhabitants of the 'old people's village' at the Zhopu Monastery. The little house belongs to the elderly woman sitting on the right of the picture (China 2005). PHOTO: PAT DEAVOLL

Bottom Malcolm Bass climbs the summit ridge of Haizi Shan while below him the Tibetan Plateau stretches away to the horizon (China 2006). PHOTO: PAT DEAVOLL

Top The only woman on the streets in Quetta (Pakistan 1986). PHOTO: BRIAN DEAVOLL

Bottom Brian Deavoll surrounded by the locals in the Quetta Bazaar, after crossing the border from Iran (Pakistan 1986). PHOTO: PAT DEAVOLL

Top Beka Brakai Chhok (Pakistan 2007). PHOTO: PAT DEAVOLL

Bottom Camp Two on Beka Brakai Chhok - Lydia Bradey does dinner (Pakistan 2007).
PHOTO: PAT DEAVOLL

Top Lydia Bradey climbing above our Camp Two site on our summit bid, Beka Brakai Chhok (Pakistan 2007). PHOTO: PAT DEAVOLL

Bottom On the summit of Wahine are, from left to right: Giampi Corona, Lorenzo Corona, Lydia Bradey and myself (Pakistan 2007). PHOTO: GIAMPI CORONA

Top Malcolm Bass on the summit ridge of Beka Brakai Chhok during my second attempt in 2008. At this point we decided the conditions were too dangerous for us to continue, and turned back (Pakistan 2008). PHOTO: PAT DEAVOLL

Bottom The view of Karim Sar from the Baltar Glacier, which I climbed alone in 2009 (Pakistan 2009). PHOTO: PAT DEAVOLL

Malcolm and Paul scrutinise our route on the West Face of Vasuki Parbat from across the Vasuki Glacier. The route follows the obvious mixed line slightly right of centre (India 2010). PHOTO: SATYA DAM

Ten hours later, Marty and I had climbed the crux of the route – a near-vertical shield of hard grey ice that Marty led quickly. I wasn't climbing well – I was feeling the exposure and the loneliness of our situation, and wished we could just finish the route and get down. I was very disappointed in myself, and wasn't sure why I felt nervous. Something wasn't right, but what?

'We're doing fine,' Marty tried to console me. 'We just need to keep working away. We'll wear this mountain down eventually.'

The further we climbed, the narrower the gully became, until we were cocooned deep in a runnel that led naturally towards the cornice ringing the summit. By 6 p.m. we were high in the runnel, and I was tired and scared. We'd climbed almost twenty pitches of tenuous hard ice. New Zealand routes are only half this length, I thought to myself as I relinquished yet another lead to Marty. Then I happened to glance down. To my dismay, a grey wall of cloud was moving up the Tokositna icefall and into the cirque. As I watched, it rolled towards Huntington and enveloped our base camp.

'Hey Marty, look,' I called shakily.

Marty paused and looked down for a minute, then climbed on without saying anything. I followed, feeling sick with apprehension. I just wanted to be back on the ground.

Shortly before midnight we arrived at the last pitch, and were together on an anchor directly under the summit cornice in the twilight gloom. The cloud layer had long since blanked out the cirque and the peaks poked above it like steep islands in a sea of grey. It was an eerie and surreal scene; what's more, the cloud now rose quickly and ominously up the gully to meet us.

'One more pitch should do it,' Marty said, as he moved off the belay.

Within minutes, I was engulfed in the cloud and he disappeared from view. It began to snow and I gave a couple of pathetic whimpers. 'God, I hate this sport,' I moaned to myself as I played out the rope. 'I'm freezing cold, I'm all alone, I need to pee and it doesn't look like we'll be back at camp for at least another twelve hours …'

Suddenly my feet were whipped out from under me. 'What the …' Scrambling up, I looked frantically around, to see the snow moving downhill in ripples, like a gentle but relentless river. There was a swishing, hissing sound. Thank goodness I'm still attached to the anchor, I thought, but what's going on? Then it dawned to me. The weight of the freshly fallen snow had triggered the release of the 10cm snow pack sitting delicately over the ice, and it was sliding off down the gully, gathering speed. The amount of sliding snow was minimal here at the top of the slope, but what would it be like at the bottom? It would have collected into a full-blown avalanche. Enough was enough.

'Marty,' I shouted as loud as I could into the gloom, 'we've gotta get outa here!'

It took Marty and me ten hours to descend back to the glacier, and we both agreed it was the most frightening experience either of us had ever had in the mountains. Up under the cornice, we considered taking shelter in a crevasse, but the prospect of being trapped for days in a storm with no bivvy gear made us think again. We *had* to get down. We began to abseil. Every few minutes the slope above released its load, and we were enveloped in a deluge of snow that clogged our noses and worked its way inside our helmets, our clothing and our packs. Building a V-thread was impossible and we were forced to use our precious ice screws as anchors; by the time we were part of the way down the mountain there were frighteningly few of these left.

'This will take us twenty abseils,' Marty said. 'What are we going to do when we run out?'

I didn't have an answer; I was concentrating on one rope length at a time, and on staying alive.

At 3 a.m. we reached the bottom of the runnel. It was a huge relief, as it had become physically impossible to withstand the strength of the rushing snow, which now had the potential to destroy our anchors and hurtle us down the mountain. In desperation, we'd hunted for places of shelter but they were few and far between. As the face spread out, the volume of the avalanches would increase, but there were also more natural features to hide behind: snow lips, small arêtes and rock buttresses that could offer a few moments of sanctuary. I looked at Marty. His face was drawn with cold and fear.

'Do you think we are going to get down alive?' I blurted.

'I don't know,' he said simply.

At least he's being honest, I thought. I'd always respected Marty's opinion; he was the most experienced of my climbing partners, and a mountain guide to boot. If anyone knew, or didn't know, it was him.

But our position improved. We were able to work away from the avalanche path and build anchors at the side of a large rock buttress. We also became used to the roaring cascades rushing past us a few metres away. A determination set in. We *were* going to make it down, come hell or high water. The bottom third of the face descended a steep, narrow gulch, and the cascades of snow flew by us not 5m away like huge airborne waves. We doggedly pushed on. By now it was daylight and still snowing heavily, but at least the midnight gloom had lifted.

'I can see the bergschrund!' Marty yelled in excitement. 'We're nearly there.'

I was so relieved to hear this I nearly burst into tears. Preparing for the last abseil, I cinched the hood of my down jacket tighter around my face and headed for the upper lip of the schrund, looking downhill over my shoulder warily.

'Watch out!' came an urgent call. I looked up to see a torrent of white and grey galloping towards me. On instinct, I jumped over the lip and slammed wildly into the upper wall of the crevasse. The torrent shot over my head – I was protected by the overhang – and I laughed out loud.

'I tricked it, Marty!' I yelled manically. 'I tricked it! I tricked it!'

Marty laughed and punched the air with his fist. We'd made it down, we'd survived.

Marty and I crawled into camp at 10 a.m., a day and a half after setting out with high hopes of making the first ascent of our mountain. We'd missed our summit by 50m but had survived a dreadful descent, and that was prize enough. We slept the rest of that day, and all the next, with short waking intervals during which one of us would cook an enormous meal. The sun came out and dried our clothes, every item of which had been wet through. Come the evening of the second day, we got up feeling recovered – or so we thought.

'How about one of Malcolm's routes on Kahiltna Queen,' Marty said.

'Sure, I'm ready,' I replied emphatically, and we left for the climb there and then, at eight in the evening.

But high in the giant couloir, surrounded by colossal orange walls pouring with spindrift, I couldn't control my emotions. I felt scared and vulnerable. I tried to tell myself it was only spindrift and that it wouldn't harm me, but the back of my mind echoed, 'What if? What if?' So it was an enormous relief when, at two in the morning, Marty said, 'I don't think we should be up here, the conditions aren't good,' and we retreated back to camp. For once I was glad to have failed.

The Kahiltna Glacier is 70km from top to toe, making it the longest in the Alaska Range. Forty-five kilometres from the terminus and at an altitude of 1600m is Kahiltna Base Camp, the drop-off point for the hundreds of climbers who set out to climb Mt Denali every year. A steady stream of hopefuls fly in from Talkeetna to land at the camp during the main climbing season of April to July. They alight from their planes, load their supplies onto plastic sleds, don snowshoes and head towards the mountain, towing their sleds behind them. The standard West Buttress route on Denali isn't technical, but it does require patience, strength and the presence of mind to deal with the weather and the effects of altitude. At any one time there can be up to a hundred tents pitched at the base camp as climbers come and go.

The North Buttress of Hunter towers over the base camp, drawing the eye to take in its spectacular steepness. What's more, any climber tackling the route comes under constant scrutiny as the camp rangers have trained a telescope on the buttress – it's a common pastime for climbers to while away the hours watching whatever hapless team happens to be struggling their way up. Marty and I flew into Kahiltna Base Camp at the height of the season. It was like a small city, a far cry from our lonely ABC in the Tokositna cirque.

The North Buttress hosts several routes, but the two most sought after are the Moonflower and Deprivation. The latter was first climbed by Scott Backes and Mark Twight in 1994, and, like the others, consists of 1200m of continuously steep, mixed ground. It was this route that Marty and I decided to try. We would go as far as the top of the buttress, and then make an abseil descent. There were a number of other teams at base camp eyeing up the North Buttress, including some big names, but the ice was thin, we were told, and to date no one had managed to get through the first rock band. Then Johnny Copp and Kelly Cordes, a couple of well-known North American climbers, made it to the last ice band on Deprivation, before being forced back by a turn in the weather. Marty and I felt like novices amongst the overconfident North Americans and wondered if we should really be there. We listened to the stories of the retreating parties and pondered our situation for a few days. In any case, we needed the rest after our trials in the Tokositna.

Four days after our arrival, British climbers Richard Cross and Jon Bracey, who like us had been quietly biding their time, headed for the bottom of the Moonflower, as yet another pair of North Americans arrived back at base camp after making little headway. Over the next twenty-four hours, Richard and Jon made it through to the first ice band, one-third of the way up the climb. They sat out a few hours on a chopped ledge and then forged ahead up the crux of the climb to the second ice band, and then on to the third.

Marty and I quietly began our preparations for leaving, carefully filling a second's pack with the majority of our equipment, and a lighter leader's pack. We would try and climb Deprivation in a single push, we decided; after all, we'd managed to climb non-stop for thirty hours on our unnamed 3511m peak and Karen and I had done the same on Huntington the year before. We'd lead the route in blocks, each taking on several pitches at a time, and we'd take bivvy bags but no sleeping bags, a stove for melting water and minimal food.

That evening, Richard and Jon made the top of the buttress and began the descent, watched closely by the humbled hordes.

'OK,' said Marty. 'Weather's good. It's now or never.'

At midnight we skied quietly out of camp, too unsure of ourselves to create any sort of fanfare. An hour later we reached the base of the buttress and stashed our skis on the down side of the bergschrund. The night was beautiful, and away down the glacier the dark bulk of Mt Foraker stood out against the dusky sky.

I'm about to embark on the highlight of my climbing career, I thought to myself. Nearly thirty years of climbing has led up to this. I knew Marty was thinking the same thing, as unspeaking we rechecked our gear and donned harness and crampons. Two hundred metres to our left, Richard and Jon were completing their last abseil and we waved and shouted our congratulations. They darted off on their skis in the half-light, calling 'Good luck! Good luck!'

The first few pitches were straightforward enough, and we moved together on the rope to the bottom of a series of narrow ice runnels. I took the lead and, after a nervous start, began to enjoy myself. It was the kind of climbing I loved and it reminded me of some of the Canadian ice routes: thin, technical and requiring a deft touch. I led the three pitches quickly, Marty following with the larger pack, and we arrived at the base of the first rock band on sunrise. A vertical chimney soared skyward from a small patch of snow: was this the crux that had turned everyone but Johnny and Kelly back? I remembered their words, 'If you can climb that gully, dude, and the weather stays good, the route's in the bag!' Best let Marty lead it, I thought.

Marty climbed the first pitch of the gully steadily, in spider style, stemming his feet on the rock rimming the sides and reaching high with his tools. But he was knocking down snow – could this be why the pitch had turned so many climbers back? Vertical unconsolidated snow is invariably hard to climb. Predictably, by the time I'd reached the halfway point on the pitch I was starting to tire. As I suspected, there was little ice, but I did my best to hook the rock with my tools and sketch my crampons on anything that gave purchase. I began to scrabble wildly, but willed myself to calm down. 'Think about what you're doing,' I chided myself. 'This isn't the steepest thing you've ever climbed.' Luckily, by the time I reached Marty's belay, I'd partially recovered and composed myself.

Marty led two more pitches in the chimney, each harder than the last. By the top of the third pitch, both of us were undeniably tired, but there'd been a shift in our psyche. The crux was done – we'd climbed the bit that had turned the other teams back. Perhaps we weren't bumbling antipodeans after all? We stopped looking back down at the ground and started looking up, up, with confidence and determination, with purpose. Now we were underneath the first of three ice bands – a sixty-degree swathe of glass that proved unforgiving and very tenuous – and by the time we reached the top in mid-afternoon a rest was called for. Hanging on an anchor, I precariously balanced our little cooker on my pack to melt some water.

'We're doing fine,' we congratulated each other. 'We're the bomb. Weather permitting, we are going to climb this.' The sky was cloudless.

By 1 a.m. the next morning, twenty-four hours after leaving the ground, we reached the top of the second ice band. I'd been leading ever since our rest, and was proud of myself – I'd been quick on the technical mixed ground between the two ice bands, and what's more, I'd loved the climbing. It was a joy, requiring finesse rather than strength, and concentration. I'd been consumed with my task and the hours had gone by in a second. There's nowhere in the world I'd rather be than here, I thought to myself as I waited for Marty to arrive at the last belay before the ice band. This is *so far* from our unnamed mountain. Please don't let anything spoil this.

I wasn't quite so keen on the three glassy pitches of the ice band, however, and by the time I'd reached the top I was starting to feel the ill effects of twenty-four hours of standing on my front points – my calves were dead, and I was in dire need of food and a cup of tea. We decided on a rest and set about chopping a ledge to sit on. Chopping ice is a tedious and time-consuming undertaking at the best of times, but when you're dog-tired it's an unappreciated trial. But eventually we were able to sit side by side, tied to the slope, and look out at the moon over Foraker, the tent smatterings at base camp, and the Kahiltna Glacier streaming away to the south in all its dusky midnight glory.

Again, I balanced the cooker on my lap to melt water, while Marty slumped against me, dozing. 'Sit up Marty, you are pushing me off,' I whined. Then I became frighteningly cold, and as Marty snored, had doubts

I would sleep. But I woke from a light slumber at four o'clock and by 5 a.m. we'd forced our reluctant bodies to begin the long traverse across the top of the second ice band. We moved together, placing ice screws as intermittent protection between us.

At the end of the traverse a wild ledge led diagonally back left and up to meet the middle section of the third ice field, and I took the lead again. Some of the jubilation of the previous day was starting to wane for both of us, and we were hankering for the summit. 'Twelve hours,' Marty had said on leaving our diminutive bivvy. 'We'll be at the top of the climbing in twelve hours.' But it was 2 a.m. by the time we'd toiled our way to the top of yet another iron-hard, polished grey ice field and we knew from there on, no matter what we did, we wouldn't regain our strength. It was just a matter of wearing the route down before it wore us down.

'Fuck, I hate these ice bands,' I said to Marty. I did, too. Although they weren't steep, they were brutal on the calves and there was absolutely no-where to take a rest – no snow to kick a step in, no rock to hang on to.

We stopped again before what has become known as the Bibler Come Again Exit, the final series of steep ramps and ice flows leading to the top. I was momentarily overcome by a wave of emotion born of tiredness.

'We ARE going to make it, aren't we Marty?'

'Of course we are,' he said, matter-of-factly. 'But why don't we have some soup before we tackle this last bit?'

I wasn't keen; I just wanted to reach the top. But his practicality won the day, and once again we got out the little cooker.

Afterwards, I felt rejuvenated, both emotionally and physically, and my heart sang as Marty headed off up the first steep pitch of the final section.

'Nearly there, nearly there,' I hummed to myself as I followed him up the gritty ice. 'Nearly there, nearly there,' as I led the next pitch of eighty-degree ice covered in powder snow. 'NEARLY THERE, NEARLY THERE,' as I belayed Marty again, up vertical rock and tenuous snow. Then the rope stopped playing out.

'Come on up,' came a faint cry.

I began to climb – a steep runnel of ice led to a 10m rock buttress covered in snow. It was vertical and difficult, and my tools clawed for purchase.

'Reach out right,' came a shout, much closer now. 'I found a good hook out right … now reach over the top, as far as you can.'

I took a final swing above my head and the tool dug deep. I ran my feet up high under me and willed my exhausted body to propel me upward. There was Marty, 3m away, beaming. I scrambled to the belay and we hugged in pure, uninhibited joy. It had taken us forty-five hours, but we'd made it.

It's widely recognised by sports physiologists today that sleep deprivation in endurance athletes can result in brain fog – a lowering of concentration levels, memory loss, hallucinations and an inability to solve problems. By the time Marty and I reached the ground again, fifty-two hours had passed since we'd first stepped out of our skis and begun the long haul up the North Buttress. Celebrating briefly on the summit, we'd forgone the opportunity to chop a ledge and rest, a task that would have taken an hour, maybe two, and instead began our descent, using Richard and Jon's V-thread anchors from their ascent of the Moonflower. I knew in myself I was severely sleep-deprived and dehydrated, and that my mind could wander from the task at hand with drastic results. It was late evening and the sun was on us. To the west, Denali stood guard, and directly down glacier Foraker was bathed in the last brilliant rays. I took in the scene but felt disconnected. I was two people, one hanging on the rope while the other looked on from above.

By 11 a.m. we'd abseiled twenty pitches, and were descending a particularly steep part of the Moonflower route called The Shaft, a thin, vertical pillar of ice no more that 45cm wide. I was free-hanging on a two-screw anchor and called for Marty to join me. He'll be ten minutes I mused, and turned to look out over the Kahiltna Glacier. The air was chilly but soft, the sky pink and mauve, there was no sound but the occasional tinkle of falling ice …

I awoke with a start as something hit me in the side. It was Marty, arriving clumsily at the belay. 'Couldn't you hear me yelling at you,' he said. I looked at him for a long moment, not comprehending. Then it dawned on me – I'd fallen asleep. Hanging by my waist against cold grey ice, feet dangling in space, thirsty beyond belief, I'd dropped off to sleep!

We reached the ground at 1 p.m. The only audience was our skis, standing upright like sentinels in the snow, and we were so tired we hardly spoke. Marty glided away down the slope intent on base camp; I was no longer in his thoughts. I skied 100m and fell over; got up painfully slowly and managed another 100m before slumping on my side.

'You've never been great at skiing in your plastic climbing boots, but not this bad,' a voice said from somewhere. I scrambled up. 'Come on, you can do it,' said the voice with an edge of anger, closer now.

I glided on, unaware of how fast or how slowly I was travelling. Base camp loomed ahead, growing larger, but slowly, so slowly. I stuttered to a halt by my tent and put my head down between my knees at the onset of a sudden rush of dizziness. Marty walked towards me with a cup of tea and a hug. Kelly and Johnny appeared, and Jon Bracey.

'Hey, the bomb, guys,' Kelly said. I thought back to 1975, when I'd climbed Mt Binser – it had been the happiest day of my life. That day had now been superseded – I'd never felt so happy.

It took Marty and me a few days to recover from our efforts on the North Buttress, during which time we did little more than sleep and eat. Then we decided Karen and Christine deserved a visit and bumped into the Ruth Glacier. They were having a grand time with a team of German mountaineers and had climbed a beautiful new route on Mt Dickie.

'We're off to the Kahiltna now,' they said, 'to take a look at Foraker.' We separated for a second time.

'See you soon in Talkeetna,' I called, as their plane roared off across the glacier.

Marty and I donned skis and sleds and headed for the confluence of the west and northwest forks of the Ruth Glacier. We wanted to climb the southwest ridge of Peak 11,300; I'd read that American alpinist Mark Twight rated the route highly and that was credential enough for us. We climbed it easily in a day and a half, bivvying high on the route the first night and summitting and descending in a storm. After Hunter we were relaxed and confident, and the weather had little effect on us. I'd never felt more a climber, more competent, more successful. Maybe I was the real thing?

But the euphoria was short-lived. Back home, nothing had changed. The dissatisfaction I felt with my life, the job I no longer enjoyed, and Andy's inability to accept my need to climb were all problems that resurrected themselves alongside my reoccuring lack of self-worth. Why was the sense of satisfaction and wholeness I'd experienced in Alaska so ephemeral? I couldn't find an answer and became morose and withdrawn, shunning friends and preferring to spend time at home with my cats. The doctor became worried, insisting on a dose of anti-depressants, and suggested I get counselling. I refused the counselling – what good would it do? – but agreed to try the medication. It had no effect. Andy and I were drifting apart – he was wrapped up in his career and his own pastimes, while I reminisced in solitude on the Alaskan trip. I wanted his support and affirmation, and he couldn't give it. Within weeks of my return I'd moved out of our home and our ten-year relationship was at an end.

CHAPTER SIX
On Top of the World

India is the cradle of the human race, the birthplace of human speech, the mother of history, the grandmother of legend, and the great grandmother of tradition.
— Mark Twain

India is mad. Not bedlam mad, bloodthirsty mad or nuclear holocaust mad, but mad in a chaotic, riotous, joyful, blindingly colourful way that distinguishes it from any other nation on earth. Nowhere else do you find such contrasts between religion, ethnicity, lifestyle and culture as you do in India. Stay a while and Indians' love of their country becomes apparent. Stay a while longer and you can't help but fall in love with India yourself.

India has one of the oldest cultures in the world and it's this that essentially gives the nation its outrageous and undeniable charm. All the trappings of the Hindu religion remain intact – the ancient temples, the sadhus, the gods, the sacred rivers and mountains, the caste system, and the festivals, marriages and religious holidays. Life in India revolves around a religion and culture that evolved more than 2500 years ago.

However, as a mountaineering nation, India has tended to draw the short straw – it's been the poor sister to Nepal and Pakistan since the advent of Himalayan climbing. The reason for this is that it has none of the 8000m peaks within its borders – the summits that these days attract the majority of climbers, intent on being the first of a nation, or a gender, the oldest, the youngest, or the most physically disadvantaged to summit Shishapangma, Cho Oyu or, of course, Everest. The Indian Himalaya, which has some of the most breathtaking peaks on earth, has been relegated to second best for no other reason than its mountains fail to meet that magic 8000m mark.

In late 1984, my husband Brian and I launched ourselves into a two-year odyssey that would see us travel overland the length of Asia and Europe, with climbing our objective. A few years earlier, Brian had spent the elective period of his medical degree in a large hospital in Patna, the poorest city in Bihar, which in turn is one of the most backward and desperate states in India. He'd come back dazed, having seen the worst of what third world medicine had to offer, but entranced with India and wanting to return. As a couple, we decided he would take two years off his medical training and we'd head off into the unknown with what money we could scrape together. I doubt any medical house surgeon today would gamble his profession on a two-year stay of absence.

In 1984 we married, and late in the year flew out for Singapore with our backpacks full of climbing gear, planning to wing it. We wanted to travel as far as we could overland, and would buy an airline ticket only when war, politics or border restrictions made it necessary. We knew we'd have limited contact with home – there was no Internet then, and only limited telephone opportunities from Asia. Mail would depend on those countries that supported American Express offices, which would act as our letter depots – we were told not to trust the post offices.

For me, the trip was a coming of age. I'd never seen anything like the highrises of Singapore or the shantytowns on the east coast of Malaysia, which simultaneously enthralled and horrified me. We headed up the Malay Peninsula, spending a couple of weeks in a dingy hotel in Penang over Christmas and the New Year while we waited for our visas for Thailand to be approved. Staying in the same dive were a mother and son from New Zealand. The boy was about seventeen and spent much of the time slumped comatose in a chair. Both he and his mother were dreadfully thin, their eyes dark, sunken smudges in their haggard faces. The mother wore a shabby blue sequinned cocktail dress that looked odd amongst the cotton hippy trousers and T-shirts favoured by the rest of the dirtbag travellers. She had badly executed breast implants.

'Heroin addicts,' Brian whispered to me the first time we encountered them in the hostel cafeteria. 'We'll meet them everywhere.' I was fascinated; I'd never met a heroin addict before.

All four of us eventually got our visas, and on the same day headed north by train, across the border into Thailand. Brian and I forgot the couple, for several months at least, until one day we were reading a UK newspaper.

'Recognise these two?' Brian said, turning a page towards me with raised eyebrows. There was the couple on the front page. Lorraine and Aaron Cohen, a Kiwi mother and son, both drug addicts and fast becoming pop heroes, were awaiting the death penalty in a Thai jail after attempting to smuggle narcotics across the Thai border early in the New Year of 1985.

Thailand passed quickly for Brian and me. We hung out on the beaches of Ko Samui, explored the golden architecture of Bangkok and stayed in tiny thatched huts in the Golden Triangle. We tried, and failed, to get coconuts out of the trees. Brian got so desperate for a good book that he stole *Sophie's Choice* from an English bookshop in Chiangmai. I was horrified.

'What were you thinking?' I yelled at him in the privacy of our hotel room. 'Do you want to spend the rest of your life in a Bangkok jail?' Even so, I enjoyed the book as much as he did.

We hopped across the border into Burma on a Burmese Airlines flight, spent a week there (at the time, tourist visas were limited to seven days) and enjoyed it so much we flew out to Dhaka with Bangladesh Air, spent just two hours in the airport and then flew back to Rangoon (Yangon) for a second go. I loved the Burmese capital, with its crumbling colonial architecture and shonky footpaths, and was especially captivated by the ancient city of Pagan (Bagan). We roamed around the sixteenth-century temples, scattered amongst the thorny scrub, on antique black pushbikes. I ate my first avocado, a luscious orb the size of a rugby ball. From the top of the temples, dream-like views of the Irrawaddy River, drifting lazily across a golden plain, stretched to the horizon. I read Somerset Maugham. We had lots of punctures.

We made it to Nepal in March 1985, and in my mind at least, this is where our journey started in earnest. Whereas other backpackers were travelling Southeast Asia with nothing much more than a hessian shoulder bag and a hooch pipe, we'd been lugging 30kg of climbing equipment apiece, marking time till we arrived in the Himalayas. The closer we got, the more excited I became.

'We have to stick to our US$5 a day budget,' I bossed Brian, 'so we can stay here for as long as we can!' Brian looked rather forlorn at the prospect of such deprivation but I was determined our limited savings would keep us away from New Zealand for two years, even if we had to starve.

For Brian, who'd made it up to Kathmandu from India during his elective stay in Patna, the city was heaven. There was western food there, he said. 'Yak steaks, lemon meringue pie, cheese, German bread, proper coffee

– even beer.' The accommodation was cheap and comfortable, the US dollar could be exchanged on the black market at an exorbitant rate in your favour, and marijuana was sold on the street. 'Life is good there,' he said, his eyes taking on a dreamy, far-away gaze.

I wasn't disappointed. I loved the city at first sight: the colour and sound of the markets, the smell of wood smoke and incense, the exotic Nepali dress, the crumbling temples and the sounds of tin whistles and barking dogs in the evenings. I even loved the good-natured squalor that pervaded everything and everywhere.

But the mountains beckoned, and within a few days we were off on our first trip. In the meantime, to the south, India was on a radical journey of its own.

On 31 October 1984, just days after Brian and I left New Zealand, Indian Prime Minister Indira Gandhi was assassinated. As we travelled we heard snippets of the unrest spreading across the subcontinent as a result, particularly in Delhi and the Punjab. The UK newspapers reported that thousands of people were dead, and that there had been terrible 'pillage, arson and rape'.

Indira came to power in 1965, succeeding her father Jawaharlal Nehru, the first Indian prime minister to take office after British Rule. After a rocky start, she substantiated her popular appeal with a major shift towards social-ist policies, but was found guilty of corruption in 1974 and arrested, along with her son Sanjay. Her Congress Party was swept back into power in 1979, unfortunately at a time when a rise in troubles in the Punjab was starting to jeopardise the country's security. When Indian forces raided the hideout of Khalistan militants in the Golden Temple in Amritsar, the deaths of civilians and damage to the temple ignited tensions in Sikh communities nationwide. Indira's own Sikh bodyguards assassinated her. The resulting violence caused the deaths of thousands. It was around this time that Brian and I left Kath-mandu for the Nepal–India border.

By the end of June 1985 we had, literally, worn ourselves out in Nepal, tak-ing on several ambitious mountain trips into what were then remote areas with little support for westerners. Scorning the use of porters (or, rather, not having the budget) and shouldering in excess of 30kg each, we prowled the mountain regions east of the Dud Khosi River in a somewhat arrogant ef-fort to avoid other westerners. Not for us the standard treks to Everest base camp or Annapurna. We deep-ended ourselves trying to get up the Barun Valley to Makalu base camp at the end of winter, experienced the loneliness of the Panch Pokhari before it developed into a major trekking route, and tried to climb a number of peaks that were too tough for us, too high. We went weeks without seeing other people. I learnt the hard way about acclimatising, suffering recurring bouts of altitude sickness every time we climbed above 6000m. Unable to carry enough food for our journeys, we were always, *always* hungry, and on our interim trips back to Kathmandu ate ourselves crazy, only to lose the kilograms on our next foray into the hills. It was a harsh but effective learning experience, and I'd never felt so satisfied. I was in the Himalaya, on a wonderful adventure with a wonderful companion. What more could I want?

But by the middle of the year we were exhausted. 'I think we should head down to India for a while – give ourselves a break. You need to spend a bit of time at a lower altitude, recover a bit,' Brian convinced me. I agreed grudgingly. In the back of my mind brewed an idea that it was my fault we were leaving. I should have done better, should have done more. The familiar self-blame was still there, waiting to surface.

But careering down to Varanasi on a cramped local bus, I began to relax again. Brian and I listened to bootlegged Bruce Springsteen tapes on our state-of-the-art Sony Walkman and puffed surreptitiously on a marijuana joint to pass the time. The border was manned by bad-tempered and officious Indian policemen who had had their fill of deadbeat hippy westerners like ourselves, and wanted nothing more than to extort a few extra rupees out of the immigration process. I didn't blame them – recreational travel was not a luxury they would ever be able to afford. When we arrived they were in the process of interrogating a Belgium tourist who didn't have a passport.

'Pay 50,000 rupees baksheesh [bribe money],' they ordered, 'or we will arrest you.'

As we stood in line waiting to be processed, Brian gave me a sudden dig in the ribs. 'What did you do with that last joint?' he whispered.

'Fuck, it's in my wallet,' I replied, horrified. 'What shall I do?'

There was nothing I could do – we were being called to the counter. A mustachioed policeman grappled his way through the contents of my backpack, and then started on my shoulder bag, which held my wallet and the offending joint. He opened my diary, took letters out of envelopes and glanced at them, took the batteries out of the Walkman and shook it. He turned the bag inside out and investigated the seams with his thumbs. The whole time

Brian and I held our breaths and sweated. Finally, the policeman picked up the wallet, gave it a perfunctory glance and replaced in my bag. 'Welcome to India, madam,' he said with a smile.

Outside the customs office we rolled our eyes at each other in relief. 'Must make a note not to do that again,' Brian said.

When we finally rolled into Varanasi, forty-eight exhausting and filthy hours later, I was stunned to attention. I thought I'd never seen such a beautiful and extraordinary city. Couched on the banks of the Ganges, Varanasi's rich ancient architecture was highlighted by a subdued orange light. Smoke from cremation sites wreathed stealthily about the temple roofs. The bathing ghats (stairs leading down to the river), swarming with brown bodies, were a scene from *Lord of the Rings*. 'I knew you'd like it,' Brian said, grinning at me with red-rimmed eyes.

Varanasi is regarded as holy, not just by Hindus, but also Buddhists and Jains, and is considered one of the oldest continuously inhabited cities in the world. Nearly 100 ghats line the river, most of them for bathing, and thousands of people can be seem splashing merrily in the Ganges at any one time. Others are used as cremation sites, and it's common to see bodies being burned on top of large piles of wood. It's also common to see bodies in the river, put there by the families who can't afford the firewood.

I could have spent weeks there. I prowled the narrow streets and bazaars of the old city, bartering for pieces of gaudy fabric while Brian stood patiently by, and perched on the steps of the ghats watching the bathers and sadhus (holy men). We went out on the river in a rowboat and I was interested, rather than horrified, when I saw the ghostly blue-white apparition of a corpse float by just beneath the surface of the water. I experimented with the food and developed an insane appreciation for Indian sweets. Yes, the crowding was unprecedented, the streets were filthy and the beggars ubiquitous, and it wasn't uncommon to see a rat galloping along the sidewalk. But remarkably, as Brian said would happen, I reached a place within myself where I could see past the filth and poverty, and there was the beauty of India.

We headed west over the next few weeks, stopping in the Muslim city of Lucknow for a few days, and then Agra to visit the Taj Mahal. In Jaipur I shopped for fake silver jewellery and took delight in the exotic skirts and pink and orange turbans of the Rajasthanis. I wished I had more money for shopping, but Brian reminded me, teasingly, of our pledge to live on US$5 a day. 'Can't break the bank,' he'd say with a twinkle in his eye, which meant, 'If you really want it, I'll buy it for you.' Even so, my pack was growing steadily with each scrap of sparkling fabric, each bright new cushion cover and each cheap wall-hanging.

As we travelled third class by train up to Delhi, packed cheerfully amongst families of farmers, and office workers, tradesmen and merchants, Brian began to feel ill. We put it down to yet another bout of giardia. But after a few days in the 45°C heat of Paharganj, the chaotic New Delhi hang-out for addicts and budget travellers, his eyes started to turn a lurid yellow-green. We were alarmed.

'Oh bloody hell,' said Brian the doctor, self-diagnosing himself with hepatitis. 'It's really contagious,' he said, and with that dashed to the nearest street-side pharmacist. He returned with a syringe and an enormous needle, cornered me and administered a shot of gamma globulin to my backside. I was still complaining weeks later.

Realising it would be hard for Brian to recover in India on our meagre budget, which precluded the cool of an air-conditioned hotel room, doctors and even bottled water, we decided to hightail it for the UK. Harried, I searched the bucket-shop travel agencies in Delhi for affordable tickets to London, settling on a black market Aeroflot flight purchased from a frightening Afghani whose shop in Old Delhi was at the far end of a dark alley. The flight deposited us in Tashkent, at the time swarming with Russian soldiers retreating from Afghanistan, then hopped us on to Moscow and, finally, London. We landed at Heathrow in the middle of the night. It was October 1985, we were broke and Brian was ill, but from the moment we stepped from that plane and felt the chill of the English autumn, we began to plan our return to Asia.

The Greater Ranges is a term made popular by alpinists in the Victorian period and is used to distinguish the high peaks of Asia from the European Alps. The term encompasses the high mountain ranges of the Himalayas – the Karakoram, Hindu Kush and Hindu Raj, Pamirs, Tien Shan, Kunlun Shan and Nyenchen Tanglha – along with various smaller ranges inside Tibet and in western China. All of these ranges have peaks over 6000m and most have peaks over 7000m, and together they are home to all of the world's 7000m-plus peaks. Climb in the Greater Ranges, and you know you've come of age as an alpinist.

During our mid-1980s Asian odyssey, our lack of finances and insight, and a Kiwi do-it-yourself ethic, meant Brian and I were as self-sufficient as we could be on our Himalayan trips. We spurned the use of porters and carried enormous packs, at times resorting to double-packing loads over the high passes when the altitude took its toll. In hindsight, this was a decision that affected us both mentally and physically – we arrived back in New Zealand at the end of 1986 seriously underweight and torridly worn out.

Decades later, after reading about the expeditions of the mountaineering greats – Chris Bonington, Maurice Herzog, Ed Hillary and Reinhold Messner – I began to wonder what it would be like to take part in an organised assault on a mountain. Even more appealing were the lightweight expeditions described by Andy Fanshawe and Stephen Venables in their 1999 book *Himalaya Alpine-style: The most challenging routes on the highest peaks.* Climbing in Alaska had introduced me to the benefits of an organised mountaineering trip, but I wanted to do more, climb higher. The Venables/Fanshawe book became something of a bible – I poured over the stories, minutely examining every photograph, every map and every chart. An ideal grew, to be part of a Himalayan expedition with all the trappings – porters, sirdar, liaison officer, cook, base camp, advanced base camp – but one where the climbers operated 'alpine style', self-sufficient on the mountain above base camp. I didn't want to climb with assistance from high-altitude porters and guides, and I wanted to climb a technical peak, not a rarefied 8000m giant.

Meeting Malcolm Bass in Alaska in 2002 and again in 2003, I realised I'd found a potential ally; someone willing to front up both financially and physically to technical multi-day alpine-style routes. When he wasn't busy working as a clinical psychologist, Malcolm had been on half a dozen expeditions to the Himalayas since the early 1990s, including a number to the Gangotri region of northern India. He was considered something of an expert on the area. Maybe he'd want another trip? Could he possibly want to climb with me? After my second season of climbing in Alaska, I plucked up the courage and approached Malcolm with the suggestion that we organise an Anglo–Kiwi expedition for 2004. To my delight, he agreed, and I became enormously excited at the prospect. Malcolm even had a peak in mind – Jankuth (or Janahut), at the head of the Gangotri Glacier, which at 30km is one of the longest glaciers in the Himalayas. Jankuth (6805m) was unclimbed, technical and very beautiful, he said. It was in the famous Garhwal region.

'A plum,' Malcolm said. 'The only reason it hasn't been climbed is because it's so bollocksing remote.'

The Garhwal is arguably the earliest explored part of the Himalayas. It was described by nineteenth-century traveller and mountaineer Tom Longstaff as 'the most beautiful country in all of Asia'. He went on to say:

> It has neither the primitive immensity of the Karakoram, the aloof dominance of Everest or the softer beauty of the Hindu Kush,' he said. 'Mountains and valleys, forests and alps birds and animals, butterflies and flowers all combine to make sum of delight unsurpassable elsewhere. The human interest is stronger than in any other mountain region of the world, for these anciently named peaks are written of in the earliest annals of the Indo-Aryan race.

Today, the Gangotri Glacier area, the popular hub of the Garhwal, remains the main arena of climbing in India. Its mainstays, Shivling, the Bhagirathi Massif and Kedar Dome, attract a yearly quota of climbers, but nothing like the numbers flocking to the Khumbu region of Nepal. The upper reaches of the glacier are rarely visited, however, because of the remoteness and inaccessibility – hence Jankuth's lack of attention and virgin status.

By April 2004, Malcolm and I had rallied together a group of like-minded individuals to come on our Jankuth expedition: Paul Figg and Andy Brown, friends of Malcolm's from the UK who were both experienced at climbing at altitude; and Marty Beare, who had never climbed in the Himalaya but wanted to give it a try. We enlisted the help of a company called Himalayan Run and Trek, fronted by a Mr Pandey, to organise our peak permit, sort out the myriad of government fees and levies, find porters for the walk in to base camp, locate a government liaison officer, employ a cook and a cook's assistant, and buy food, basecamp tents, pots, pans, tables, chairs, and so on. The other option was for us to deal with these logistics ourselves, but as Malcolm pointed out, with India's fetish for bureaucracy, it was much easier and cheaper in the long run to have a company do it for us. By the end of August we were set to go … and I was very hyped up! I hadn't climbed at altitude for many years and knew that, at nearly 7000m, Jankuth was a big unknown for me.

Arriving in Delhi after nearly two decades, the city seemed unchanged, the wonderfully familiar colours, sounds and smells that are distinctly India washing over me in an exuberant wave. It seemed just yesterday that Brian and I had been there. But when I tried to find the budget hotel we'd frequented in Paharganj, or the dingy restaurant that had served our favourite *masala dosa*, there was no sign of them. There were fewer signs, too of the hippies – both the drug addicts who'd sold their passports to feed their habit, and the long-term bottom-budget giardia-ridden travellers who had been away from home for years. Western travellers now seemed more affluent, better clothed, better fed and more short term.

Two long days' drive in our half-size private bus got the team to Gangotri, a funky little town in the Uttarkashi district of the state of Uttarakhand. Large swathes of the road were scoured by flooding, and we had to push the bus hundreds of metres at a time through the mud. The town was at the end of the road, perched precariously across the banks of the headwaters of the Ganges River and surrounded by large granite spires. Gangotri is a Hindu pilgrim destination focused around a small but very lovely white marble temple to the goddess Ganga, built by a Nepalese general in the early eighteenth century. The whole town closes down for the winter, when many of the sadhus – who are a head-turning feature of the town – migrate down to the warmth of the plains. Thirty kilometres up a well-worn foot track is the terminus of the Gangotri Glacier; this is where many of the pilgrims head to, as bathing in the water rushing from the glacier is a holy ritual.

We began our walk in to base camp after spending two days sorting porter loads and enjoying the company of the jovial and bizarre locals. Marty, who'd initially been a little taken aback by India, was beginning to relax. 'I've just had the weirdest experience,' he told us one afternoon. He'd been approached by an elderly gentleman wearing a long orange robe, leather sandals with thick socks and a woollen balaclava pulled down around his face. Perched on his nose was the thickest pair of bottle-lensed glasses, through which he'd peered up at Marty with unabashed interest. 'I thought he was a sadhu at first,' Marty spluttered, 'but then he started to talk to me about the 1997 Westpac New Zealand takeover of the Bank of Melbourne. Turns out he's a banker from Bombay.'

Another extraordinary character was an elderly gentleman called Mountain Baba or Swami Sundaranand, who had been one of India's premier mountaineers in his youth, as well as a yogi, sadhu and photographer. We visited him at the suggestion of our liaison officer, Chandra. Mountain Baba sat in front of us in the familiar orange robe and a woollen cardigan, his legs crossed beneath him and smiling benignly. He blessed our expedition by raising his hand and nodding sagely. Beside me, Malcolm hissed, 'Look at that photo.' On the wall was a large photo of a youthful Mountain Baba in a contorted yoga pose displaying an astounding set of abdominal muscles. It was an outrageous picture and none of us could take our eyes off it, much to Chandra's embarrassment. Mountain Baba told us that when winter arrived he'd head to Delhi to deliver a series of corporate lectures, and had done so in various countries around the world, including the USA. Then he sold us copies of his beautifully produced coffee-table book of photos of the Gangotri area at US$75 a pop. To me, he epitomised all the anomalies that are India.

Out on the trail, thirty-five porters carried our equipment. They were all young men from western Nepal, fleeing the persecution of the Maoists, and despite being tiny many carried double loads in excess of 45kg. 'When winter comes we will go to the plains to work in road gangs,' the leader said. 'Then we'll come back here next summer.' They laughed and giggled day in, day out, and kept us all awake at night playing endless games of poker. I became known respectfully as 'Madaaaam', and they were always trying to do things for me – take down my tent, help me on with my pack, dry out my shoes – but I was uneasy with the memsahib role.

By the third day we'd climbed to 4200m, and established a base camp on Sunderban meadow at the junction of the Kirti and Gangotri glaciers – a lonely, windswept spot frequented only by bharals, the native mountain sheep of the Himalaya and Karakoram. We pitched the cook tent and the mess tent, and then our own satellite tents in orbit around them. The weather was superb and the surroundings magnificent – the South Face of Shivling reared above the Kirti Glacier, the Bhagirathi Massif sat across to our left, and up the valley was a wild, magnificent peak called Karchakund.

But Jankuth was nowhere in sight, still 18km away at the head of the glacier. After the porters had relinquished their loads and headed for the road end, the five of us were left with the task of stocking an advanced base camp (ABC) beneath the mountain. We headed enthusiastically up the Gangotri Glacier for a day trip, each carrying a large pack of supplies, which we deposited on the glacial moraine at what we ignominiously called 'Dump Camp'. Unfortunately for Dump Camp, a metre of snow fell overnight and the little EV 2 tent full of food first disappeared, then collapsed, under the weight of it. It was Malcolm's tent. 'Two broken poles,' he grumbled in his Yorkshire accent. 'Bollocks. Bollocks. Bollocks.'

Not only that, but the snowfall saw the demise of our mess tent, and for the rest of the expedition the five of us, plus our cook Hera and his assistant, all shared the same communal space when we were around base camp. 'Oh well, makes for extra warmth,' said Malcolm, and he was right – it was nice sitting beside Hera's kerosene stove.

After a couple of rest and acclimatisation days, we settled seriously into the task. It took five days of ferrying loads to establish ABC, and it was a process I found demoralising as I was always hundreds of metres behind the men, plodding along on my snowshoes in a world of my own, weighed down by a 30kg pack. I'd also found it hard leaving the relative luxuries of base camp in what had turned into a mixed, cold weather pattern, knowing it could be up to a month before we returned. Every afternoon, large, dark cumulus clouds spilled over the range and by 3 p.m. it was snowing. A cold wind blasted down the glacier, picking up the snow and hurling it in our faces. We would pitch camp in a storm and wake to a fine day, only for the bad weather to return in the afternoon.

Jankuth wasn't visible until we were almost at our ABC site at the junction of the Gangotri and Miandi Barmak, less than 3km from the base of the mountain. 'There it is, finally,' Marty yelled, flapping his arms in excitement, as I puffed up beside him. 'It's quite high,' he said in the next breath, and it was too, towering above anything else in the vicinity – a steep, elegant pyramid, with alternating bands of pinkish granite and blue ice cliffs tumbling down its western side. It took no more than a cursory glance for us to realise there was no easy route to climb, but any lingering thoughts of base-camp luxury flew from my mind. I would die, just DIE to be the first person to climb that, I thought to myself, with a secret smile on my face, and I knew Marty was thinking the same thing.

Our ABC wasn't particularly salubrious – just two tents pitched on the snow at the edge of the glacier – but the location was glorious in its remoteness. At the head of the glacier were the peaks of the Chaukhamba Massif, all above 7000m and ringing what is undoubtedly one of the great mountain cirques of the world. Karchakund stood wild and handsome across the glacier, while almost 20km down valley, the now diminished shape of Shivling dominated the horizon. All memory of the endless snowshoeing and heavy loads disappeared; I was just so glad to be there. I could hardly believe it – I was in the Himalayas and about to try a first ascent. Things couldn't have been better.

Malcolm, Andy and Paul had already been to the base of the Jankuth to scope a route and returned excited. 'We've chosen a Scottish mixed line,' they told us. 'The rock looks fantastic. It should be well protected from avalanche.'

Marty and I wandered up the next day and settled on a typically Kiwi route – a huge snow and ice lead that would deposit us into threatened terrain but, given good snow conditions, would get us quickly up the 1200m to the summit ridge. There we'd be safe, and it would just be a matter of traversing the ridge to the summit. It would take two days to climb the face and another two days to traverse the ridge and reach the summit, we figured. With the three days needed for the descent, that made a total of seven days on the mountain. Then we'd be back at the glacier, triumphant.

'Reminds me a bit of the Caroline Face,' Marty remarked. 'There's potential danger there, but at least it will be a fast ascent.'

Two days later, all five of us were sitting at the base of the West Face, nervously awaiting take-off. We were at 5200m, 1700m below the summit. Our gear was strewn about in semi-organised piles and the afternoon was gruellingly hot.

'This is it,' Malcolm said. 'Who knows, in a few days' time we could be on the summit?'

The rest of us mumbled in agreement, trying to contain our excitement. Was I really going to climb an unclimbed mountain, I thought to myself? I couldn't control my emotions – tense and grumpy one minute, wired with anticipation the next.

But, like clockwork, the familiar purple clouds rolled in that afternoon and it began to snow. We waited an hour, then Malcolm, Paul and Andy, crowded into the diminutive EV 2 with its hastily mended poles, decided to head back to their larger tent at ABC.

'We'll need to let the face clear of snow for a day anyway,' they said. 'No point waiting here. We're too squashed. Bye.'

Marty and I waited out the night, during which we were almost engulfed in a large avalanche churning down the face. The wind blast flattened the tent and we only just got the door shut in time to prevent an influx of snow. Alarmed, we joined the others.

Another two days passed and Marty and I returned. The other three had headed back to Dump Camp for more supplies. We peered apprehensively up at the face through the binoculars; the sky was a deceptive blue, the mountain had shed its cloak of fresh snow and everything sparkled in the stillness. Jankuth was begging to be climbed.

'What do you think, mountain guide?' I said to Marty, hopping from one foot to the other.

'OK, let's do it,' he said, forthright. 'Let's leave tonight. Second time lucky.'

At 11 p.m. the stars were glittering in the crystal-clear sky and the temperature was -20°C. The gas cooker stuttered, then came to life. I tried to eat some muesli but nerves had me empty my plate into the snow. I managed a lukewarm cup of tea. Then we packed the tent and headed into the night.

During that first day on the mountain we wallowed in deep, cold snow up to our thighs, making painfully slow progress. I was constantly anxious and felt very 'out there', with just Marty and me on the mountain and 18km from base camp, which in turn was three days' walk from the road end. Even the town of Gangotri had limited telephone facilities and no Internet access. What if one of us was injured? Who would get us down? What if we were hit by an avalanche?

'Do you think the snow pack is safe?' I asked Marty repeatedly, painfully aware that two of our friends had died in avalanches six months before.

'I think it's OK,' he would say, poking at the snow pack with his ice axe.

After twelve hours of struggle we arrived, very tired, at a vague snow rib 700m above the glacier. Higher up, the steadily steepening slope narrowed into a series of ice flutings. To our left was an imposing set of ice cliffs and a truly colossal granite pillar. Realising there'd be no camp spots until the ridge a further 500m above, we chose to pitch our little red tent on the snow rib, guessing it would afford some protection from avalanches. I set about slowly digging a platform with my ice axe, stomping with my boots and stopping every few minutes for breath while Marty scuttled around taking photos. Then I stopped and looked around.

'Bloody hell, this is great,' I realised. The weather was perfect. The symmetrical summit of Swachand (6600m) commanded the west, and behind was the tip of Satopanth, more than 7000m high. The Gangotri rolled lazily down around the corner, and over squat Miandi Parbat I could see the blue-green foothills of the Himalayas. Maybe I could see the plains? One billion people, out there somewhere, living their lives. Far below were the Brits, tiny dots were moving up to the camp at the bottom of the face. I waved and shouted.

'They'll never hear you,' Marty pointed out.

I bet they're waving and shouting too, I thought. A relaxing afternoon rolled out in front of us – after all the hard work, we were on our way to making a first ascent of a Himalayan mountain. My God. If I wasn't the luckiest, the happiest person in the world.

We couldn't replicate our 11 p.m. start of the night before; in fact, we didn't get going until 6 a.m., moving slowly upward with the sun into the severe chill. The terrain steepened and soon we were pitching seventy-degree ice, heading towards the flutings. These turned out to be 10m high, and negotiating them was difficult. We began hauling the leader's pack as the angle and altitude sapped our strength. It was also very cold, and although I was wearing all my clothing – including my down jacket – I couldn't get warm. After six ice pitches we moved right onto a defined snow arête, and once again hit deep snow. By now I was beyond exhausted and chilled to the bone, and Marty took over the lead, plugging deep steps and shovelling away a couple of feet of snow to place ice screws. I was worried we'd climbed too quickly – 1200m in two days. A textbook ascent is 300m per day for optimum acclimatisation. Was I feeling the initial effects of altitude sickness? Please no.

The sun was sinking as we hit the 6500m summit ridge at 6 p.m., and all around us the mountains were appearing and then disappearing amid towering cumulus clouds. Swords of light streaked across the sky and a strong, bitter wind carried angry snowflakes through the air. The Chaukhambas were within touching distance and far down the valley was Shivling; we were now higher than its summit. Lightning began to flash in the encroaching dark, followed by crackling peals of thunder. We hastily scraped out a tent platform. What was the weather doing? What would the night bring?

Cooking dinner in the tent, I was hit by a sudden urge to vomit. My temples began to throb and my vision blurred. 'Oh fuck'. I knew what was happening: the first stages of acute mountain sickness (AMS). I couldn't believe it. I curled in my sleeping bag in misery – my summit. I beseeched (anybody) that I'd feel better in the morning.

Meanwhile, 500m below us, Malcolm, Andy and Paul were having their own drama. They'd left their camp that morning and had climbed 650m of mixed ground to a site on a small ledge slightly above and to the right of where Marty and I had camped the night before. They'd had a good day – step-plugging was less arduous shared between three and the mixed ground was challenging but fun. Crowded into the EV 2, they tried to get some rest. The weather worried them though – what were those dark clouds? By 9 p.m. it was snowing. Lightning flashed, illuminating the Chaukhambas in electric blue, and the three men felt very exposed. By midnight, small avalanches were threatening to push their tent off the ledge. What to do? Stay and risk being hit by a large avalanche, or abseil off the ledge into the dark? They realised their position was extremely dangerous, and fighting panic made the decision to retreat. In the dark and snow, they headed down.

In the meantime, Marty and I were frightened by the thunderstorm but, camped above the main cloud layer, missed the worst of the snowfall. We woke to a frigid, clear morning – a perfect climbing day. But I was no better – my head throbbed alarmingly and I could eat nothing. Marty convinced me that we should stay put for another twelve hours in the hope I'd improve, so we settled back in our sleeping bags.

Sometime during the following night, Marty really began to worry as I was deteriorating. There'd be no way he could get me off the mountain if I collapsed, he realised. He fed me dexamethasone, a strong steroid, but to no effect. My head was imploding, I was unable to keep food down, and unable to think straight or sleep.

'You're weak, you're hopeless, get up, get up, get going,' I told myself over and over. 'Your chance to climb this mountain is slipping away.' But a dreadful lassitude had invaded my body and part of me just wanted to be home.

The next morning, Marty gently convinced me that we needed to go down. 'Look where we are – it's so remote and we are so far out on a limb here. Eighteen kilometres from base camp, and that's three days from the road end. The situation is really serious.'

'No we can't go down! Why aren't things different? Why is this happening to me?' I railed against my physiology and sobbed out loud as I staggered around packing the tent. I was heartbroken. I desperately wanted my summit. But I was putting us both in danger. We began the long rappel back down the West Face.

Anyone who has suffered an altitude-related illness will never forget the pounding headache, the nausea, the fatigue, the insomnia. Coupled with being far from home, high on a mountain in less than comfortable surroundings, AMS can be a painful, lonely and despairing experience.

AMS is essentially the effect on humans of exposure to low partial pressure of oxygen at high altitude. It presents as a series of symptoms much as I have described – something like a very bad bout of flu or a hangover. It can progress to high-altitude pulmonary oedema (HAPE) or high-altitude cerebral oedema (HACE) if not treated. It's impossible to determine who will be affected by altitude sickness and the causes are still not fully understood. What is known is that the percentage of oxygen in air (21 per cent) remains almost unchanged up to 20,000m. But the air pressure itself (the number of molecules of both oxygen and nitrogen per volume of air) drops as altitude increases. Consequently, the amount of oxygen available to sustain mental and physical ability decreases above 3000m. Contributing factors include dehydration due to the higher rate of water vapour loss from the lungs at higher altitudes, the rate of ascent and individual susceptibility.

The most serious symptoms of altitude sickness arise from oedema (fluid accumulation in the tissues of the body). At very high altitude, HAPE results from fluid build-up in the lungs, which in turn prevents effective oxygen exchange. As the condition becomes more severe, the level of oxygen in the bloodstream decreases, which can lead to cyanosis and eventually death. HACE is the result of swelling of brain tissue from fluid leakage. It usually occurs after a week or more at high altitude and, in severe instances, can lead to death. In both HAPE and HACE it is necessary for the sufferer to get to a lower altitude immediately – not easy if the way up the mountain has been difficult or the weather bad.

I have often wondered to what stage my AMS had developed high on the summit ridge of Jankuth. It wasn't HAPE or HACE, I knew this much, but I was very ill. Doing some reading on the subject, I came across an article called 'Outdoor Action Guide to High Altitude: Acclimatization and illness' by Rick Curtis from Princeton University. It seemed to sum me up:

> Moderate AMS … includes severe headache that is *not* relieved by medication, nausea and vomiting, increasing weakness and fatigue, shortness of breath and decreased coordination. Normal activity is difficult although the person may still be able to walk on their own. At this stage only advanced medications or descent can reverse the problem. Descent even a few hundred feet may help and definite improvements will be seen in descents of 1000–2000 feet.

By the time Marty and I had abseiled four rope lengths my headache was waning. After ten rope lengths it was gone, although I still felt desperately weak. It was dark by the time we reached the glacier, but we continued to ABC knowing the others would be worried. I shambled along in the halo of my head torch, too tired and too dispirited to think.

Up ahead, a light appeared. It bobbed up and down, zigzagged here and there, and then a Yorkshire voice called, 'Bollocks. Am I glad to see you two.' Malcolm loomed out of the dark and I promptly burst into tears.

'We had to turn back, it was my entire fault, we would've made the top if it wasn't for me, it's all my fault,' I sobbed. Poor Malcolm, I was inconsolable.

Would we have made the top if I hadn't come down with AMS? Probably. But we may not have made it down. Sometime in the night a severe snowstorm moved in and we crawled out of the tents at ABC the next morning to find over a metre of new snow on the ground. Malcolm, Paul and Andy decided to hightail it for base camp but, needing a rest day, Marty and I stayed put. The following morning we packed up camp and, shouldering enormous packs, headed down the glacier into the blizzard – blinding snow, angry gusts of wind and zero visibility. At ten o'clock that night we made it to the haven of base camp, where the others were waiting for us with a huge meal, a bottle of whisky and a general feeling of, 'OK, we didn't make the summit but well done everyone, we gave it our best shot.'

The storm lasted for over a week – it was the first of the winter, Chandra said – and the temperature plummeted. Marty and I were both in agreement that, had we pushed on to the summit, we would have been caught by the storm on the descent and perished on that high, lonely ridge at the far end of the Gangotri. A sobering thought, but one that brought a small amount of relief from the self-blame that absorbed me. Slowly, I began to see the expedition in a new light. I'd learnt more about my reaction to altitude and would plan my acclimatisation better next time. I'd been to the remote end of one of the longest glaciers in the Himalaya. I had climbed steep, high, technical ground with a heavy pack on, and climbed it well. I'd been to within 300m of the top of an unclimbed peak. I'd spent six weeks in India, one of the most fascinating countries on earth. Wasn't that enough? In many ways it was, but the sense of failure still lingered in the background. I thought back to my travels with Brian in the 1980s. I was climbing in a different league now.

Twenty years earlier, Brian had recovered from his bout of hepatitis in London and, after topping up our flagging funds, we'd made our way back overland through Europe, then Turkey, Iran, Pakistan and India, to reach Kathmandu in the beginning of February 1986. It took us seven arduous weeks of local buses and trains, but we found the noisy, friendly little city unchanged and a haven after our long, isolated journey. Almost immediately we set off on a six-week foray into the mountains – possibly a mistake, because I was constantly ill. Not with altitude sickness this time, but with malaria, which we calculated I'd picked up in southern Iran. I was treated for the disease in Lahore, Pakistan, some weeks later and partially recovered but never really regained my fitness. We spent from May until September in the Karakoram doing several very ambitious high-pass traverses and climbs, again forgoing porters, carrying enormous loads and compromising on food.

After nearly four months in Pakistan I contracted pleurisy, and we had to turn back from a trip into the Baltoro Glacier because of my relentless cough and high temperature. No amount of rest restored me to health. When Brian, a 90kg rugby forward in New Zealand, reached 70kg, we reluctantly realised that we needed to take it a bit easier. But by then I was deeply in love with the Karakoram mountains – there was so much more I wanted to see and do. Perhaps I just needed to try harder? Were we getting soft? Couldn't we rally for just one more trip?

'No! We're done here,' Brian said.

We crossed the border to India and settled on a houseboat to recuperate in the lovely Kashmiri town of Srinagar. To Brian's delight, Australia and India were due to play each other in a one-day cricket test. There was some wonderful shopping to be had – traditional carpets, Kashmir shawls, lacquerware – but I couldn't relax and remained discontent. Again, I hadn't performed in the mountains the way I'd wanted to, and the disappointment I felt in myself failed to dissipate on arrival back home, almost two years from the day we left for Singapore. Brian threw himself headlong into his flagging medical career, quickly returned to his former weight, and seemed happy and satisfied with his lot. I wasn't, and struggled to find a reason to be in New Zealand. I'd failed as an alpinist, and was about to fail as a doctor's wife. I wanted to be far away, back in Asia. I slumped into a depression no amount of medication or counselling would shift, and by the middle of 1988 our marriage had foundered.

It would be decades before I could appreciate just what Brian and I had achieved. We'd spent the best part of two years in the mountains of the Himalaya and Karakoram, taken on self-sufficient two-man trips that drove us to the end of our physical and emotional endurance, and travelled thousands of kilometres overland through countries at war that were letting in few western visitors. We'd lived on the minimum of money. We'd made the most of those two years, experienced them to the fullest, been in each other's pockets relentlessly but remained the best of companions. If only I'd realised the quality of our relationship at the time. But I was blinkered by a sense of failure and a flagging self-worth.

It was September 2007. Three years had passed since the Jankuth trip and I'd since become something of an old hand at expeditions to the Greater Ranges. For two consecutive years I'd climbed successfully in western China, one of the last bastions of unclimbed mountains in the world. Earlier in 2007 I'd been to Pakistan for what turned out to be an unsuccessful but very fun expedition with Lydia Bradey. I'd been back in New Zealand just six weeks before heading to India with Paul Hersey and Shelley Graham, a married couple from Dunedin, and Scottish climber Bruce Normand.

Bruce and I tried repeatedly to get another permit for Jankuth, but failed. In the intervening three years the Uttaranchal State Government had decided to add their permit and peak fee to the fee required by the Indian Mountaineering Federation (IMF). The IMF was happy to give us a permit, but the state government turned us down, for no other reason than our peak wasn't on their list of mountains for climbing – something no doubt down to the fact that Jankuth was (a) unclimbed, and (b) unknown because of its remoteness and lack of attention. Jankuth was unfinished business for me, but we eventually gave up and applied for the unclimbed southeast ridge of Karchakund, a beautiful, wild peak dominating the middle reaches of the Gangotri Glacier. Karchakund was climbed by a British team via the north ridge in 1987, but had not been touched since. The southeast ridge was the impressive but very difficult-looking line visible from our 2004 advanced base camp. I thought it a worthy target and one that was bound to attract the ever necessary funding. After much effort on the part of Himalayan Run and Trek, we were granted the permit.

In the two decades since Brian and I had trekked back and forth across northern India, the subcontinent had continued on its erratic political and social journey. Governments had come and gone, borders and territory were disputed. After Indira Gandhi's assassination in 1984, the Congress Party chose her son Rajiv as the next prime minister. At forty, he was the youngest national political leader ever, and his youth was seen as an asset in the eyes of a population tired of government inefficiency and corruption. Rajiv lead Congress to its largest majority ever, reaping the sympathy vote from his mother's assassination. In 1987, he brokered an agreement between the government of Sri Lanka and the Tamil rebels who had been tearing the island apart for over a decade. Indian troops were sent to enforce the agreement, resulting in outbreaks of violence that ultimately ended the fighting but killed thousands of Indian soldiers. Then on 21 May 1991, while Rajiv Gandhi campaigned in Tamil Nadu on behalf of his Congress Party, a Liberation Tigers of Tamil Eelam female suicide bomber assassinated him.

In the following years leading up to the end of the twentieth century, the Indian economy was opened to global trade and investment. By the time of my expeditions, the nation was finally being looked upon as a potential superpower.

At the end of August our team of four united in Delhi. We were something of an unknown to each other. Bruce and I had met once before in New Zealand, and we had climbed the Coxcomb Ridge of Mt Aspiring together in glorious weather and in quick time. Paul I knew as a talented author but not as a climber. He and Shelley were keen to try an expedition to India and, if nothing else, I knew they would be good company. But from the moment we met up in the YWCA in Delhi, a seed began to grow in the back of my mind. Was this expedition a mistake?

Bruce arrived from Switzerland sometime in the middle of the night, short-tempered and disgruntled, and with little time for the rest of us or our staff. Six weeks beforehand, he'd reached the summit of K2, the world's second-highest mountain, without oxygen, a remarkable feat of alpinism and athleticism. He'd been back to Switzerland briefly for rest, then come straight back to India. Granted, he was very tired and I was willing to cut him some slack. Paul and Shelley, in India for the first time, were wide-eyed and requiring some direction, but happy to be there. I was still jaded from my trip to Pakistan in June, and felt overly responsible for the expedition and a bit homesick.

A few days later we were in Gangotri. The town was as quaint as ever and Shelley and Paul were delighted with the temple, the sadhus and the massive granite spikes hogging the skyline. Bruce kept to himself, and went off on a long walk while the rest of us sorted the equipment and food into porter loads. On the last day of August we set off on the walk to base camp in clear weather with our entourage of porters, liaison officer Samal, cook Saran and cook's assistant Kanaia. We arrived at Sudenbam three days later. Nothing had changed – even the bharals were still there.

This time I was determined to acclimatise to the altitude before setting foot on Karchakund and suggested to the others that we head part of the way up Kedar Dome (6900m), the great white hulk of easy-angled slopes towering over the camp. I pointed out that it was impossible to acclimatise on the Gangotri Glacier because it's so flat, and suggested instead that we could have some staged camps on Kedar, up to 6000m. Everyone agreed that this was a good idea, although Paul, who was already suffering from the altitude, was less enthusiastic.

Several days later we were camped on the northern slopes, Paul and Shelley a few hundred metres below Bruce and me. To the north were spectacular views of the granite towers of Thalay Sagar, Meru and Shivling. Twice Bruce and I had been up to 6200m in glorious weather, then retreated to our camp at 5500m to sleep. I felt fine on the climb, but had several bad nights with a splitting headache and little appetite – it was tempting to head down, but I stuck it out. The means will justify the end, I will be super-acclimatised, I convinced myself.

Meanwhile, Bruce's mood had improved; he seemed happier in the mountains and was good company as we relaxed at our top campsite. I queried him endlessly on K2 – how did he feel up there? Was it cold? What about all the other climbers?

'Idiots,' he said, 'idiots the lot of them.' There were climbers there who should never have been 'within a hundred miles of the mountain,' he said, and was particularly scornful of a Korean climber who had needed two porters to carry her oxygen. 'Tourons,' he called them, 'who rely too heavily on the porters and know little of what high-altitude climbing is all about.' I was fascinated by the conversation, but wondered if he wasn't being a little harsh.

In the meantime, the weather couldn't have been better and Karchakund beckoned white and beautiful up the glacier. Back at base camp, Bruce and I had a good day together, caching some food and equipment under the southeast ridge and studying our route and the best way to access it. I began to feel more optimistic.

After ten days, the team deemed itself acclimatised, organised and ready to climb. All four of us departed for Karchakund laden down with heavy packs, and were waved off by Samal, Saran and Kanaia, who would settle in to listen to a one-day cricket test series on their little transistor and await our return. Bruce and I set up a gritty and uncomfortable advanced base camp on the moraine under the imposing East Face of Karchakund, and the next day wandered further up the glacier to scope out a potential route on the South Face for Paul and Shelley. We were dallying behind, looking at the southeast ridge from different angles, when we saw Paul and Shelley heading back toward us, looking glum

'It looks awful. The icefall is really dangerous. Bummer. I think we like the look of that mountain over there instead,' Paul said, waving his ice axe at Yeonbuk, a lovely but moderate peak to our left.

'Why not?' Bruce said. 'No one is going to know what we climb way up here,' he added, meaning that the ascent would be illegal and unreportable.

Paul shrugged. 'Fine by us,' he said

At three o'clock the next morning Bruce and I packed up our tiny First-Light tent, stumbled across the moraine, and settled into a steady trudge up the rock-strewn lower slopes of Karchakund's East Face. Bruce quickly pulled away from me in the dark. I followed the erratic blink of his head torch, feeling out of touch and a bit uneasy, and I wondered just how much say I would have on the way this climb panned out. Bruce was a strong character and a far better climber than I was, there was no doubt about that. He was enormously fit and acclimatised, as anyone who'd just climbed the second-highest mountain in the world would be. Our route was very difficult. Was I out of my depth here?

Up ahead, the first rays of sun were peeping through a small rocky col on the southeast ridge proper and glinting off the shiny grey ice on the slope below. I was plucking up the courage to ask for the rope when Bruce stopped in front of me. 'I think I'd like the rope on,' he said to my surprise, getting ready to lead.

I followed his pitch slowly, feeling the weight of my pack. Then my lead came, and I headed upward then right to cross a small gully. As I built an anchor from two ice screws I glanced down at Bruce. He was gazing away across the glacier, and looked bored. What's he thinking, I wondered. That he's been lumped with a lemon for a partner? That he's glad he didn't have me as a partner on K2? I knew I was going slowly – I was only just controlling a reoccurring knee injury with double doses of codeine and ibuprofen. But we moved on steadily, alternating the remaining six ice pitches, and arrived at the col in time for a late lunch.

As we ate, iron-grey clouds began to build in the north behind Shivling. They were the first clouds we'd seen since our arrival, ten days ago. 'What you think they mean?' Bruce said, indicating with his Clif Bar.

'I wonder if it's the end of our good weather?' I replied, recalling the unpredictable and stormy weather we'd had in 2004. 'I hope not.'

Bruce looked gloomily away and said nothing.

After lunch, Bruce shed his pack and scrambled off to check out the next section of the route – some steep rock climbing that would take us to the west, then back up a broad gully to the ridge again. On his return, we glanced again at the rapidly increasing clouds, then Bruce indicated back at the ridge. 'OK, let's go,' he said, and we climbed on, although I knew he too was glancing periodically over his shoulder at the building mass as the afternoon wore on. That night we set up camp on a small snow platform, cooked dinner, and settled in to see what the weather would do.

Dawn arrived to reveal several inches of snow surrounding the tent and, during breakfast, what remaining blue sky there was faded out. The snow began to fall heavily – thick, wet flakes from a now leaden sky. What to do? We sat in the tent for the next few hours, taking it in turns to look out and report on the state of the weather. By 11 a.m. almost 30cm of snow had piled against the sides of the tent.

'Time to go down,' said Bruce. I hastily agreed, and as we V-threaded our way down off the col, all I could think was how glad I was Bruce had been first to voice the decision to turn back, not me.

The next week passed in a blur of dissatisfaction. By the time Bruce and I arrived back at base camp, 60cm of snow lay over the ground. It continued to fall heavily for seven days and the temperature plummeted. Bruce and I hunkered down in our tents to wait it out, but Paul and Shelley, unused to expedition procedure and the vagaries of Himalayan weather, thought the trip was over. They couldn't grasp the concept of using the time to rest, recuperate and psyche up for the next attempt. Often this is a part of an expedition I enjoy, especially if I have had a period of intense physical activity beforehand and have plenty of climbing time left. The weather is beyond my control, and it offers a chance to read, which I love but have limited time to do at home. This time, however, I felt responsible for the pair and couldn't relax.

Just as tempers were starting to fray and tolerance for the bad weather was at its limit, the sun returned. Spirits rose, including my own, and plans for heading back up the glacier were hatched. Bruce and I headed off on our snowshoes at four o'clock the next morning with the temperature around -15°C. Paul and Shelley, who'd rehatched quiet plans to attempt Yeonbuk, waited until daylight. We'd said our good lucks and goodbyes the night before. 'See you in a few days, guys.'

Back at the base of Karchakund we looked up at our route. The rock steps were now plastered in snow and the hanging ice faces pillowed with white – everything was poised to avalanche. I knew instinctively that I didn't want to go back up, and wondered anxiously what Bruce's reaction would be when I said as much.

'Well that's that then, this route is out of condition,' he said, before I could open my mouth. I said a silent prayer of thanks.

'Why don't we go round and take a look at the South Face?' I suggested. 'The route Paul and Shelley were originally going to try.' Bruce nodded thoughtfully, and we trudged on in the bright sunshine for another couple of hours, as always Bruce far in the lead.

The way on to the South Face lay up a tumultuous icefall, and within minutes of scoping the route through the binoculars we'd concurred with Paul and Shelley's decision. There was no way we were going up there! As we watched, a large serac collapsed with a whoomph! Bruce sat on his pack looking sullen and distant.

What to do now? It didn't look like Karchakund was going to happen. Maybe we should head to the north side for a look? Or had we wasted enough time on this mountain – should we throw in the towel and go home? Part of me wanted to, and then I imagined how I'd feel arriving home without at least trying to climb something. I couldn't call our first attempt a proper try. Could something be salvaged from the trip? I looked around.

Several kilometres away across the glacier, on the north side of the Miandi Barmak, was a peak of about 6500m. Off its western flank flowed a steep icefall about 500m high. Unlike the icefalls plummeting down the western side of the Gangotri, which were steep and angry, could this one be climbed? And if we climbed it, maybe we could summit the peak via that steep spur on the right? I looked again and again, tracing the route up the icefall, across the cwm and up the slopes to the summit ridge, unwilling to draw Bruce's attention to the mountain until I was absolutely sure it was a realistic prospect.

'What do you think of that nice-looking peak over there? I remember from the guidebook it hasn't been climbed. And look, that icefall looks manageable. Maybe we could give it a try?' I held my breath while Bruce peered through the binoculars, expressionless for several minutes.

'Not a bad proposition,' he finally said, in his thick Scots accent.

That night we camped very close to the site of the 2004 Jankuth advanced base camp, but there was no evidence of our team ever having been there. The spot was as lonely as ever and I kept peering across at the base of Yeonbuk, hoping to see the comforting yellow of Bruce and Shelley's tent. But they didn't seem to be there. Directly above us rose the icefall. The bottom two-thirds looked relatively free of hazard, but the top third was a prickly mass of tottering seracs and deep blue crevasses.

Just two days and we could be on top, I told myself. Then another three days and we'll be back at base camp. Then it's just the walk out and drive back to Delhi and this expedition will be over. The time will pass and it will be worth it because we'll have climbed something. I just need to keep it together for a few more days.

The next morning we left in the dark and plodded slowly up the lower reaches of the icefall, looping easily through the slots. As the dawn broke the terrain became more problematic and we roped up to tackle the steep, more crevassed sections. Even so, mid-afternoon saw us topping out in the broad cwm and settling on a campsite in a sheltered hollow. There was a cold easterly wind blowing, which picked up eddies of snow and flung them in our faces. Over the ridge to the southwest were the Himalayan foothills, dark blue, hazy and distant. The cwm was cupped on one side by a dinosaur's tail of sharp granite pinnacles and behind by another icefall. Jankuth towered over the southern rim. It was a stunningly beautiful place. We passed the rest of the afternoon uneasily watching the weather.

The day before the push for the summit is always a stressful time in an expedition. The whole journey has led to this; the organisation, fundraising, bureaucratic hassles, acclimatisation and load-carrying all culminate at this one point in time, which could be jeopardised at any moment by the weather. An overnight snowstorm, and the expedition will have been for nothing – especially if time is running short, as it was for Bruce and me. We needed to be back at base camp in four days to meet the porters, begin the walk out and, ultimately, catch our flights home. If we were going to climb the mountain, it was tomorrow or never. Just keep it going, I told myself – it will be worth it.

We left our camp at 3 a.m. in exquisite cold. To my surprise, I was feeling fit and acclimatised as I followed the beam of my head torch up, always up. Bruce, as ever, was out in front. After several hundred metres we broached the lip of a col leading over into the Miandi Barmak and felt a frigid blast of wind. The sun began to rise.

'I'm not sure about those clouds over there,' Bruce mused. I hadn't noticed them and turned around in surprise. From over the Chaukhambas foreboding streams of high cloud were whipping across the pale sky. Oh no! Please give us just a few more hours I prayed, then tried to put the clouds out of my mind.

We roped up for several pitches of ice, climbing above the massive icefall that tottered over our camp. At any other time I would have enjoyed the climbing, but I couldn't stop looking behind at the building mass of grey. The wind increased, the clouds moved faster, and I put my down jacket on over the rest of my clothing, shivering despite the physical effort. By noon the summit reared above us, but the slopes leading up to it were steep and gunmetal grey with ancient ice.

'Might be better to traverse across to the left and see if we can get onto the summit ridge that way,' Bruce said, pulling his hood hard around his face. I followed in his wake. We were so close now; we could pull this off if only the weather would hold a few more hours.

At 4 p.m. the summit ridge disappeared in the swirling cloud and it began to snow lightly. Blasts of wind rushed up the slope from the Swachand Barmak, buffeting us with ice granules. The glacier below had long disappeared and I stopped looking for Paul and Shelley. Hunching our way along the ridge, we butted up against a steep ice pyramid topped with a cone of rock that appeared fleetingly through gaps in the cloud. As Bruce led up a steep pitch I hoped with everything that this was the summit, but after half a rope length he'd disappeared into the grey and I was left alone and unknowing. The wind tugged and bullied the rope as I crouched in the bergschrund, hunting for shelter. Finally, I heard a faint cry. 'Come on up.'

The final pitch led up a small gully ... to where? I tucked my head further inside my down hood, and front-pointed doggedly on. Suddenly, there was no more up. I was standing on a small table top of snow, alone at 6500m, snow pummelling my face as the wind pushed me double. I was on the top, 1100m above our camp in the cwm, 1700m above the glacier. We'd beaten the weather. I shouted into the wind with joy and relief. Now we could go home.

At the time of writing in 2010, India's population topped 1.18 billion, making it the second largest on earth. It is also going through a historic transformation to become a global power, and has the world at its feet. But there are two Indias. While one India is on a rapid development trajectory, the other has 300 million people living below the poverty line. Most of these come from small villages and rely on agriculture for their livelihood. They work on the land seven days a week just to stay alive, earning less than US$1.25 a day. Recreation is an unknown concept to them.

Driving back to Delhi in our private bus, I gazed out of the window for mile after mile. Men worked their crops with their animals, women and girls carried water in earthen pots, children in rags stared back at me. How could I ever justify climbing a mountain to these people? How could I explain the money and time spent satisfying my own ego to someone whose life revolves around simply staying alive? How could I even explain the concept of recreation to someone who has neither the time nor the money for such a luxury?

This expedition was the first during which I questioned my motives for travelling half the world for the sake of climbing a mountain. Was there any purpose to it, other than my own satisfaction? A sport such as cricket gives pleasure to millions of fans, particularly in India. It connects people from different cultures across the world, and supports a sense of nationalism and pride. High-altitude mountaineering satisfies none of these. Bruce and I made the first ascent of a lovely peak against the odds, but so what?

CHAPTER SEVEN
The Ultimate Price

Death is part of all our lives. Whether we like it or not, it is bound to happen. Instead of avoiding thinking about it, it is better to understand its meaning. We all have the same body, the same human flesh, and therefore we will all die. There is a big difference, of course, between natural death and accidental death, but basically death will come sooner or later. If from the beginning your attitude is 'Yes, death is part of our lives', then it may be easier to face.

– Dalai Lama

When people think of Tibet, they usually imagine a remote and mysterious land of high steppes, mountains and snow, inhabited by a gentle Buddhist population of nomadic yak herders and burgundy-clad monks, and with an ancient culture of literature and monasteries, that has become one of the great tragedies of the modern day. More than a million people died as a result of the Chinese occupation of Tibet during the 1950s, and although international awareness of what took place has grown over the last half century, what is less well known is that there was a fierce armed resistance against the invaders, particularly in the eastern Tibetan region of Kham. Here, groups of men, retaining a warrior-like quality of old, banded together to oppose the Chinese by force. Although they were ultimately unsuccessful, these guerrillas, riding on horseback and often equipped with outdated weapons, put up a good fight. They let the so-called People's Liberation Army (PLA) know what the majority of Tibetans felt about their presence. This Khampa uprising is now a matter of history. In 1950, following their defeat of the Kuamintang, the PLA entered western Kham, overcame it and merged it into the Tibetan Autonomous Region. The eastern side was joined to the Chinese province of Sichuan, the border between the two formed by the Yangtze

River. The region's rugged mountain ranges are, in fact, the far eastern edge of the Himalayas.

In 2005, quite by chance, I came across a book called *Buddha's Warriors: The story of the CIA-backed Tibetan Freedom Fighters, the Chinese invasion and the ultimate fall of Tibet* by Mikel Dunham. Out of idle curiosity I bought the book, but by the time I'd finished its 400 pages I had determined that the region of Kham was a must-visit. Unlike the western area of Tibet, with its popular 8000m peaks, to me Kham was a mystery. It held romance, it had unexplored mountain ranges, unclimbed peaks and hidden river valleys, and it was home to a race of people whose persona was at odds with the typical Buddhist demeanour of peace and acquiescence.

I delved further and found the publications of an elderly Japanese academic called Tomatsu Nakamura. By 2005, Nakamura had made as many as twenty-five journeys into Kham and was considered one of the great explorers of modern time. He had just published *East of the Himalayas – to the Alps of Tibet*, and luckily for me, he had written it in English.

At the time I was suffering a serious bout of depression, triggered by a break-up with Marty Beare not long after the Indian Jankuth expedition in 2004. After fifteen years as friends and climbing partners Marty and I had fallen suddenly into a relationship, which sadly foundered after only eighteen months. I was very ill, but clung to normality by attempting to complete a journalism qualification extramurally, while holding down a full-time job as a journalist (my first) with a small community newspaper. I was terribly overcommitted, was drinking too much and eating nothing, surviving on calories from the alcohol and a heavy dose of anti-depressants. Journalism was to be my new career, offering an end to the eighteen years I'd spent teaching outdoor education for a living. I was tired of outdoor education – the concept of teaching people the basics of recreation had begun to feel, ironically, groundless and trite. I wanted a career where I could make some social contribution.

But another expedition! That would really give me something to look forward to. I asked Karen McNeill what she thought of the idea, and she was immediately on board. Karen had been asked to speak to the National Geographic Society in Washington – a real honour – and what better than to speak of an expedition to one of the most significant unclimbed mountain regions on earth today?

In the middle of *East of the Himalayas* was a series of colour plates of (then) unclimbed peaks, one of which showed the north face of a steep, bold, very white peak called Xiashe (5833m). Xiashe (pronounced 'Zza-sha') lies on the Tibetan Plateau three long days' drive west of the Sichuan capital of Chengdu. It's in the Shaluli Shan (Shaluli Range) and rises above the southern fringe of the Zhopu pasture, a vast golden plain dotted with nomadic yak herders' tents and yaks. During the Chinese invasion, the herders rode out against the PLA tanks on horseback, wielding their swords. It must have been quite a sight. Nakamura's book said that a large monastery overlooks a beautiful lake on the northern edge of the pasture that is full of holy trout. The side valleys are forested in juniper, deodars and rhododendrons. To me it sounded like heaven.

Karen and I decided we'd attempt the first ascent of Xiashe, which at the time had had one former try by a team of Koreans. We thought it looked beautiful, and within our capabilities. But we also found out that a team of British climbers would be vying for the first ascent and would likely be there at the same time. This stirred a sense of competition in us. First, however, we had to get a peak permit.

Aware of my fragile and overcommitted state, Karen took over the expedition organisation and sourced an agent in Chengdu called Zhenleng (Lenny) Cheng, who got us a permit from the Ganzi Tibetan Autonomous Prefecture Mountaineering Association for the sum of US$1500; a cheap fee to pay for an unclimbed peak in Asia. She also applied for, and won, a US$7000 Shipton–Tilman Award from W. L. Gore (Gore-Tex), and after adding to that a number of smaller grants our finances were sorted. Karen's Mountain Hardwear sponsorship meant that she was always clothed in the latest in women-specific outdoor clothing and always had the latest tent. She was also getting a financial stipend from the company to fund her climbing. I was very jealous. 'I'll see what gear I can get for you,' she said. 'Make a list of what you want!' I did.

Six weeks out from our planned departure for China, doctors and counsellors persuaded me to spend some time in the psychiatric ward of Dunedin Hospital. 'You aren't coping,' they persuaded me, even though I thought I was. 'You need to have your medication properly monitored; you need to get some proper rest. If you don't agree to go, we will have you committed.'

I was appalled. I had worked so hard to manage my new job, plus the hour-long drive each way to get to it, and the ongoing study that kept me up until the early hours of the morning. Being busy had seemed the best way to cope with my dark state. 'And you can't possibly go to China while you are this ill,' I was told. But the three-week 'break' turned out to be just what I'd needed. My sisters visited, the staff was both practical and compassionate, and I was allowed to go off to the local gym every day. I returned home rested, with a new medication regime and in a somewhat better state of mind.

In September 2005, I left New Zealand for China. I remember boarding the Thai Airways flight out of Auckland with a small suitcase full of anti-depressant medication, sobbing uncontrollably because Marty hadn't rung to say goodbye. I left my family and friends consumed with worry, but there was no doubt in my mind that I was doing the right thing. Climbing was the only thing that was going to make me feel truly better.

Karen was waiting for me at Chengdu airport with the irrepressible Lenny Cheng. Standing just 155cm tall at most, and looking decades younger than his fifty-three years, Lenny bounced into my life like a court jester. Driving down the wide boulevards towards the city, he chatted non-stop as I peered around in amazement – here was a modern city of 14 million people and I'd never heard of it? Arriving at our hostel in downtown Chengdu, Karen dumped several armloads of Mountain Hardwear clothing, a virgin sleeping bag and a beautiful new tent in my lap, and I spent an hour of bliss stepping in and out of my new wardrobe. I felt I'd come of age – an American company thought I was worth supporting. I felt a flutter of optimism.

The next day we set off in a battered Range Rover, heading west along a six-lane highway, which soon became four lanes, then barely two as we entered the Daxue Shan range and followed the Dartsedo River to the delightful city of Kangding. As we purred along the highway, I couldn't stay awake – months of insomnia was taking its toll – but as we arrived in Kangding I began to wake up.

'Hey, check out this place, man,' Karen said in her pseudo Canadian accent. 'It looks aaawsome.'

The small city, wedged in a deep valley on the steppes of eastern Tibet, ringed by 4500m peaks and with a galloping river splitting its CBD, was closed off to westerners until recently. It's now the gateway to the Chinese Ganzi Autonomous Region of Sichuan but used to be the frontier between ancient China and mysterious Tibet. Karen and I thought it charming. Smartly dressed Chinese wielding mobile phones mingled with young Tibetan girls in jeans and heels, while older women in traditional long Tibetan aprons, with red strands of cotton yarn braided across the tops of their foreheads, sold yak butter on the pavement. Khampa men in sheepskin tunics and Stetson hats, long knives belted at the waist, lounged across the seats of their motorbikes in kerbside groups. School was just out, and dozens of children in matching English-style uniforms were making their way home along the footpaths. We thought the Khampa dress exotic and the men enormously attractive. We raced around the souvenir shops and up the German cableway to the local monastery before it got dark. We noticed the chill drop in temperature and wondered what base camp would be like at 4200m.

The following morning we drove straight up onto the Tibetan Plateau, zigzagging 2000m up to the first pass in an hour and a half – too much altitude gain for my system. Struggling out of the Range Rover to look at the view, I had a thumping headache Panadol wouldn't shift.

'Poor Patria,' Lenny sympathised, and brought me a cup of tea from a funny little stall. His solicitation was genuine and Patria, his version of Patricia, stuck. Despite the headache, I found the view breathtaking: range after range of brown hills rolling away to eternity, interspersed here and there by white peaks that seemed ethereally suspended in the air. One in particular, was massive.

'Gongga Shan,' Lenny said with a wide grin. 'Ha killed many, many climba!'

He was right. At 7556m Gongga Shan (or Minya Konka) collects all the weather moving west across southern China and has a reputation for repulsing most who come to climb it, and killing around 20 per cent.

'You need at least ten weeks if you are going to climb Gongga Shan,' said Lenny, 'to wait out the weather. Ver, ver dangerous!' Another grin.

After eighteen hours of bone-crunching discomfort we rattled over the last of three 4500m passes and rolled down a slope into the town of Litang. If Kangding had entranced us, Litang, we both agreed, had to be the grooviest town ever! At 4200m it claims to be the highest 'city' in the world and its streets offer unparalleled people-watching opportunities. It was like no other place either of us had ever been, with tall, swarthy Khampa men in embroidered hats and *chuba*, or sheepskin-lined coats with extra-long sleeves; women with hair down to their waists decked out in a festive profusion of gaudy turquoise and silver jewellery; and dirty urchins with streaming noses running carefree in the cold, rarefied air.

In the middle of the town was a large square decorated with, of all things, life-sized plastic palm trees. Locals sat under them chatting, completely oblivious to the anomaly. A long boulevard of the trees led down to the edge of town, where it petered out into the brown steppe. Every second door off the street seemingly opened to a pool hall, and outside each was a muddle of motorbikes and tethered horses, as brightly decorated as each other in bits of tinsel and red ribbon. The 'cowboys' slouched, played pool, or roared up and down the street on their motorbikes, their long, shining black hair streaming out from under their Stetsons.

Karen and I bought some of the chunky jewellery favoured by the women and paraded it down the street to the delight of the locals. We ogled the men and egged each other on to get their photographs. Karen was bolder than I in this respect.

'Can't we take a couple of them with us?' she giggled. 'Oh man!' For the first time in months, I laughed and laughed. I was having a good time. It was fun being there with Karen. The troubles of home were fading.

Then it was back on the road.

Eighteen hours later we finally reached the headwaters of the Zhopu River and drove onto the Zhopu pasture. We'd changed from the Range Rover to an ancient American jeep, more suitable for negotiating the last 80km of muddy track from the diabolically awful hamlet, lodged in the bottom of a dark, damp gorge, where we'd spent the previous night. Every house there had a large, fierce, mangy Tibetan mastiff chained to the front door; the streets were wall-to-wall mud, and the same mud covered the surly inhabitants. We spent a frigid night in a basic guesthouse, unwilling to venture out too far, before leaving the main Kangding–Lhasa highway.

'It's like something from the Middle Ages,' Karen said, screwing up her face. 'I'm surprised no one's in the stocks.'

The Zhopu pasture was a complete contrast, spread out before us like a huge golden carpet. At over 4000m, it was bordered on the north by a range of granite peaks and on the south by a number of snow-covered mountains, one of which was Xiashe. We were all – Lenny included – enormously happy to arrive at last, as three sixteen-hours days on the roughest road imaginable had taken their toll.

The track stuttered off across the pasture to the Zhopu monastery, but somehow we had to head back east to the base of our mountain. The area was new to Lenny, but our Tibetan driver nonchalantly wheeled off the track and began heading across the grass, dodging swamps and the black tent encampments of nomadic yak herders. Karen and I pressed our noses to the glass. The camps were deserted but for the odd woman with a small child clinging to her legs and a skinny but formidable mastiff hurling itself in a frenzy against a pegged rope as we passed. Far up on the sides of the hills we could see yaks dotted like flies, and here and there the figure of a yak herder.

Nomadic yak herders are known as *drokpa*, Lenny told us, and make up about 25 per cent of the Tibetan population, or in some counties as much as 90 per cent. There are an estimated two million people in the Tibet Autonomous Region and other Tibetan areas that practise some form of nomadic lifestyle. Most are nomadic only in the summer; in winter, they live in houses in the lower valleys and have been doing this for centuries. The nomads carry their possessions from camp to camp by horse, by yak or, these days, by truck. A typical nomad has 50 yaks, perhaps 300 sheep and half a dozen horses, and might earn US$100–300 a year. It is the weather, particularly the rainfall, that determines whether nomads have a good year or a bad one. If there's a good rainy season, pastures are lush and there is plenty of feed for the animals, but the down side to the rain is that too much makes it difficult to dry yak dung, which is essential for cooking as the altitude at which the nomads live is far above the tree (firewood) line.

A hard winter can kill stock. The worst winter snows in fifty years occurred in 1996, when an estimated 1.2 million yaks, sheep and goats perished, affecting about 80,000 Tibetan herders. Lenny told us that piles of animals could be seen on the sides of the roads and desperate Tibetans were breaking into the cars of foreigners (Chinese) looking for food. These days in some parts of Tibet, nomads are encouraged to fence off their pastures to prevent overgrazing and erosion, and to switch from subsistence herding to industrial livestock production. The nomad families that go along with this sign long-term contracts for state-owned land, and are given money for fencing and access to yak sperm banks. Those that don't agree with the government's wishes face harsh fines.

Even more extreme is the Chinese 'comfortable housing programme', which since 1999 has seen the Chinese government relocate some 250,000 nomads (nearly one-tenth of the population) into new 'socialist villages' close to the main roads. Settlement policies vary and the effect on the social fabric of the nomadic communities is complex. In many places they have been encouraged to give up their animals, leading to reduced income and a rise in alcoholism and other social problems. Nomads are also ill-equipped to compete with Chinese migrant workers for jobs. The government claims the scheme enables the herders to have access to schools, jobs and healthcare, but human rights activists tell a different story. They say peasants must take out loans of several thousands of dollars to pay for the houses (which cost an average of US$6000), and don't have the right to challenge or refuse participation in the scheme. They also say that the relocation scheme has generated a social resentment amongst the Tibetans and will eventually lead to the final extinction of the Tibetan culture.

'Tibetan way of life ver important,' Lenny said. He was one of a growing number of Chinese who valued the Tibetan culture and had some comprehension of its fragility. Not only was he widely read on the subject, he also spoke Tibetan. As we drove Lenny would shout noisy greetings to his Tibetan friends, who replied in form. He was even good friends with one of the leading monks in the Litang county – quite an honour apparently.

After an hour of wheeling and skidding across the pasture, we turned south up a side valley, and suddenly the North Face of Xiashe – 2000m of steep snow, rock and bulbous icefalls – reared above us. Our first thought was one of dismay. The whole face was scarred with avalanches and the black trails of rockfalls, making it appear to be a completely different mountain to the one in Nakamura's book. It looked far too dangerous, possibly beyond our capabilities, and we pondered the situation as we set up a base camp at 4100m beside a small stream, under the scrutiny of a bunch of boys who'd appeared from nowhere, dressed in burgundy robes like mini Tibetan monks. 'Novice monks,' Lenny explained. (These boys and their yak herds were to become regular visitors to our camp. The animals would wander through, grazing lazily and tripping over our tent pegs.)

The following evening, after a day of looking at the mountain from a number of different angles, and both of us suffering mild headaches and lack of breath from the altitude, the sky darkened and it began to snow. The inclement weather continued all the following day, confining us to our tents. I read *The Bookseller of Kabul* in a single hit. Lenny revealed his cooking skills, presenting us with fabulous Sichuan meals far surpassing anything I'd eaten on an expedition before. On the third day we woke to find the skies clear and Xiashe transformed under several feet of fresh snow – the first snow of the coming winter, Lenny told us.

We were enchanted! 'Gee!' said Karen. 'This is what we need.' Here was the beautiful white peak we'd expected. We headed excitedly up the valley with a load of food and equipment, and set up a cache at the toe of the small glacier directly under the North Face. But two more days of unsettled weather laid another 60cm of snow at base camp, and progress once again ground to a halt. We began to wonder if we had the strength to lay siege to the face under all the new snow. Perhaps we would be better off following the long and convoluted east ridge – at least it would be free of avalanche hazard. The other option was the southwest ridge, which would involve a long trudge through deep snow to the head of the glacier and an ascent of the ridge from there. We dithered, unable to commit to either route.

But on the evening of our fifth night at base camp we were harshly galvanised into action by the arrival of three British climbers. We had known that Ed Douglas, Duncan Tunstall and Tom Prentice were going to turn up, but had managed to push their inevitable arrival to the back of our minds. Now, suddenly, our first ascent was under threat. The three invaded our camp like a whirlwind and we were initially stunned by their size.

'They're enormous,' Karen whispered to me as the three descended from their 4WD vehicle. "They must be at least 6'6". How on earth are we going to compete with them?'

They had enormous thighs, all the better for plugging steps in waist-deep snow, and shoulders as broad as a rugby players. But when Tom pointed out, 'Hey, I'm only 5'10" and I have really skinny legs,' we were incredulous until we realised our misconception was the result of having spent two weeks in the company of a race of people whose average height was just over 5ft (150cm). We'd become unused to 'normal'-sized people. We laughed uproariously at our stupidity.

It was good to have the Brits around – we swapped climbing stories, played cards and tried to drink abominable Tibetan liquor. We knew Ed from his formidable reputation as a journalist and writer. Tom was the editor for Scottish Alpine Club and Duncan seemed an all-round life and soul type. They seemed to appreciate Lenny's cooking as much as we did.

Karen and I eventually set off on a four-day acclimatisation sortie up to the 5200m col at the head of the glacier running under the North Face. Getting there was extremely hard work in the deep fresh snow – even in snowshoes we were sinking up to our thighs. Although I was feeling a lot happier at this stage, my poor health had left me unfit and weak, so Karen did most of the work. I began to realise what a debt I owed both Karen and Lenny for setting me on the road towards some form of equilibrium. I couldn't have asked for two better companions; we laughed together constantly and I knew intuitively that coming to China had been the right thing to do.

After reaching the col we returned to base camp for a day of rest before our summit bid. The Brits in the meantime had had an acclimatisation day on a smaller mountain and declared themselves ready to attempt the North Face in a couple of days. Although there was no outward competition, Karen and I girded our loins.

'Hey man, this is our mountain!' Karen muttered to me in her Kiwi-Canadian accent. 'We were here first.'

We knew we were the weaker team, and inevitably settled on the south-west ridge as our route because, although it wasn't the most technical, it afforded us the best chance of a summit. We loaded up our packs, planning to leave the following morning, and spent the last night at base camp playing poker with the crew, in a state of heightened anticipation.

Snow was falling lightly when we set off at around 7 a.m., making our way up the valley to the forested area where we'd left our cache. We passed the site of a now abandoned nomad's tent camp. The ground was strewn with, of all things, old shoes. Up on the glacier we struck deep snow and, struggling and cursing with our loads, made the decision to double-pack to the col. We carried a half-load up onto the glacier, sinking to our knees in cold powder, then returned to the moraine and spent the night there. The next afternoon saw us in a desperate situation as we tried to negotiate the final slope, at times having to burrow a way clear with the snow shovel. We eventually got a load to the top, but had to return the next morning for a second. We spent the afternoon peering at the route through the binoculars while a bitterly cold wind relentlessly buffeted the tent. The binoculars told us we'd have to drop 200m in height to avoid a ridiculously pinnacled piece of ridge line, allowing us to sidle round to the base of the broad South Face. We'd go up that, hit the ridge again and race for the summit.

That night the gale shook the tent harder than ever, and it was very cold. My thermometer read -20°C at 9 p.m., and I made us hot-water bottles from our Nalgene drink containers. Getting up at midnight was awful, and it took us ages to pack up and head off as the wind continued to hammer the tent. We secured it as best we could and crossed our fingers that it would be there on our return. Karen had a headache and said she felt bad-tempered and lethargic, although I didn't notice. 'Sometimes I hate this sport,' she said. 'But funny how the bad bits fade when you get back home. Then you just wish you were back there again.'

The descent off the ridge was simple enough and got us out of the gale, but in the pitch black we didn't know where to start up the face. Our head torches seemed woefully inadequate, and after trudging back and forth we eventually got fed up.

'Why don't we just try going up that way?' I said to Karen grumpily.

'What else can we do?' she agreed. 'We can't sit here until daylight, we'll freeze to death.'

We began to front-point upwards with no idea of the terrain above and all the while the wind bombarded us with ice pellets and threatened to tear the rope from our hands. 'I really, *really* need to do something about my feet,' Karen said after a short time, so we built an anchor and hung on it while she carefully removed her boots one at a time and massaged her toes.

'This isn't working,' she said, putting the boots back on. 'Let's try and light the friggin' cooker, see if a hot drink helps.' But the cooker wouldn't light, as the wind was too strong. By now we'd wasted an hour, and if anything were even colder than before, despite being cocooned in our down jackets and insulated pants. We gave up on the cooker, figuring we were at risk of frostbite standing waiting, and climbed on.

After a short while I heard a clank and a rattle and looked down, alarmed. 'Oh crap, one of my crampons has fallen off,' I squawked at Karen, perching on one foot and looking anxiously around me. There was no sign of it within the halo of my head torch.

'It must have fallen,' Karen said, 'I'll lower you down.'

I went slowly backward down the hill, and after 20m came across the crampon, lodged on a small lump of ice. 'Phew, lucky,' I said, relieved, as I put it back on.

At 5 a.m. the gusts got perceptively stronger and we felt the updraft from the north side, indicating the ridge line. The gale increased and, suspecting a cornice, we kept off the ridge, sidling carefully south and up as the sky began to lighten. Then, with a flash, the sun burst over the horizon and lit up the summit – very close now. Half an hour later we were on the top, and there were no other footprints. We were first.

'We're the first!' Karen yelled. 'We're the bomb! This mountain's ours, man.'

We whooped and hugged and leapt around punching the air. We threw snow in the air and watched it stream away like a long pennant to the south. Then we lay on our stomachs and peered carefully down the North Face. There were no Brits climbing towards us. We laughed and laughed with the craziness of it all.

Our descent back down the ridge in the daylight went quickly. We had some concern about avalanches on the South Face, but decided to try to forget about them. Before long we were at the base, and for the first time in days the wind dropped. We lounged around in the relative -5°C heat, finally got the stove going for a cup of tea and ate a packet of ToffeePops I'd brought along for Karen. 'They're my favourite, 'she said, 'and one of my great regrets of leaving New Zealand.'

The warmth was blissful. But the hike back up to the ridge line was hard work in the melting snow, as we sank down to the rock beneath. We finally arrived back at the tent around 5 p.m.

'Man, I'm so very, very happy,' Karen said. I was too.

That night the wind picked up again and blasted the tent with ice crystals. The nylon sides flattened against our faces and there was little sleep to be had. On top of this I developed an altitude-related headache and by morning was vomiting. So it was a relief to drop down to the shelter of the glacier where the wind and my AMS symptoms abated. We danced along under the North Face, where Ed and Duncan could be seen heading up the lower slopes, wallowing in the deep snow.

Back at base camp, Lenny was delighted with the efforts of his 'wimin' charges; obviously it was in his best interests for his clients to be successful. He cooked us a gorgeous meal of chilli yak meat, tuna and onion salad, pickled fried pork and Sichuan green vegetables, topped off with a celebratory bottle of Chinese red wine. Tom, who had decided not to accompany the other two, seemed really happy for us, and we appreciated his good humour and kind words.

Over the next two days we all watched Ed and Duncan through the binoculars on the North Face. It was an amazing feat of climbing. On the third night the two were just below the summit when night fell, and they sat out the darkness on a small ledge with the tent wrapped around them. They reached the summit the next morning and followed our footsteps down the South Face. When confronted with the climb up to the col, they were both so exhausted that they contemplated walking south to the Tibet–Sichuan highway, which would have put them roughly 200km away from base camp. Fortunately, good sense prevailed and they arrived back at camp the next night, very tired but in the best of spirits, knowing they'd pulled off a remarkable ascent.

When we weren't watching the boys' progress, Karen and I were umming and ahhing over what to do with the remaining eight days we had up our sleeves. From the top of Xiashe we'd seen a good-looking peak towering over the western end of the pasture. Lenny told us it was unclimbed, but to try it we would have to pay the requisite peak fee of US$1500 to the Ganzi Tibetan Autonomous Prefecture Mountaineering Association. We anguished over whether to use subterfuge and tell Lenny we were going for a 'trek' in the general direction of the peak, then give it a shot, or whether to pay up and do it legitimately. Tom patiently listened to us tossing around the options, changing plans on the hour and generally being hopeless. In the end we decided we couldn't cheat Lenny – he had been a wonderful guide and had become a true friend – and said we'd pay the fee and asked him to get us to the base of the mountain.

The next day the old American jeep appeared from nowhere and we bounced 20km across the pasture towards the mountain until a rough stream barred our way. 'We'll meet you at the monastery in a week,' said Lenny, and the jeep roared off, leaving Karen and me standing on the bank surrounded by our gear, wondering exactly where the monastery was.

'Let's worry about that logistic later,' said Karen, as we waded across the stream. Climbing west into a hanging valley, we met a sweet but desperately poor herder couple with a very dirty young child. They invited us to their tent and it was obvious this little girl meant the world to her doting parents. The valley was also quite beautiful; dark green deciduous forest surrounded a grassy meadow dotted with multi-coloured yaks, and a clear stream ran across the northern side. Is their lifestyle as simplistic and idyllic as it seems, I wondered. And what future is there for this little girl, who will have no education and who may never leave the Zhopu pasture? Will she be happy with her lot?

The family pointed us in the right direction and we hiked over a forested ridge. Dropping down to the base of a steep little glacier, we spent a peaceful night sleeping under the stars. I felt content, but my thoughts kept returning to the family. Could I be satisfied with their lifestyle? Maybe if I'd known no different I would be.

Two days later we'd made it to the bottom of the steep slope we hoped would take us up onto the summit ridge of our chosen mountain (we didn't know if it had a name). Camping at the base of a dirty grey ice cliff, we went to bed in deteriorating weather. By 9 p.m. it was snowing heavily and we were uneasy; by midnight, spindrift avalanches threatened to engulf the tent, and we were really scared.

'We have to get out of here!' screeched Karen, after one particularly heavy deluge reduced the tent's footprint by half and forced her onto my lap. Enough was enough. We crawled out of the tent, shoved everything willy-nilly into our packs, and shuffled as fast as the dark and blizzard would allow us along a ledge and down a nasty snowed-up couloir. Finally, with profound relief, we found a safe campsite under a rocky overhang.

It snowed persistently for the next four days – heavy, wet flakes that imploded on our nylon roof and forced us to dig out the little tent on the hour. We read the one book we had between us (a Jane Austen), ate the remainder of the food and endlessly discussed the reasons for my depression.

We played I-spy and twenty questions, we discussed clothes and mutual friends in New Zealand, and we got bored. Then it occurred to us that we had only two days to go before we had to meet Lenny at the mysterious monastery to start the long drive back to Chengdu. Considering we didn't really know where the monastery was, we had to leave!

Back on level ground, the Zhopu pasture had been transformed under 60cm of snow into a beautiful white realm. The yak herders had gone, packing up their tents and moving their herds down the valley for the winter. As we trudged towards the monastery in the now clearing weather, we listened to … complete silence. There was not a puff of wind, not a bark from a dog, not a call from a bird. It was a magical moment in a magical part of the world. How lucky I was to have experienced such a moment, I thought to myself. How glad I was I'd come to China.

Lenny was overjoyed to see us. He was comfortably ensconced in the old people's village attached to the monastery, but was starting to worry about his charges. Often when elderly Tibetans are widowed, they go to live near a monastery with other elderly widows, spending their days in prayer, doing charitable works and socialising. After spending two nights camped in a lovely old woman's back yard, it seemed to Karen and me an idyllic way to spend a retirement.

On the three-day drive back to Chengdu we were given a taste of just how harsh the Tibetan winter could be. We drove into a blizzard with the temperature well below -10°C, and broke down twice. We spent a frigid night in Litang, discovering to our amazement that the town had an Internet café. In Kangding we were in for a treat – to celebrate our first ascent of Xiashe, the top officials of the Ganzi Tibetan Autonomous Prefecture Mountaineering Association shouted us a night in the flashest hotel the town had to offer and took us out for a Sichuan banquet, a very riotous affair during which Karen and I were well and truly outdone by our hosts. 'These guys sure know how to party,' Karen said after yet another toast in our honour.

Back in Chengdu, we shopped for earrings in the Tibetan market and I bartered for dried yak meat, hoping against hope I'd get it home through New Zealand customs. Karen was the first to leave, flying out on a Singapore Airlines flight at ten o'clock in the morning. She'd become my support and my confidante, had helped me laugh and see a future less bleak, and I didn't want her to leave. But I never realised this would be the last time I would see her – waving as she walked through the departure gate, a small figure with a mass of dark curly hair and a winning smile.

Back home, I moved to a new job with a community paper in Wanaka and things began to mend. I kept insanely busy, putting far more energy into the job than was warranted, despite an editor who didn't seem to like me and an unhealthy relationship between the staff and the local entrepreneurial owner.

In the meantime, Karen was planning her most ambitious climbing project yet: the first female team ascent, with Sue Nott, of the notorious Infinite Spur route on the South Face of Mt Foraker in Alaska. At 5300m, Foraker is the second-highest peak in the Alaska Range, and the 2700m Infinite Spur is one of the hardest mountaineering routes in North America. By 2006, it had seen only seven ascents in almost thirty years, all by world-class two-man teams. No women had ever attempted it.

I rang Karen the day before she left for Alaska to wish her good luck. I made her promise to take care and back off the route if she felt out of her depth. She was light-hearted and happy.

'I think we can do it,' she said. 'Why shouldn't we? We've got the skills. The only thing that might slow us is the size of our packs.' Both Karen and Sue were small women, hardly weighing 100kg between them, but intended to apply the same approach as had seen them succeed on Mt Denali's Cassin Ridge – slow, steady and safe.

They started up the route on 14 May 2006, carrying approximately twelve days of food and fuel. North American climbers Will Mayo and Max Turgeon, retreating from a line to the right of the Infinite Spur, met Karen and Sue at the base of the route. They were carrying huge packs, the men said, and had hoped to be back at base camp in ten days.

A week later, another North American climber, Mark Westman, who had climbed the Infinite Spur in 2001, flew over the South Face and spotted tracks at the bottom of the arête. He saw no one on the route, but was unconcerned; by their own estimates, Karen and Sue still had several more days of climbing before they finished the route, let alone started the long descent. But later that day the weather turned for the worse, producing eight continuous days of blizzard. From the 25th to the 28th, gusts as strong as 110kph were clocked at the 4300m camp on neighbouring Mt McKinley, and more than 160kph higher on the mountain. Foraker was swathed in enormous, impenetrable lenticular clouds.

On 29 May, Will Mayo got a good look at the upper half of the Infinite Spur from a plane but saw no tracks or climbers. The pilot and owner of Talkeetna Air Taxis, Paul Roderick, was alarmed that there was no trace of the women. Back in Talkeetna, he contacted park ranger Daryl Millar and voiced his concern. Millar took stock of the information he'd been given – the weather, Sue and Karen's abilities, and the route – and on the 31st launched a full-scale search and rescue.

I was spending the weekend rock climbing when I got a message from Kim Czizmazia, Karen's friend in Canmore. 'Karen and Sue are missing,' she said. 'They are a week overdue – people are getting worried.'

I was stunned. Why had I assumed they'd be fine? I leapt on the Internet and read the headlines: 'North American Climbers Nott and McNeill Lost on Alaskan Mountain'. No mention was made of Karen's Kiwi heritage, so it was no wonder it hadn't hit the papers in New Zealand.

I called Karen's family, talking for an hour with sister, Wendy, reassuring her not to give up hope at this point. The two of them were hugely experienced, and had probably just holed up somewhere waiting for the weather to clear, I told her. 'Don't lose heart. They will be fine.' I agreed to handle the media in New Zealand, should their disappearance become news here.

Back in Alaska, a Lama helicopter was dispatched to fly over the route. The pilot spotted tracks at 4200m but no sign of the climbers. The next day, Westman was flown up and discovered Sue's pack, pad and sleeping bag low on the route. These were collected by the helicopter's electronic grabber and flown back to Talkeetna. Signs indicated that the equipment had been sitting in position for several days; the radio was inside the pack, still working but unused. Rescuers concluded that the pack had been inadvertently dropped or blown off the route.

Later that day, the Lama flew searchers over the lower section of the route. Nothing. A fixed wing scoped the standard descent routes off the mountain – the Sultana and Southeast ridges. Nothing. Two searchers were stationed at 2400m adjacent the Infinite Spur with a powerful spotting scope. Nothing.

By now Karen's family were making rapid plans to travel to Alaska, and I agreed to put out a press release to the media once they'd left the country. I wasn't sure how to do this, but my editor suggested I contact *The Press* in Christchurch and offer to write up the story. 'Make sure they agree to pay you,' he said. I was furious with his lack of sensitivity.

I wrote the story, which made the front page of *The Press* the next day, accompanied by one of my favourite pictures of Karen drinking tea at Xiashe base camp. I was immediately bombarded by journalists from radio, television and newspapers. I told the story again and again. In the meantime I was calling Canada daily, sometimes twice daily, in the hope of hearing some positive news. My friend Barry Blanchard was blunt. 'I think they're gone, darlin',' he said. I angrily brushed off his comment.

At the time, the media had just finished dealing with the death of British climber David Sharp on Mt Everest. David had suffered a lingering and solitary demise high on the mountain while dozens of so-called climbers and their guides walked past him, their intent on reaching the summit consuming all humanitarian thought of saving his life. I was determined that Karen and Sue's fate should not be confused with David's, and made a few enemies within the Everest fraternity in the process.

'These women were climbing one of the most serious mountaineering routes in the world, were there because of experience gained over decades of climbing "alpine style" on some of the toughest mountains in the world,' I told the media. 'The Everest summitteers were there because they had money, not skills. They'd paid to be assisted to the top by Nepalese Sherpas and professional mountain guides, and had little understanding of the vast wealth of experience needed to become a world-class alpinist.' I wanted the public to see the difference between the Everest climbers and Karen and Sue.

Back in Talkeetna the search efforts continued, but hopes were fading. Sue's family arrived and Karen's were on their way with Kim. On 4 June, three weeks after the pair had started up the route, the Lama flew four separate sorties, spotting tracks at 4750m and 4800m. The next day, more tracks were discovered at 5000m and 5060m, and the focus of the search shifted to the summit. The women had obviously made it to the top of the Infinite Spur, completing the route, and had reached the broad summit slopes. But by 8 June no more signs had been found. Then the bad weather moved in again. The winds howled.

My birthday was on 12 June and I was run ragged with the waiting, the media attention and my boss, who could not understand why I was so distracted. Much to his chagrin, I left work early and went home. I sat on the deck in the weak winter sunshine stroking my little cat Rinki, who smiled sweetly up at me. I knew it was over.

The phone rang. It was Kim. 'They've called the search off,' she said. 'The facts no longer add up. They'll have been without food and gas [for melting water] for two weeks. They only have one sleeping bag. There's been a week of really high winds. There's no chance they will still be alive. The search is transitioning into a "limited search" – a body recovery, not a live rescue.'

I sat with Rinki and cried and cried.

What happened to Sue and Karen? To this day their bodies have never been found, but there has been some speculation. The lost pack was probably dropped as there was no blood on it. The searchers were convinced that they saw footprints high on the summit, but saw no such tracks on the descent. Well-informed conjecture is that they dropped the pack by accident at 3500m and aborted the climb. However, instead of descending they decided to go up and then down a much easier route, but died in the attempt and are likely to lie in a snow cave near the summit.

After thirty years of climbing, I'd known many people who had died in the mountains; adding them up, they came to dozens. But there'd been no one like Karen – to her I applied the same fundamental reassurance I did to myself: 'It'll never happen to me.'

According to psychological studies, there is a basic assumption that people are motivated to protect themselves from harm. But this doesn't take into account paradoxical behaviour such as skydiving, bungy-jumping or mountaineering, where the individual enjoys the experience of being at risk and makes a conscious choice that the enjoyment of the thrill outweighs the risk. The person feels in control of the decision – even if the decision is to abandon oneself to the feeling of being temporarily out of control. Why an individual would persist in such irrational behaviour is a seemingly unanswerable question. Psychologist Albert Menninger said, 'The extraordinary propensity of the human being to join hands with external forces in an attack upon his own existence is one of the most remarkable of biological phenomena.'

But rather than inspiring me to put mountaineering aside, as Karen's family and friends expected me to do, I became more determined than ever to continue climbing. Karen was the toughest, most resilient person I'd ever known – that was her strength. She wouldn't expect me to give away the mountains. And I still couldn't let go of the premise: 'It'll never happen to me.'

It was déjà vu: the same galloping stream, the same handsome Khampa men and hip teenagers, the same Chinese entrepreneurs with their cellphones.

The only thing that had changed in Kangding, a year after Karen and I had headed through to the Zhopu pasture, was my climbing partner.

I had tempted Malcolm Bass to China with the possible first ascent of Haizi Shan, an unclimbed peak of 5833m in the Daxue Shan range, a day's drive north of the Kangding. No fewer than ten expeditions had tried Haizi over the past decade but, for one reason or another, none had been successful.

'Ver menee climba try, menee fail,' said Lenny, whose *joie de vivre* had been somewhat tempered by news of Karen's death.

I felt I'd come a long way since my previous visit to China. I'd battled to change careers and was now a trained journalist with a full-time reporting job. I'd even been tasked with editing the paper for short periods and was proud to be given this responsibility. I'd done my best to put Marty behind me and was making a concerted effort to avoid him in the small-town environs of Wanaka. And for the first time in my life I was on a medication regime for depression which, to my delight, seemed to be working. I had a future – an exciting future. I'd even accepted the medication as long term. 'Why fight it if it's helping,' my counsellor had convinced me. 'Depression is far more common than you think,' she added. And I was slowly, very slowly coming to terms with Karen's death. I was ready to go climbing.

Malcolm shared my enchantment with Kangding. 'It's like a Tibetan version of Chamonix,' he said, as we prowled the gift shops. He almost bought a plate with a picture of a Red Army soldier on it before deciding that it would be anti-Tibet. He loved the Khampas in their exotic dress but couldn't appreciate the men quite as Karen had done. He was excited about the trip and fun to be with, even if he was suffering from some form of stomach ailment picked up in our five days in Chengdu.

The trip had almost come to an early demise. I'd travelled through Bangkok's new Suvarnabhumi airport en route to Chengdu the day it opened. Everything was chaos, including the baggage-handling department. Not surprisingly, my bags arrived in Chengdu four days after I did – a tense time spent bombarding Thai Airways with queries and wondering how on earth we were going to replace my climbing equipment in a city of 14 million people but no outdoor store. Fortunately, we found a gym and a swimming pool in a large hotel close to our backpackers', and managed to work off some of the frustration.

Climbing up to the first pass in our 4WD, I felt the familiar altitude headache settling in, and by the time we got to the second pass, after traversing the western flanks of Haizi Shan, I had a full-blown migraine. Lenny fussed and was sweet. 'Poor Patria,' he kept saying. But my headache momentarily evaporated when we caught the first glimpse of Haizi Shan through a brief parting in the clouds. It was (and still is to this day) one of the most beautiful peaks I'd ever seen; not overwhelming like a Karakoram peak, but ethereal and elegant, rising out of an autumn forest landscape resembling North America, and with streams running off its slopes reminiscent of New Zealand's West Coast. Our base camp was to be in the forest next to a small river. Yaks grazed in the clearings and beautiful Tibetan boys with long, shining, dark hair and almond eyes rode past on their horses.

'There could be trout in that river,' said Malcolm, leaping from the jeep.

Malcolm and I were in agreement: the mountain was an alpinist's dream, with a number of lovely snow ridges leading up to the summit pyramid, some of which had been tried by previous hopefuls, some not. It was the untried 1500m North Face that took our fancy – steep, but with the potential to take us directly to the summit. That was if we could negotiate our way onto the lower slopes. Two things threatened this: first, a 400m-high granite cliff running the width of the lower face; and second, an impenetrable morass of low-growing rhododendron forest, dense, hostile and scratchy. We pottered up and down the broad yak herders' track on the opposite side of the valley, chatting with the locals as they sat with their animals and straining to get glimpses through the trees of a potential access route onto the face.

A deep, steep ravine appeared to carve its way through the middle of the cliff, draining a broad cwm at about 4500m. It was full of snow, which in turn was sprinkled with rockfall. Far up on the face, at about 5600m, was a truly colossal ice cliff. It took only a glance for us to realise a regular scenario: the ice cliff, periodically 'calving', would set an avalanche free-falling down the face. The avalanche would momentarily slow as it wound through the easy angle of the cwm, then pick up speed again as it cascaded wildly into the gully and whooshed frantically downward, to ricochet gleefully out the bottom and eventually grind to an exhausted halt in the creek bed. We tossed up the alternatives – be scratched to death by rhododendron or dice with the avalanches in the ravine. We chose the avalanches, and the next day carted our first load up the gully to our advanced base camp.

'I'm glad no one's watching us doing this,' said Malcolm. 'We'd be struck off the sensible climber list!'

After a week we'd climbed up through the gully three more times to acclimatise and stock our camp, and had survived. On the second trip we'd only just exited the bottom when we heard a loud roar above us. Scrambling hastily out of the creek bed, we turned in time to see a huge plume of snow billow from the cwm and tumble into the top of the ravine. 'Bollocks! Here it comes,' shrieked Malcolm, as the mass of snow spurted out the bottom and rolled to a halt beneath us. We burst into nervous laughter.

Overall, however, everything was going extremely smoothly, and after a couple of days' rest we deemed ourselves ready for our summit bid. In the meantime, Lenny and his offsider, Amping, were enjoying basecamp life – the beautiful setting, the good weather and the constant stream of visitors from the local yak herder population. There were always half a dozen Khampa men sitting around the campfire drinking tea. Amping, who was tall, broad and good-looking, prided himself in being a 'full-blood Khampa'. He had a beautiful baritone and could often be persuaded to sing a Khampa folk song. He was in training to become an employee of the Ganzi Tibetan Autonomous Prefecture Mountaineering Association and could cook a fine yak meat curry. I learnt a few years later that he'd become the president of the association.

There was even a little basecamp drama, in the form of a posse of policemen who arrived to investigate the theft of some local yaks. They drank tea at the camp and then headed off to a high valley, leaving one member who was suffering from blisters behind with us. Late in the evening, the sound of gunfire echoed around the mountains. There was a pause, then more urgent shots, then another volley. The abandoned policeman leapt to his feet and set off up the hill at a shuffling lope.

'What's happening, Lenny?'

'Oh! Policemen shoot yak thiefs dead,' Lenny exclaimed, with eyes like saucers.

'Really!' Our eyes were like saucers too.

Amping looked wildly up the hill, grasping the handle of the vicious-looking knife sheathed at his waist, seething with anticipation.

Despite the excitement, Malcolm and I felt fit and acclimatised. We spent a rest day discovering the whereabouts of a beautiful natural hot spring on a bleak and eerie pass about two hours' walk from camp. Steam from the springs hung suspended in the air while the tattered remains of Tibetan prayer flags fluttered from stunted trees, dwarfed by the towering flanks of Haizi Shan. We splashed happily, but it was a surreal, lonely spot.

After a brief snowfall, we left base camp for the last time on 16 October, climbing easily up to our camp in the cwm. An avalanche from high above had missed the camp by mere metres, but we were hopeful conditions would be safe for our summit attempt. We were joined by a little animal rather like a furry guinea pig, which appeared and then disappeared amongst the boulders. Malcolm later identified it as a hyrax. We spent a good hour trying to persuade it to sit still for a photograph.

The next day we continued up through a deep, cold snow pack to 5000m, dug out a safe tent platform on a narrow, exposed spur and nervously sat out a thunderstorm that rattled helter-skelter around the evening skies. Somehow I managed to burn a sizeable hole in the roof of the tent with the gas cooker, much to Malcolm's consternation. His expletives echoed around the mountains with the thunder for several minutes. Fortunately, neither the thunder nor Malcolm's swearing turned out to be a threat, and by four o'clock the next morning we'd packed for the climb and were off, Malcolm leading up and outward into a broad mixed gully in the dark.

We were a little tentative to start with, but gained confidence as the sun began to rise. The snow pack proved more stable, and the rock and ice more protectable, than we'd initially thought, and the pitches flowed one into the next until at 2 p.m. we were hit by a blast of cold, spindrift-saturated air rolling off the summit ridge. Both weary, we crouched beneath the cornice, snacked, and then threw on another layer of clothing and goggles before launching up the final 300m snow ridge to the summit. The clouds came and went with the wind, giving elusive but breathtaking views of the Tibetan steppe. We caught flashes of the plateau to the north and west, and the Daxue Shan range, dominated by the monstrous Gongga Shan, to the south.

This is so very, very beautiful, I thought. Unlike any other mountain view I've ever seen. The plateau goes on for ever. And it's such a huge unknown.

I ran out a final, shambling rope pitch and then huddled on the summit in the wind, waiting for Malcolm to join me. I looked down – there was our base camp, where Lenny and Amping would be watching us through the binoculars. Somewhere out east was the vast realm of China, where 1.3 billion people were going about their daily lives, virtually unknown to the rest of the world. And to the west? To the west was Xiashe, where a year ago Karen and I had experienced an almost identical situation – a lonely, wind-blown summit, the vast Tibetan steppe stretching away below us, the exultation of summitting an unclimbed peak tempered with the worry of descending, of wanting to be back on the ground. I was overcome with sadness. Karen, what happened? Why didn't you make it down? Did you think you were invincible? Did it happen quickly or, God forbid, did you have time to contemplate your own death? I'd probably never know.

Then Malcolm was beside me. We shook hands and took our summit photo, huddling together in front of the hand-held camera. We argued about the names of the peaks in the distance, waved gratuitously to Lenny and Amping, then turned to the descent. Our smiles were as wide as the Tibetan steppe below us.

CHAPTER EIGHT

The Mighty Karakoram

Once climbers have been to Pakistan, they don't go back to Nepal. Nepalese mountains are more feminine. Our mountains are men.

– Nazir Sabir

If there is any one country that's captured my heart and imagination, fuelled my desire to travel, explore and climb, it's Pakistan. To this day, this Islamic republic, a mix of federally administered states and lawless tribal areas, continues to intrigue me despite representing some of the harshest physical landscape and most unfathomable culture on earth. I travelled to Pakistan three times to climb in the late 2000s. Reeling from the after-effects of 9/11, the country was in political and economic chaos, but for me there was, and still is, something magnetic about the place.

When I was twelve, to ease the angst of my first few months at boarding school my grandmother inundated me with reading material. This included a book called *The Lotus and the Wind*, by John Masters. In it a nineteenth-century British espionage agent becomes embroiled in the struggle between Great Britain and Russia over control of India, and, of course, what is now Pakistan was then part of India. My hero was Lieutenant Robin Savage, who uncovered a plot by Russian agents to invade India through Afghanistan. Accompanied by his faithful Gurkha orderly, he rode into the wilds of Central Asia to save the British Empire single-handedly. On the front cover was a sketch of Lieutenant Savage on horseback dressed as a native Pashtun. He cut a dashing and romantic figure. The backdrop was the Karakoram mountains – huge, empty and uncompromising. Reading the book I'd forget my homesickness, and when I got to the last page I knew that one day I'd go to the Karakoram.

For those who aren't aware, the vast Karakoram massif stretches 600km across the northern reaches of Pakistan, from Afghanistan to India, and is home to most of the highest mountains in the world (despite the general misconception that Nepal has this honour). You don't go to the Karakoram if you are looking for another Nepal, with its cheerful tea-houses, bumbling yaks, greenery and tourists. Aridity and grandeur set the Karakoram apart. The range receives little rain and, as many of its valleys are virtually high-altitude deserts, it's largely uninhabited. It is also the most heavily glaciated part of the world outside of the polar regions, with five glaciers extending more than 60km in length. The range is bound on the northeast by the Tibetan Plateau, and the north by the Wakhan Corridor in Afghanistan. Off the western end lies the Hindu Raj Range, and beyond this the Hindu Kush of Eric Newby and Alexander the Great fame. The southern boundary is formed by the massive Indus River, which separates the Karakoram from the northwestern end of the Himalayan Range proper. The overall impression is one of emptiness and colossal scale. There's a spot on the Karakoram Highway where a traveller can stand at the junction of the Karakoram, Himalayan and Hindu Kush ranges, the three highest mountain ranges in the world. How romantic, how wild and how incredible is that?

But as starkly beautiful and as extreme as this country is, it has suffered more than its share of political and humanitarian distress since its inception in 1947, when it gained its independence from the British Crown. Independence resulted in wide spread rioting and the deaths of an estimated 100,000 people as millions of Muslims migrated to East and West Pakistan and millions of Hindus and Sikhs migrated to India. In 1948 the First Kashmir War with India enabled Pakistan to gain administration rights to one-third of Kashmir, and a second war in 1965, and then a third, led to the secession of East Pakistan and the birth of Bangladesh in 1971.

Zulfikar Ali Bhutto of the Pakistan People's Party (PPP) ruled Pakistan from 1972 until 1977 when he was deposed and executed by General Zia-ul-Haq, who became the country's third military president. Zia's martial-law administration gradually reversed the socialist policies of the previous government and strict Islamic (Sharia) law was introduced in 1978, often cited as contributing to the religious fundamentalism seen in Pakistan today.

With Zia's controversial death in a plane crash in 1988, Benazir Bhutto, daughter of Zulfikar Ali Bhutto, was elected as the country's first female prime minister. Over the next decade she alternated power with Nawaz

Sharif as the country's political and economic situation worsened. After a *coup d'état* in 1999 General Pervez Musharraf assumed power and in 2001 named himself president. While his economic reforms bore results, his liberal views on reforming Sharia practice met with resistance from the religious extremists who were gaining influential ground after 9/11. The extremists also objected to Musharraf's political and military alliance with the US, including his support of the 2001 invasion of Afghanistan. Musharraf survived several assassination attempts by terrorist groups and after the Afghan invasion he sent thousands of troops into the hills of Waziristan in search of Osama bin Laden.

After an eight-year exile in London Benazir Bhutto returned to Pakistan in 2007 to prepare for the parliamentary elections in 2008. As she travelled to a rally in Karachi two suicide bombers attempted to assassinate her. She escaped unharmed but 136 people were killed.

In late November 2007 Musharraf retired from the army and was sworn in for a second presidential term. Shortly afterwards Benazir Bhutto was shot dead by a terrorist as she was leaving an election rally in Rawalpindi, along with twenty others. The elections, delayed by five weeks, were finally held on 18 February 2008, and Pakistan's two main opposition parties won the majority of the seats and formed a new coalition government. In August, the government moved for the impeachment of Musharraf who announced that he would resign after nine years in office. In the presidential election that followed, Asif Ali Zardari, Benazir's husband, was elected president.

The first time I visited Pakistan was early in 1986, and I arrived not by air or from India, but across the border from Iran. At the time, General Zia had just lifted martial law, holding non-partial elections and hand-picking Muhammad Khan Junejo to be the new prime minister. Iran was in the midst of the Khomeini-driven revolution and at war with Iraq, fighting over the oil-rich Faw Peninsula.

Brian and I had spent the last months of 1985 in the UK. While Brian recovered from his bout of hepatitis, I'd done my best to top up our flagging funds. In February 1986, flush, healthy and gagging to get back to Asia, we'd jumped on the famous 'magic bus' to Istanbul and launched ourselves east into the unknown. At the time, few nationalities were gaining access to Iran, but New Zealand still maintained trade relations with the beleaguered country and Kiwis were amongst the lucky few (along with the Japanese and Irish) who could get a four-week transit visa.

Crossing from Turkey into Iran proved problematic as there was no public transport between the two countries. But after waiting in the chilly eastern Turkish city of Erzurum for a few days, by chance we stumbled across a busload of Iranians heading back to Tehran. They'd been to Ankara trying to get visas to live in any country but their own and were happy to have us on board. We spent the best part of twelve nocturnal hours at the border in negotiation with tired and fractious immigrations officials, before setting out on the thirty-six-hour journey to Tehran. Every few miles the bus was stopped by Khomeini's Revolutionary Guard, who proved to be nothing more than teenage thugs. They'd order the Iranians roughly off the bus and search their bags, but showed little interest in Brian and I. As we headed east, a lone Kurd sang folk songs and danced in the aisle to enthusiastic applause. Hoardings along the road showed crude pictures of beheaded American and Russian soldiers, and the landscape was bleak, wintry and mountainous. I struck up a conversation with a woman who before the revolution had lectured English literature at Tehran University. 'Now all I'm allowed to do is teach primary students,' she said sadly.

To our surprise, our stay in Iran was a delight. Tehran, with its rooftop anti-aircraft installations and abandoned traffic system, streets full of drifting snow and women clad in black chadors, was a little overwhelming, but the charity of the locals soon made up for this. For three days we were run around the huge, chaotic city by two young men in a beaten-up orange VW Beetle. They'd initially exchanged our US dollars for rials at the outrageous black market rate of one to 600 (a scary procedure done down a back alley), before becoming our self-appointed tour guides. With wads of cash but nothing to spend it on, we visited their families, their friends, their local hang-outs and all the 'tourist spots'. We were welcomed numerous times by strangers in the street. It was fun and, as a female in an Islamic country, I found I could cope with the imposition of having to wear a garment not dissimilar to a dressing gown and a large unmanageable scarf around my head.

But over everything and everyone hung the black cloud of war, and most houses had photos posted on the walls and gateways of the young men, sons, brothers and husbands who'd been killed in the fight with Iraq. Those who'd survived a tour of duty risked being conscripted into the military for the second time, and didn't expect to live. 'Can you help me get a visa to come and live in your beautiful country?' we were asked time and time again. The Revolutionary Guard was everywhere, as were scary posters of the Ayatollah Khomeini on huge billboards and loudspeakers yelling out his equally scary deliberations, usually positioned directly outside our hotel room. There was an 8 p.m. curfew, after which no one was allowed on the street. Food was basic and scarce, and there were no other westerners. The only postcards featured the Ayatollah's head and shoulders on a blood-red background. I sent them to everyone and I've kept a couple to this day.

By the time we reached the southern crossing into Pakistan four weeks and several thousand kilometres later, however, we'd relaxed into revolutionary Iran and were sad to leave. Apart from a tense moment in Isfahan when I'd almost been arrested for photographing a large anti-aircraft gun silhouetted against the sunset ('What a great shot, but why is that garrison of soldiers running in our direction, Brian?'), we'd been treated like royalty by a handsome, curious and welcoming population.

We were also sad to leave Iran's comfortable public transport, as we bumped across the desert from the border to the southern Pakistani town of Quetta, sitting on our packs in a ramshackle bus with no windows and no seats. The road through the desolate Baluchistan desert was no more than a rough track, the only inhabitants nomadic camel herders and Afghan refugees in lonely tent camps fleeing the war with Russia. As a western woman I was scowled at and then ignored. At one point the bus drove off without me when I was taking an urgent pee, and it was only at Brian's desperate insistence that the driver turned back. I read in our Lonely Planet guide that husbands in Quetta had the right to kill their wives if they were seen talking to a man outside of their immediate family. We arrived in the city at five in the morning, filthy, exhausted and a bit scared.

Fortunately, this unfavourable introduction to Pakistan didn't leave a lasting impression. Overnight, someone set up a vegetable stall against our street-side hotel door and we laughed hysterically as we crawled out into the market under the vendor's feet. As we roamed around the streets I soon noticed the lack of other woman. They were confined to their homes, or the fields, remote and unknowable. I felt very foreign.

We travelled on to Lahore by train, treating ourselves to first class. Having our own compartment was luxurious, the experience spoilt only by the sight of a man who minutes earlier had been run over by a train. He was dragged legless along the platform by two policemen, screaming in anguish. We crossed into India and travelled on to Nepal, and then in July 1986 doubled back to Pakistan intent on travelling up the famous Karakoram Highway to the mountains, to trek and climb. Eventually, winter and illness forced us back to India to rest up in Srinagar, by which time the Karakoram Mountains had become firmly entrenched in my psyche. To me, these enormous, solitary mountains had so much more appeal than the gentler and more verdant Himalayas. I couldn't explain why, I just knew they did.

Around the time of Musharraf's formal election as President of Pakistan, SPARC put up a colossal NZ$100,000 grant to fund a Kiwi expedition to anywhere on earth, and the New Zealand outdoor world sat up and took note. SPARC's aim was 'to encourage all Kiwis to seek challenges, be active, and take advantage of New Zealand's unique outdoor environment', and it received almost a hundred applications for expeditions ranging from climbing to caving to hot-air ballooning. Competition was rife, and speculation as to who was going to get the grant fuelled heated conversations for months to come.

I slaved for weeks over a proposal to take a team of eight to Pakistan to climb the magnificent Golden Peak of Spantik (7027m). Brian and I had been close to Spantik in 1986, when we'd made an ascent of a smaller mountain called Girgindal (6200m) above the Sumayar Bar Glacier, near the northern town of Karimabad. I'd gawped across at the peak, which at the time was still unclimbed, and thought I'd never seen anything so gobsmacking in my life. I wondered if I'd ever be good enough, or have the opportunity, to tackle such a mountain. Would I even get the chance to go back to Pakistan? Well hopefully SPARC would give me the opportunity now.

This was the first time I'd tried to organise a proper mountaineering expedition, and apart from being handicapped by a complete lack of computing skills, I realised before long that I was enjoying the process. I liaised with famous climbers – the first ascensionists of Spantik, celebrated British climbers Mick Fowler and Victor Saunders, and the second ascensionist, Marko Prezelj, one of the top climbers in the world today. I contacted the famous expedition outfitter Nazir Sabir Expeditions for quotes. I costed airfares and porters, liaison officers, dehydrated food and peak permits – all the trappings of the mountaineering expeditions I'd read about in my favourite books. When I didn't get the award I was disappointed, but not unduly so because I knew I'd learnt a valuable process.

So when the SPARC grant came up for grabs again in 2006 (this time the NZ$100,000 was to be split amongst several teams), I knew just what to do. In the interim, I'd raised the funds for my expeditions to Alaska, India and China, and was aware that my best chance of winning the money was to target an unclimbed peak. But how to find a suitable peak? I decided to ask Bruce Normand, who'd climbed in Pakistan many times. He sent me a publication by German academic Wolfgang Heichel. Wolfgang had documented the status of every mountain in the western Karakoram, and in his book I came across an unclimbed peak called Beka Brakai Chhok (7012m). My chosen partner in crime was my friend Lydia Bradey (I also thought an all-women expedition more likely to be an award-winner), and we decided at once that this lovely Matterhorn-ish peak was the one for us. So when SPARC granted us NZ$15,000 we were both tremendously excited. I'd won funding before, but never anything like this. To top it off, I applied for, and was granted, a Shipton–Tilman Award and a sizeable Mount Everest Foundation grant. In all, we had over NZ$22,000 to spend on our expedition. Lydia and I were in heaven.

We flew into Islamabad, the capital of Pakistan, in the beginning of June 2007, but from the outset I realised something had changed since my visits in the 1980s. Lydia and I were the only westerners on the flight from Bangkok, our fellow passengers all Islamic men, bearded and wearing white skullcaps and the traditional *shalwar kameez*. We both had memories of the days when tourists and climbers poured into the country in their thousands, by plane, overland from India and even via Iran as I had. The assassination of Indira Ghandi, the Sikh uprising in the Punjab, the Afghani–Russian war and even the troubles in Kashmir had all failed to dampen a western enthusiasm in the mid-1980s for exploring every untamed corner of Pakistan. So where were all the tourists now?

On our first night in the capital we were taken to dinner by Nazir Sabir, founder of Nazir Sabir Expeditions, the company organising the logistics and support for our trip. Nazir was accompanied by a handsome middle-aged Pakistani called Shukrullah Baig, who was to be our guide. The pair took us to the Marriott Hotel, which did a fine western-style buffet.

Nazir is a world-renowned mountaineer in his own right, with many first ascents under his belt. He was in his fifties, exuded vitality, was charming and liberal in his thinking, and a great raconteur. At the time of our trip, he was also the president of the Pakistan Alpine Club, which sets the fees for foreign climbing expeditions. Nazir was dedicated to attracting overseas climbers back to the Karakoram and was in the throes of organising a group of female alpinists from the USA to run a mountaineering course for young Pakistani women. Lydia and I immediately related to him as a fellow climber. Nazir explained how post-9/11 shockwaves had decimated Pakistan's once thriving tourism and climbing industries, and how tourist operators, carpet-sellers and trekking companies alike were all struggling to make a living from the few westerners who, like us, still came.

'Islamic fundamentalism is everywhere since 9/11,' he told us, 'but most especially in the North-West Frontier Province. Bloody Talibans.' Islamabad had remained largely free of strife, he added, but he thought it only a matter of time before the 'bloody Talibans' made their presence felt in the capital's pleasant leafy streets.

The next day, after a meeting with the higher echelons of the Pakistan Alpine Club, we headed north along the Karakoram Highway, clad in the obligatory headscarf, long-sleeved shirt and floppy trousers. I remembered my dressing gown arrangement of twenty-five years before and hoped I looked slightly more sophisticated now. Lydia and I babbled on in excitement while Baig and our driver gave us perplexed glances through the rear-view mirror.

We discovered that Nazir was right about the rise in Islamic fervour. The small towns were heavy on glowering men with 'mullah' beards (Sharia law forbids men to shave), who more often than not directed their disapproval at us. Local women were confined to their homes and conspicuous by their absence. Walking in the small town of Besham, which I recalled from the 1980s as a dirty but cheerful place on the banks of the Indus ten hours north of Islamabad, we clutched our headscarves tight under our chins and soon scuttled back to our hotel.

By now we were travelling through the most wild and arid section of the Indus Valley. The temperature was in the forties and we were glad of our air-conditioned 4WD – a far cry from the way Brian and I had travelled, I reflected, on the backs of trucks, jammed into public buses for interminable journeys, and once even perched on the wheel arch of a tractor for several hours.

Nanga Parbat (8125m) came into view, a shimmering white mass rising above the searing heat of the valley. The peak is known by alpinists as the 'killer mountain' and is the highest single mountain in the world, in that its not joined to any other mountain. We passed the point at which the Diamir River, draining the Diamir Face of Nanga Parbat, converged with the Indus. I remembered Brian and I staggering down this valley after a ten-day circumnavigation of Nanga Parbat in '86. Crossing the Mazeno Gah, we'd travelled down the Diamir Glacier to a small, squalid hamlet populated by a surly group of men sporting rifles and bandoliers of ammunition. They'd demanded 'medicine', matches and salt, and, becoming frightened, we'd left. We were hurrying towards the river when several teenage boys suddenly appeared out of the trees. They sprinted towards us across the meadow, shouting for us to stop. Running with them was ... what? A dog?

Nervously, I called out, 'Brian, I'm scared. Wait!' The black creature loped powerfully along, and as the group got closer I could see that it was somehow running easily on its knees and the backs of its hands, rather as a chimpanzee would. Was it a dog? No, it was a filthy, terribly deformed man, his stunted legs folded grotesquely beneath him, his arms and shoulders abnormally large and muscular.

Brian began to sprint, his long, skinny legs moving further away from me by the second. Our billy, tied to the back of his pack, made a loud clanking noise with each stride. For a moment I stood frozen with horror. I couldn't move, I couldn't breathe. Then I ran. With my 30kg pack, I ran like the wind.

'They're troublesome up that valley,' said Baig from the front seat. 'Lawless and tribal. Shoot tourists, rape women.'

The following day our entourage reached the Hunza Valley and we began to see women in pretty *shalwar kameez*, some even bare-headed, walking in the small towns, either with their husbands or in happy, chattering groups. Baig explained that Hunza is predominantly populated by Ismaili Muslims, who practise the most moderate form of Islam.

'I'm Ismaili myself,' he told us, with a big grin. 'We Ismailis are very liberal, and we are very, very tolerant of tourists and western woman.'

The Ismaili constitution is based on an allegiance to Imam Prince Karim Aga Khan, he said. The Aga Khan is particularly interested in eliminating poverty and advancing the status of women. His values have given rise to a tolerance of western ideals amongst the Hunza people that has remained steady despite the resurgence of fundamentalism in Pakistan as a whole. He has established hospitals, universities, community centres and irrigation schemes in Hunza, and is adored by everyone, including Baig. Nonetheless, the Aga Khan prefers to live in Switzerland.

By now we were right amongst the mountains and I began to recognise the peaks around us: Haramosh, Rakaposhi, Diran, Spantik. More memories flooded back, of Brian and I walking the length of the Sumayar Bar Glacier to stand under the magnificent Golden Peak of Spantik. Back in 1986 it was still unclimbed, but a year later Victor Saunders and Mick Fowler made the first ascent, a climb decades ahead of its time. Brian and I camped under the mountain beside a small glacial meltwater pool. A group of local yak herders came out of their way to warn us of a large bear that was attacking shepherds and killing stock. That night we lay in our tent, ice axes at the ready by our sides.

Sometime in the early hours of the morning I was woken by a soft grunt, then a scraping sound outside the tent. I nudged Brian. 'What's that?' I whispered.

'How do I know?' Brian replied, still half asleep.

Silence. Then another grunt and the sound of something padding softly around the tent. I prodded Brian in the ribs; that woke him. Neither of us dared breathe as the footfalls continued, around and around, occasionally interrupted by a breathy snort. Then whatever it was started to lap lazily from the pool. Lap, lap, lap, lap. Then the noise stopped.

Brian sat up slowly, ice axe in one hand, and slowly pulled back the tent flap. He peeped outside into the moonlight. After a while he murmured softly, 'It's gone'.

The morning after, I went to collect water from the pool. Around the muddy edge were paw prints – enormous paw prints with pronounced claw indentations. I trotted back to Brian with the news, partly excited, partly horrified.

'Well, we aren't staying here tonight,' he said, matter-of-factly. We took photos of the prints alongside a matchbox for scale, and packed up

The night before Lydia and I began our walk into base camp, we stayed in the tiny village of Bar. The moment we leapt from our jeep (after three days travel we needed to leap) we were surrounded by a ring of grubby, shrieking boys, whose fathers (soon to be our porters) formed an outer ring behind them. They pushed closer and closer, intrigued by our cameras, our watches and Lydia's vibrant red hair. Eventually we spotted a group of diminutive girls hiding behind a boulder, peeking out from under their headscarves and giggling. The boys were ordered back to the classroom by their teacher, and the girls crept closer.

'Come on, come here,' we encouraged, as if we were calling a litter of kittens. Eventually, one of the older girls walked up to us with a baby on her hip.

'Would you like to come and see my cow?' she asked us in almost perfect English.

'Yes,' we said, and soon we were a noisy team of various ages, walking up a steep path to view a small scruffy calf housed in a dark stone shed, with Baig reluctantly bringing up the rear.

'Would you like to come to my house for some tea?' the girl said.

'Madams don't you dare,' Baig jumped in quickly. 'You will be sick in the stomach and unable to climb your mountain.' We grouched, but knew he was right. Food poisoning has been the downfall of plenty of climbing expeditions.

As we got to know Baig, we came to realise that his primary goal in life was to give his six children, including the three girls, the best education possible. He was doing well – the three oldest were studying masters degrees at southern universities – but since 9/11 his work had dried up and his income had become sadly reduced. He admitted ours was the first all-female expedition he had been in charge of, and he was nervous. But as the expedition went on we became firm friends, and he gave Lydia and me a glimpse of a modern Islam at odds with the current western perception. Not only did Baig herald the education and social liberation of women, like Nazir he detested the influence of the mullahs (religious leaders) in Pakistan's politics and felt the then current government's alignment with the USA to be a positive step.

Lydia and I were extremely glad of Baig's company the next night, when our thirty-five porters staged a sit-down strike in lieu of a significant pay rise. Bruce Normand had warned us, 'Those Nagars, they're bastards, expect trouble from them.' Our porters were from the Nagar region, but I'd thought the warning uncharitable and pushed it to the back of my mind. However, it took hours of negotiation on Baig's part and a promise of an extra day's wages for our party to be on its way again. While these negotiations were underway, Lydia and I stayed out of sight in our tent, swigging whisky to celebrate my forty-eighth birthday.

'Thank goodness Baig's here, we'd be hopeless at this,' we giggled. We knew that as western woman we couldn't have resolved the porter situation ourselves.

Despite our problems, our first sight of Beka Brakai Chhok was magical. One minute we were trudging up the moraine of the Baltar Glacier in the heat, the next we rounded a corner to be confronted by the mountain, its summit a glinting white pyramid far above us.

'Golly! Is it bigger than you expected?' Lydia stammered.

I stood and looked. Our base camp would be at 4500m and the summit is just over 7000m. We had to climb 2500m to reach the summit. That was a huge elevation gain to make at altitude, and even tougher for a team of only two. Had we bitten off more than we could chew? As we set up base camp and made a plan for our assault over the next few days, we found ourselves pausing often to look up at the peak and wonder.

Base camp was a dream. Perched at the V-junction of the East and West Baltar glaciers, it was the one splash of green in an otherwise white, black and grey landscape. The grass was knee-high and lush with flowers. A freshwater spring shot out from under the scree 50m from the cook tent, and a beautiful tarn, warmed by the sun and complete with little crawly things, was at our disposal for some modest swimming. At night we sat in the cook tent, chattering and joking, and testing Baig's English with his enormous English–Urdu dictionary. We saw omnipotent 'signs' of our imminent success everywhere: in a 'P' of rocks on the far side of the valley, in a small yellow bird we called 'Scary Canary that Flitted around Base Camp', in a spire the shape of New Zealand on the horizon. 'It's a sign,' one of us would crow, whenever we recognised an imagined omen.

But how were we to climb the mountain? First, we had to negotiate a 5km stretch of moraine-strewn glacier to reach its base. Then we had to get enough food and supplies onto the lower slopes to sustain a summit push. We had to decide on a route, and we had to acclimatise to the altitude. We set about making a number of sorties up the glacier to establish the best way through the lumps and humps of ice and moraine. We carried up food, tents and equipment. And we decided on a route: we'd climb the South Face until it converged with the main south-east ridge, follow that to a formidable rock buttress at 6000m, and then romp up the ice slopes leading to the final summit pyramid. It was steep but we thought it was within our capabilities. All we could do was give it a try. After stocking what we grandly called advanced base camp (a rock cairn on the glacier three hours from base camp), Camp 1 (a small snow platform at 5000m) and Camp 2 (another snow platform on a sharp arête at 5500m) over the next ten days, we retreated to base camp for a much earned rest, where to our surprise, we discovered we had visitors

If we'd been climbing one of the popular peaks in Pakistan's Baltoro area, like Gasherbrum I or K2, meeting other mountaineers wouldn't have surprised us, but ours was a remote peak and few westerners had been to the area. Giampaolo and Lorenzo Corona were two well-known Italian climbing brothers. Giampi was small, very tanned and a driven climber, with several oxygen-free 8000m ascents under his belt. The older brother, Lorenzo, was built like a Greek god but had none of Giampi's intensity. Both were very handsome and were dressed in the smartest outdoor clothing. Accompanying them was their guide, Noori, who was a friend of Baig's, their cook, Masur, and two chickens, to be eaten at a later date. Noori was very large, wore a voluminous white *shalwar kameez* and moved around base camp like a sailing ship in full canvas. Giampi and Lorenzo intended to make the first ascent of a nasty-looking 6200m peak above base camp. They were chatty and friendly despite the language difference, and seemed to appreciate our company. The next morning I noticed Lydia was wearing make-up. I, meanwhile, felt frumpy. But for two days we had a lovely time with the Italians at our shared base camp, swimming in the little lake and drinking coffee from their chic portable espresso machine.

All too soon, however, it was time for Lydia and me to head off on our summit push. We left base camp somewhat apprehensively on 24 June with large packs, the Italians kissing us enthusiastically on both cheeks and the Pakistanis solemnly shaking our hands. We slogged the five hours up the glacier to the base of the mountain for the last time and climbed an annoyingly gruelling 500m scree slope to reach our Camp 1 stash. From here we had a spectacular view of Hachinder Chhish, its massive gothic spires belying the fact that a Japanese team had made an ascent of the mountain in 1982. We were happy, ensconced in our little First Light tent overlooking the glacier, with base camp a tiny green triangle in the distance. We were finally on our way.

'This is just so cool,' said Lydia. 'Who would have believed six months ago that we would be climbing a virgin peak in Pakistan?' Ahead of us was a huge unknown, but we felt confident that, if the weather was in our favour, we would climb Beka Brakai Chhok.

The next day we puffed and staggered under our loads up a steep slope of rotten snow and ice to the site of Camp 2, perched precariously at 5500m on a sharp arête. The camp overlooked an evil drop into a large and active icefall, and as we set about constructing a platform for the tent the icefall groaned and thumped. But once we were inside, we forgot about the racket and had a comfortable night, laughing and prattling into the wee hours about potential mates for our single girlfriends.

We'd optimistically planned for a pre-dawn start, hoping to camp the next night at 6000m on a huge ice mushroom we'd cutely named Big Blob. Back at base camp, Baig, hearing us discussing Big Blob and ever conscious of improving his English, had asked us, 'What is this "blob"?'

Lydia had demonstrated by squeezing a little mound of sunscreen into her hand. 'See, this is a "blob", Baig.'

At that moment Noori sailed across camp, looking his portly best. 'Ahh,' said Baig, patting his stomach. 'So! Noori is blob?'

Packing up a campsite when you are at risk of dropping your kit into the abyss always takes longer than you think, and it was daybreak by the time we finally left Camp 2, moving up the first unconsolidated snow slope. It was hard work and it took over two hours to negotiate the first 300m to reach a small rock outcrop. Here we had the choice of continuing up a steep, winding snow arête of rotten snow, or abseiling across a rocky gully and ascending via a vague spur to the grey ice face below Big Blob. We decided on the latter, and abseiled three pitches sideways into the gully.

Unfortunately, we arrived just as the sun was hitting the head of the gully several hundred metres above us and avalanches like small freight trains began to roar down. By the time we reached the bottom of the gully they were coming regularly every five minutes. We dithered a bit, then made a very nervous crossing, one at a time, hoping to catch a lull between the avalanches. By the time we reached the far side we were on edge and fractious with each other, all the more so when we discovered we then needed to climb some complicated mixed ground to reach the base of the spur. After a number of false starts I led a difficult pitch and then we were there. Lydia bravely Jumared after me, hauling my pack – it was hard work for her. It was also late in the afternoon, we were tired, and it was dawning on us that we weren't going to reach Big Blob.

It took us two hours to chop enough of the hard grey ice to create a platform big enough to pitch the tent, and the finished result was far from satisfactory. Our position was airy to say the least, but magnificent in its improbability. Directly above us hung the magnificent Batura Wall, ranging the length of the Batura peaks, one of which stood at 7500m and at the time was the highest unclimbed mountain in the world. As the sun went down, the wall turned pink, then purple, before fading into the dusk. All around us were unclimbed mountains, and even those below 6000m looked to be technically difficult. Our peaceful basecamp triangle of green had receded to a tiny speck. This was no place for novices, we decided. Had we taken on too much? After spending several hours melting water – an essential part of a multi-day ascent – we slept, somewhat snugly, waking the next morning to find it snowing lightly.

'Onwards and upwards,' Lydia pronounced.

Big Blob hung tantalisingly close, separated from us by a seventy-degree slope of grey ice. Lydia headed up the first pitch, and I could hear her periodic yelps as she was pummelled by small yet fast-moving avalanches of spindrift. After an hour it was my turn to climb, and I seconded slowly after her feeling tired and irritable, arriving at the belay close to tears.

'Don't worry,' Lydia said, 'I'll lead again. You led all day yesterday.'

I stood on the belay ledge, which was just big enough for the front third of each foot, feeling extremely sorry for myself, as Lydia made her way methodically up into the gloom. I could hear her muttering as she placed ice screws. After another hour she climbed into a green ice cave formed by the underside of Big Blob and I followed at glacial pace. I thought I was going to be sick.

'I'm not feeling so good, I wonder if we can make a camp here?' I said.

'Cripes, not here! We're in the bowels of Big Blob. What if it all collapses?' Lydia snapped.

It was a preposterous place to a camp, I had to agree with her, and I led off up the next steep ice pitch *sans* pack, intending to haul it after me. Without it I felt infinitely better, and I pulled over the lip onto the top of Big Blob in a far more positive frame of mind. I attached myself to a couple of ice screws and yelled for Lydia to come on up. As she climbed towards me I looked around, realising just how amazing our position was. Big Blob did indeed offer luxurious camping, with a flat area the size of a squash court. The Batura Wall was less than a kilometre away. In the distance to the east I could see the summits of Shishpare and Diran towering above the Hunza Valley. Rakaposhi had appeared over the range to the south. Knowing there'd be no more campsites like this on the mountain, we decided to park up for the night.

But whatever comfort Big Blob offered was ruined, as overnight I became ill with altitude sickness. My head pounded and I began to vomit – I was extremely miserable.

'Why does this always happen to me?' I wailed, 'It's not fair.'

Lydia dosed me with every item of medication in the first-aid kit but nothing helped. Come morning – which dawned clear and calm – it was obvious we were going nowhere and I spent the day in an altitude-related coma, willing the headache to go, while Lydia bemoaned the waste of a fine day. I was angry with her, as I thought she knew me well enough to realise that if I could have gone on I would have. The headache refused to budge and I headed into a second night of acute discomfort.

The next morning we had to decide on a course of action as my symptoms were showing no signs of abating. We were also dangerously low on gas to melt snow for water. Cooking was a luxury we could do without, but water was imperative. It would take us another three days to summit, we calculated, then three days to descend back to the base of the mountain. Six days on two gas cylinders? We calculated again. Nothing stacked up. We had to go down. Abseiling off the top of Big Blob, I was distraught, feeling that it was my fault we were heading down, regardless of our gas situation.

By the time we reached the site of Camp 3 my headache was starting to go, and when we arrived at Camp 2, late in the day, it was gone, but I was helpless with fatigue. After a good night's sleep, however, and my first food in three days, I rallied as we descended to the glacier and made our way back to base camp. As we walked we began to analyse our attempt and came to the realisation that we were actually quite happy with what we had done. We'd made some mistakes, but we'd given a 7000m mountain our best shot, climbing steep technical ground with heavy packs, and overcoming problems with route finding, poor campsites and illness.

'I think we've done good,' Lydia said, and I agreed with her. The two of us arrived back at base camp in high spirits eight days after leaving, and were welcomed by the team with hugs and a special meal of the two chickens, courtesy of the Italians. It was good to be back.

In the meantime, Giampi and Lorenzo had given up on their original project because of avalanche hazard, had tried to follow us on Beka Brakai but deferred on that, and were now intending to climb a smaller virgin peak in the West Baltar Glacier. They wanted our company on the mountain. 'Pleez. Leed-ya! Pat. Come weez us!'

Lydia and I ummed and ahhed. We were keen on getting up a lovely 6000m mountain above base camp called Baktoshi Peak. 'But maybe we should,' Lydia said. 'It'll be fun.' We agreed to go.

To my surprise, I felt pleasantly fit climbing up the glacier to our camp in the West Baltar. As we ascended the 1300m to the summit the next day, I raced along after Giampi, while Lydia and Lorenzo trailed in our wake. Sitting on the summit in a joyful huddle was great fun. We took silly photos, then argued over whether to call the peak Maria, after Giampi and Lorenzo's mother (the only constant woman in Giampi's life, he told us), or Wahine (Maori for 'woman'). Lydia and I won out.

'We'll be leaving a little piece of Kiwiana here,' Lydia said with a grin. Wahine Shah it was.

During our month in the mountains, Nazir's prediction for Islamabad came true. President Musharraf's troops stormed the Red Mosque and a hundred supposed fundamentalists were shot. A suicide bomb killed another twenty people outside the High Court. Even a Harry Potter book launch was targeted. The populace was in shock. This sort of thing happened regularly in other cities like Peshawar and Karachi, but not in the pleasant capital.

Baig urged Lydia and me to stay away from large hotels and shopping centres – areas that could be targeted by suicide bombers. Strangers in the street approached us and apologised for the 'situation', hoping we would return to Islamabad in happier times.

As our plane headed down the runway, it wasn't our failure on Beka Brakai Chhok I was thinking of, nor getting home back to normality; I was thinking of Baig and his family. For six weeks we'd given Baig a livelihood, but what would he do now? Would this recent spate of violence mean even fewer visitors to Pakistan? We were leaving Baig and his family behind, but to what future?

Despite the increasing levels of violence in Pakistan, the pull of the Karakoram wouldn't let me go. Even within a few weeks of arriving home, Beka Brakai Chhok was playing on my mind. Lydia and I hadn't climbed the mountain, but to my surprise the remorse I'd felt when we'd turned back didn't escalate into quite the level of self-blame or failure I'd come to expect. The peak was just unfinished business, no more than that, and I wanted another chance to be back amongst those arid and uncompromising mountains.

The following year, in 2008, Malcolm Bass came up with the proposal that we try a new route on the South Face of Denali. Perhaps sensing my restlessness, he then suggested, 'How about another go at Beka Brakai? I've always wanted to go to Pakistan.'

Had he been 12,000km closer I would have kissed him. Within ten months of leaving, I was back in Islamabad.

Between my two Pakistan visits I'd been on the trip to the Indian Garhwal with Bruce, Paul and Shelley (see Chapter 6), and as part of its legacy was nervous of the commitment ahead. Was I incapable of getting on with people any more? Was I just a silly old has-been who should give the expedition game away to younger climbers? Should I take up something else, like painting? And my knees, which had pained me on Beka Brakai Chhok, and even more so in India, hadn't improved. An MRI scan had shown advanced arthritis in both, with little cartilage left in the joints – bone was rubbing on bone. 'How on earth can you walk on those knees, let alone climb?' the doctor had said. I was shocked – surely this wasn't happening to me. But I knew I'd get through another expedition on painkillers.

The political situation in Pakistan had deteriorated in the intervening months. Malcolm, who arrived in Islamabad a few hours ahead of me, was settling into his hotel room when he heard a big whoomph! The floor jumped and the windows rattled and shook. 'There was a silence, then lots of shouting,' he said. 'Sirens came from every direction.'

A suicide bomber had blown himself and nineteen others to smithereens outside the Danish Embassy, just minutes from the hotel. Wide-eyed, Malcolm rang his wife, Donna, before the BBC got hold of the news. He was still wide-eyed when I arrived. 'I'm going to take this place a bit more seriously,' he said.

Dear Baig gave me a big hug at the airport and, ever conscious of our safety, hustled us through the formalities with the Pakistan Alpine Club and out of town as soon as he could. He would have liked us to fly to Gilgit, but with no flights available, once again we drove north via the Karakoram Highway. I didn't mind at all, as I'd come to love the drive. Baig was also apprehensive of the Bar porters after the previous year's furore, and had organised for several policemen to be present while the loads were being issued. I recognised most porter faces and was pleased when, to a man, they greeted me with a handshake. But their affability didn't dissuade them from demanding a goat to eat, a day into the trek to base camp, which at US$100 must have been the most expensive goat in the Karakoram. Baig made a deal that if they got us to base camp in three days rather than four, we would buy the goat – it was that or go nowhere.

Despite the hassles, the walk in was glorious, and Malcolm and I both agreed that the shepherd village of Baltar Meadow was one of the most beautiful places we'd ever seen. Resting outside our tent, we cheered on the porters as they played a game of 'foot-polo' against the local shepherds. To our envy, they galloped back and forth across the alluvial fan wielding their willow polo sticks, seemingly oblivious of the altitude. 'Lucky bastards,' Malcolm said, as he lay flat on his back on the grass.

Arriving at base camp I was pleased to see nothing had changed – the lake, the wildflowers, the summit of Beka Brakai Chhok lit up against the blue. I pitched my tent in the same spot. I was very happy.

After a couple of days spent wandering on the glacier, we decided to climb Baktoshi Peak (6000m) to acclimatise and also to allow us to scope a route on Beka Brakai. Staring through the binoculars, it didn't take long to decide on a different route to that of the previous year in order to avoid the difficult rock buttress above Big Blob. Lydia and I had always known that the buttress (had we reached it) was going to be the crux of the climb, and although the line Malcolm and I chose – up an enormous icefall to meet the southwest ridge – had none of the aesthetic appeal of the southeast ridge, perhaps it was the line of least resistance?

Up on Baktoshi I went through my usual acclimatisation purgatory, spending two days at 5500m feeling absolutely awful. But I resisted the urge to hightail it back to base camp, and fortunately this proved worthwhile, as I remained free of altitude headaches for the rest of the expedition. Despite the way I felt, it was grand to be up there, with views of Wahine Shah and the other now familiar mountains. Malcolm, too, seemed thrilled with our situation and I often found myself watching for his reaction, hoping he would see in the place what I did.

Back at base camp we packed and planned, packed and planned, trimming our loads down to a minimum of seven days' food (which would stretch out to ten if necessary), ten days' gas (so we could always melt snow) and minimal clothing. Malcolm, who's bastard-hard, packed hardly any clothing. Food consisted of a few dehydration packs, protein bars, liquid carbohydrate sachets and instant porridge. Our expedition chicken, whom we'd named Chook-Chook and became rather fond of, clucked and pecked domestically around our feet as we worked. Our goat, missing his goat friend at Baltar Meadow, also seemed to want our company and chewed lazily on our packs and bootlaces. When it couldn't be put off any longer, we farewelled Baig and our cook Jawed, and headed out of base camp for the last time. I began to feel anxious. God forbid, what if I failed again? And if I did fail again, would I be able to show my face back at home?

On the first night we put in a comfortable camp on a small terrace at the base of the icefall. It was a perfect site, and as we sat on our packs in the snow cooking instant mashed potato on our little gas cooker, we agreed there was nowhere we'd rather be. The Batura Wall glowed in the last of the sun, and below us the glacier wound lazily down to base camp. The weather was superb, and as dusk fell and the stars came out we continued to sit, watching the silhouettes of the mountains as they faded into the dark.

The pristine weather continued for three more days as we methodically worked our way up the icefall. The climbing was varied and interesting – moderate snow slopes interspersed with steep pitches of ice, which we vied with each other to lead. Everything seemed to be in our favour – our packs felt manageable and snow conditions were infinitely better than those Lydia and I had experienced the year before. We moved quickly and found fortuitous and beautiful ledges to camp on each night. Our only setback came on day three, when Malcolm took a big, scary fall.

We'd encountered a short, very steep pitch of ice, which I led, leaving my pack at the bottom to haul later. Struggling to find a good anchor, I resorted to tying off two ice screws at the back of a steep little gully, then burrowed myself into the snow in an effort to create a bit more drag should Malcolm fall. Unbeknownst to me, Malcolm started up the pitch with his own pack on his back, and mine dangling off his harness. Grunts and expletives wafted up the cliff towards me as I slowly took in the rope. To his credit, Malcolm got to the soggy, overhanging finish, but then pitched out backwards with a loud squawk. His weight pulled me out over the gully – I was hanging suspended in space, his full weight on my belay device. Meanwhile, Malcolm was also hanging in space, upside down. Flummoxed by surprise and indecision, I hung there, doing nothing.

'Malcolm, are you OK? What's going on?' I yelled. Nothing. I glanced anxiously behind me at the two ice screws; the full force of the sun's rays seemed to be concentrated on them alone. What should I do? I yelled louder, and after what seemed like an eternity the rope jerked and jerked again. There was a pause, and then more jerks. Finally, a lime-green Reactor ice tool appeared over the lip and started jabbing at the snow, followed by an arm and then a helmet. Eventually, Malcolm's head popped up.

'Bollocks,' he said, with a shaky grin. 'That was exciting.'

On the evening of the fourth day we were poised for our final push for the top, camped at 6100m on the downside of the bergschrund, a dozen steep pitches beneath the summit ridge. We prepared eagerly for summit day, melting water, counting out the last of the protein bars and checking our equipment. We'd go for the summit, 900m above us, in a single push, taking only the stove and our down jackets. We hoped to be back at camp in less than twenty-four hours. We fizzed with excitement, setting the alarm for midnight. I tried to sleep, but couldn't – it was make or break time for me. Two years of preparation, anticipation and hype all boiled down to the next few hours.

But sometime during the night the barometric pressure plummeted and it started to snow. The alarm woke us at 1 a.m. and we peered out of the tent door into the gloom.

'Never mind, we've got plenty of time, plenty of food and gas,' Malcolm said. 'We'll get our chance.' We set the alarm to wake us in a few hours, and went back to sleep.

What we didn't realise then was that this was the start of a week-long pattern of snowstorms that would see us set the alarm each evening, only to wake in the dark to a blizzard. We'd reset for an hour later, then an hour later again, but to no avail. The days and nights passed in a blur of waiting and anxiety, and our reserves dwindled. We read the one book we had between us, then resorted to dozing or chatting idly. On day seven we made a pact: regardless of how long we had to wait, we'd ration our food and gas and hunker down till an opportunity to go for the summit eventuated. But by day ten we were almost out of food and getting seriously demoralised. Malcolm was missing his wife and was regretting subjecting her to the stress of being an alpinist's 'widow', while I felt the opportunity to climb Beka Brakai slipping from my grasp. How would I cope with failing twice, I kept asking myself.

Then, on the evening of the twelfth day, the clouds rolled away and the peaks unfurled, raising our spirits. 'It's now or never,' said Malcolm. 'Let's eat the last of the porridge, and go tonight.' I was fraught with anticipation.

By 1 a.m. we were front-pointing in bright moonlight up the slopes leading to the summit ridge. It was very cold and we were both encased in our down jackets, hoods up. We hit the ridge with the sunrise, and thought we were at about 6400m. To our left, the ridge took a terribly convoluted path to the summit of Dariyo Sar about a kilometre away; to our right the summit of Beka Brakai Chhok hung tantalisingly close.

'This next bit looks really hard,' Malcolm called up to me as I peered ahead. The 500m of ridge line in front was badly corniced and the snow frothy and unconsolidated. I took a step forward. My foot broke through the ridge and I lurched myself backward with fright, then inched forward again. Through the hole my boot had left I could see a glacier, shady and moraine-strewn, thousands of feet below. I moved carefully down and away from the high point of the ridge and began sidling, wondering whether Malcolm would have the presence of mind to throw himself down the opposite side of the ridge if I did break through. That's what the textbooks say you should do. After a couple of hundred metres we reached a large snow feature shaped like a mushroom, and I built a dubious anchor in the aerated snow and prepared to belay Malcolm, who then moved over the mushroom and out of sight. After half an hour the rope stopped moving. I waited. All was quiet – not a breath of wind, nothing. The rope jerked out erratically for another few feet, then stopped again. At long last there came a faint cry.

'What was that, Malcooolm?'

'Bollocks! I can't climb this. I'm coming back. It's too dangerous. I can't justify this for Donna's sake. It's not worth it for me.'

My heart sank – I knew that if Malcolm couldn't climb the ridge, then neither could I. The seven days of waiting, the lack of food, the anxiety … it had all been for nothing. I had to agree with Malcolm – that the danger couldn't justify the summit – but this couldn't allay the misery of having failed on the mountain twice.

Two-and-half days later, we were back at base camp, feeling nothing but relief to be down. Baig and Jawed were very glad to see us as we were almost a week overdue and they had been worried. I threw up Jawed's first meal of pakoras and orange squash, but by the time the porters arrived for the walk out to Bar village, Malcolm and I had eaten our way back to health.

A week later we were back in the Islamabad heat and our failure began to register on me acutely. I didn't want to go home. What would they say, my friends, my family, sponsors, the Kiwi climbing community? Malcolm did his best to restore my spirits.

'Lots of famous climbers fail two or three times on climbs,' he said. 'Look at Mark Twight. Look at Nick Bullock. Look at Greg Child. Or Pete Takeda and Dave Sheldon – they tried the Shark Fin three times and didn't get up it.'

He was right, of course, but regardless, my mood plummeted. On arriving home, I avoided family and friends, and self-consciously closed down any conversations about the trip.

It wasn't until the television brought the news of the assassination of Benazir Bhutto shortly after Christmas that I began to put things in perspective. Millions of Pakistanis had pinned their hopes on Benazir restoring their country to normality. She had promised political and economic stability and a better future … and then she was dead. My failure was nothing compared to their loss. How selfish, how unforgivably self-indulgent I had been to take myself and Beka Brakai Chhok so seriously. I decided to look on the expedition in a new light. After all, I'd learned an invaluable lesson – that I could push myself physically and mentally far further than I'd thought possible. After going without food for days, Malcolm and I hadn't beaten an immediate retreat at the first sign of improving weather. We'd held it together and gone up!

After Malcolm and I returned to our respective homes, celebrated Italian alpinists Simone Moro and Hervé Barmasse climbed Beka Brakai – or so they thought. Shortly after their ascent, it was announced (by whom I don't know) that the true summit lay further along the ridge to the north. In fact, quite a lot further along, making an ascent of the mountain an even longer and harder proposition.

CHAPTER NINE

Moral Dilemmas

We commenced plugging up in foot-deep steps with a thin wind crust on top and precious little belay for the ice-axe. It was altogether most unsatisfactory and whenever I felt feelings of fear regarding it I'd say to myself: 'Forget it! This is Everest and you've got to take a few risks'.

– Sir Edmund Hilary

After two failures on Beka Brakai Chhok, my friends and family were non-plussed when, at the beginning of 2009, I announced I'd be going back to Pakistan for a third successive year.

'What on earth do you see in that country?' I was asked time and time again. 'What about the Taliban? What about the suicide bombers? Aren't you worried about being kidnapped? Surely it's too risky to travel there at the moment.'

'I think it's a fantastic place,' I'd reply with a shrug, on the defence, not bothering to extrapolate further. 'And don't worry. It's a different mountain this time.'

I'd first caught sight of Karim Sar (6180m) in 2007, when Lydia and I, along with Giampi and Lorenzo, were goofing around on the summit of Wa-hine Shah (see Chapter 8). From our elevated huddle we could see a lovely ice-capped peak to the south, which Lorenzo identified as the one his friend Ivo Ferrari was, at that very point in time, attempting to climb with two mates. Lorenzo even had the expedition postcard (a trend among European climbers is to produce a nice postcard advertising their expedition). I took photos and stored the peak away in the back of my mind.

In early 2009, SPARC announced the winners of their third Hillary Expedition Grant, and I was lucky enough to be awarded NZ$10,000 for a proposal to lead a team of four on an ascent of a beautiful mountain called Kampire Dior (7143m), in the far north of Pakistan's North-West Frontier Province. It was to be a remote, lengthy and ambitious undertaking: the trip involved walking for a week up the Batura Glacier, and making the first ascent of a route about which I could find little information. By now I'd put Beka Brakai Chhok in perspective and was confident my two failures on that peak wouldn't affect my judgement. I was sure Kampire Dior could be done. I was also confident that I would have recovered in time from having a right knee replacement, which had happened shortly after my arrival home from Pakistan the previous year. Hundreds of hours in the gym had seen me make rapid progress back to normal, and I had almost put the operation from my mind. It was time to move on.

Right from the start, however, the expedition proved fraught with problems. First, Lydia Bradey and her partner Dean Staples pulled out. The timing was wrong for them, they said, as they were off to Nepal to guide Everest in the pre-monsoon period. Then in April, the Taliban invaded the Swat Valley, a beautiful area in northwest Pakistan adjacent the Afghan border, and the military retaliated. Wary of becoming tangled up in the insurgence, the third member of the team reneged. I managed to enlist a replacement, Paul Hersey, who had been with me on the trip to India in 2007 (see Chapter 6). Paul had just published his second mountaineering book, was well on his way to becoming an established author and was contemplating writing a novel. He's a great conversationalist and I was looking forward to his company.

However, when it was pointed out that Kampire Dior was only a stone's throw from Afghanistan, and we would therefore need a government security officer to accompany us at our own, somewhat expensive, cost, I realised we needed to change plan. I remembered Karim Sar and emailed the world expert on the region, Wolfgang Heichel, to establish its status. 'Still unclimbed,' he said! 'A perfect alternative.'

In May, a month out from our New Zealand exodus, things really began to hot up in Swat. The military were now fighting the Taliban house to house in the provincial capital of Mingora, and two million civilians were fleeing south towards Peshawar on the military's recommendation. Of these, some 160,000 were interned in refugee camps to the north of the city while the remainder spread themselves throughout Peshawar, Rawalpindi and Islamabad. The infrastructure of the cities was coming under immense pressure as the refugees sourced accommodation, jobs, and schools for their children.

To make things worse, members of the Taliban were infiltrating the refugee migration, and urban suicide bombings were becoming more and more commonplace. The government was in disarray under the new president. To top it all, the Taliban were posting assassinations of military personnel on YouTube, and the parts of the population that had previously supported the insurgents now began to hate them with a vengeance. Trying to justify this expedition to family and friends became harder and harder.

Ignoring government travel warnings, Paul and I flew into Islamabad on 5 June. I realised immediately that things had changed for the worse in the ensuing months since my last visit. Soldiers with AK47s now lined the streets, manned roadblocks and searched passing cars for bombs. The grandiose area around the Parliament Buildings and President's Residence was off limits, barricaded with coils of barbed wire and armed installations, as was the Marriott Hotel, scene of our post-expedition feasting in the past. The Marriott had been targeted by a suicide bomber a few months before, killing sixty-five guests and staff, and I wondered which of the charming waiters I'd got to know by sight were now dead. A wary population had emptied the streets; even the giant Faisal Mosque was quiet, with only a few visitors like ourselves willing to wander its spacious terraces. Shukrullah Baig, who was acting as guide again on this trip, saw us as targets for every kidnapper, suicide bomber and insurgent in Central Asia, and wouldn't let us out of his sight.

We left the city after twenty-four hours and drove north up the Karakoram Highway against a tide of refugees, on foot or crammed onto the backs of trucks, heading south away from Swat. Near Chattar Plain, a huge traffic jam brought us to a halt. Refugees spilt out from the backs of trucks onto the dusty road and lorry drivers leant on their horns – it was chaos. After an hour or two of waiting, news swept down the line of traffic that a bridge up ahead had been bombed only hours before by the Taliban. As we bumped across the rocky stream bed I looked back at the remains of the small bridge, a large, raw hole deforming its far side, and for a moment I felt very foreign and a long way from home.

We bypassed seedy Besham and continued north to Chilas before Baig felt comfortable to stop. The next day, he breathed a nervous sigh of relief when we reached the relative safety of Gilgit, and began to smile again. '*As-Salamu alaykum*,' he called to his friends through the window of the jeep.

I took Paul into the bazaar and outfitted him in the local *shalwar kameez*. He charmed the shop owner by hanging on his words. 'Sir, you need a larger size. I think this brown will suit you better. And now you need this hat. Ah! Now you look like a Pakistani.'

Three days later, our party was settled at base camp beside the Shilinbar Glacier, under the southeast face of Karim Sar. The porters, from the village of Budelas, were a comparative delight and the walk in, although steep and strenuous for the unacclimatised, a pleasure thanks to their good nature and kindness. The loads were carried by little brown donkeys with huge soft ears, and their noisy antics kept the team laughing. Baig stood on a rock and conducted the 'donkey orchestra' with a stick. But our jaws dropped at the first sight of the south side of Karim Sar. The enormous face was a complex mass of steep snow slopes, hanging glaciers and granite rock bands, all culminating in a summit ice cap. With an elevation of 2600m it would be the largest face I'd ever climbed. I knew we had our work cut out if we were going to make the summit.

A week later, Paul and I arrived back at base camp, cold and damp after an extended acclimatisation sortie to the head of the glacier. Summer was late to arrive and we'd moved slowly in bleak, unsettled weather, Paul struggling with the altitude. My fiftieth birthday had come and gone, but I'd kept it to myself, not wanting any attention. I felt anxious about Paul's motivation, knowing that if we were to summit, everything had to be in our favour. At base camp he came down with an unknown illness, recovered after a few days, but then to my dismay decided he didn't want to climb. I was dumbfounded. Why? The organising, the fundraising, the last-minute scraping together of money – was it all to go to waste because of a sinus infection? Obviously the climb was of little importance to Paul, I thought, and we argued heatedly.

'Sponsors would understand if we have to abandon the climb because I've been sick,' Paul claimed.

I retorted, 'Everyone gets colds and viruses on expeditions, you can't let this jeopardise a costly trip to the far side of the world.'

We couldn't agree and, amid bouts of private tears, I made a decision. I would climb the mountain alone. Then, realising I was scared of the prospect, I succumbed to some angst-ridden, sleepless nights. Baig, to his credit, understood my dilemma.

'Paul is frightened,' he said. 'If I had the skills I would come with you, Pat.'

On the morning of my departure for the summit I felt bad-tempered and lethargic. To climb this huge and complex face alone; what was I thinking?

My age, my gender, my titanium knee, my non-existent success rate in Pakistan – everything was stacked against me. Maybe we should just go home? Maybe I should give up this game and take up something else?

Then at breakfast, to my utmost surprise, Paul made an announcement. 'Hey, I'm feeling a bit guilty,' he said. 'What say I come up to advanced base camp as support? I can be back-up.'

I was momentarily stunned and then gave way to a huge wave of relief and elation. Thank goodness, I wouldn't be on my own after all – Paul would be watching me, and that in itself would be enough. Maybe I *could* climb Karim Sar, after all there was no reason why not. I was fifty, but that meant I had more than thirty years of mountaineering experience behind me. I was female, but aren't women supposed to have better endurance? Yes, I had a titanium knee, but titanium is very strong. And yes, I'd failed twice on Beka Brakai, but surely that meant I deserved a success this time?

Moving up the icefall, Paul seemed to climb with a new speed and confidence. 'I feel good,' he said, surprised, 'perhaps I'm finally acclimatising.'

We spent the afternoon at our ABC in separate worlds, Paul reading and dozing while I sorted my gear. I filled my pack, then emptied it and sorted the gear again, scoped the mountain through my binoculars, then scoped the mountain again. I decided that the best route followed a large gully for 500m until it converged with a steep icefall. If I could get up a short rock band I'd be able to climb the icefall on the right-hand side until it broadened into a large cirque. A curving ridge seemed to run to the right out of the cirque until it hit a triangular rock buttress. If I went right again to circumnavigate this, I'd be on the summit ridge. A short traverse and, *voilà*, the top. If I was prepared to put in two 1000m days I could be back at our ABC and Paul in a mere three days.

At four o'clock the next morning I was ready to go. The night before, Paul had offered to come part of the way up the gully to belay me through the rock band, but I knew as he lay blinking in his sleeping bag that he was regretting saying this. Nonetheless, he moved quickly away from me in the dark, as I struggled up the gully behind him carrying several days' food and all my equipment.

We reached the rock band on daylight, and I looked up. Fuck, I thought. All I could see was a row of towering ice cliffs ringing the cirque a kilometre above. The thought of spending the next three days underneath them weakened my knees – I needed a back-up plan. The gully continued left for several hundred metres to a small col. On the right-hand side hovered another huge set of ice cliffs, but they looked fairly stable – there was none of the telltale ice debris on the slopes below. My only option was to continue up the gully and hope another line to the summit revealed itself. Then to my astonishment, Paul announced he would continue, despite having no overnight gear.

'I can sleep in your yellow New Zealand Mountain Safety Council pack liner,' he said, 'and wear all the spare clothes.'

I didn't argue. I wanted his company. Plus he could carry some of the gear.

I reached the col at 3 p.m., and after eating some peanuts began to clear a tent platform for the FirstLight tent. The sky was a clear, pale blue and the view astounding. To the south was the now familiar sight of Rakaposhi shimmering in the afternoon haze, while further east ... why, there was Sangamarmar! Far in the distance I could see the Hispar Glacier, which twenty-five years before Brian and I had stumbled down in a fug of heat, dehydration and hunger. After an hour I started to wonder about Paul, and trudged back down the gully to catch a glimpse of him. He was negotiating a tricky little rock band a couple of hundred metres below and seemed tired. He looked up, waved, and then indicated down the mountain with his whole arm.

'What's he doing?' I wondered. 'Is he heading down? What about the rest of the gear? Does that mean I have to go down and collect it?'

I decided the best thing to do was to continue with the tent platform, and walked back up to it. Forty-five minutes later, Paul arrived, completely spent but with a big grin on his face.

'I can't believe I've made it this far! Man! I'm so pleased,' he said. We hugged for the joy of just being there. But by nine o'clock I was again gripped with apprehension as Paul shivered with cold. Several hours later it became obvious sleep wasn't going to happen, so I decided to get up and get going. My head thumped and eating breakfast was out of the question, and in any case I knew that Paul, who was by now exhausted with the cold, could do with my sleeping bag. I stepped outside to a myriad of stars. This was it, I told myself. I won't rush anything, I'll just be steady and keep going. I took a deep affirming breath and headed into the night.

The first obstacle, a small granite rock band covered in loose, dry snow, almost flummoxed me. I bridged up a shallow gully for a few metres as the sky began to lighten, had an 'I can't do this' moment, and climbed back down.

'Thwarted only an hour from the tent,' I scolded myself out loud. 'Come on! Get on with it.' I gathered myself to try again and this time made the

20m to the top. Above me, a snow slope glowing pink from the eastern sky led to a 100m-high granite cliff. I headed right to circumvent this, then scurried back to the left when I realised I would have to traverse a steep rock gully with a deep, dark drop into the icefall below our camp – the icefall we'd climbed alongside the day before. I tried to calm down. 'You can always turn back,' I told myself reassuringly. 'What's that quote? "There are old climbers and bold climbers but no old bold climbers".'

Two ice cliffs dominated the skyline to the left, and between them was a steep runnel of snow about 100m high. I front-pointed up the runnel and forty minutes later popped out into the sunlight, finding myself in the cwm ringed by huge seracs I'd seen the day before. The cliffs seemed quiet, but it was early, and as there were plenty of big ice blocks strewn around to suggest their fragility, I decided to climb up onto the broad right-hand ice rib to get out of the firing line.

I tried to hurry, but as the snow started to soften in the sun my progress was glacial. I'm knackered, I realised despondently, and I've only been on the go for a few hours. Fuck. But up on the rib conditions improved, and as I picked up speed I regained my mojo. It occurred to me, possibly for the first time, that I had a real chance of summitting. Had I just been playing with the idea of climbing Karim Sar, I wondered? Making a token attempt to appease my own ego? I stopped and looked at the summit. It didn't look so far away now.

After climbing several hundred metres of moderate ground, and negotiating some big crevasses, the large rock band forming the base of the summit pyramid loomed above. From base camp this looked to be surmountable on the left, but to do this I'd have to traverse a long section of steep ice above a breathtaking drop into the Bar Glacier. I set off across the traverse but stopped after 50m. The void below seemed overwhelmingly hostile and my right leg jerked with fright. 'I can't do this! I'm too scared,' I told myself, and tentatively front-pointed back to safety. I stopped again. Did I really want to go on?

If I did go on I would have to drop 100m, traverse right under the rock band and try to summit from the east side. I pigeon-holed nervously down and started sidling left; again, the exposure was alarming, and with every step loose snow whooshed out from under my crampons and gathered speed until it shot over the ice cliffs below. After several minutes of double-kicking each foot I realised I was holding my breath. 'Breathe. Breathe with each kick,' I chanted. 'Don't think about where you are. The risk will be worth it.

You can't make the first ascent of a mountain solo without exposing yourself to some risk.'

After what seemed like an eternity, the traverse ended and I was able to start climbing back up towards the ridge line. By now the sun was high, and I wondered what Paul was doing, almost 1000m below. I was feeling very tired.

At midday I hit the summit ridge above the East Face and could see the top. I'd been on the go for over nine hours, but now the only thing between me and the summit seemed to be a seventy-degree ice slope leading up to the last small snow step. 'Am I really going to climb this mountain?' I asked myself again. 'I can easily abseil that ice slope on V-threads so there's nothing to stop me going on.'

I started up the ice tentatively, with no rope, no ice screws and a 1500m drop into the head of the Shitinbar Glacier below me. 'Come on, you've so-loed far steeper ice than this,' I grumbled. 'Just think of the summit, nothing else. The summit.'

The ice slope rounded off at the ridge and I was looking once again into the gloomy Bar Glacier. The summit was an easy 100m wander away. Only 100m? Five minutes later I was on the top. I placed two ice screws, attached myself, and slumped in a heap. I looked around. I felt no elation – nothing but fatigue. A slight breeze fanned my cheek and my shadow cast a long shape on the glazed snow in front of me. I looked around.

To the northeast was the Batura Wall – it seemed like an old friend. Beside it was Beka Brakai Chhok, although disappointingly its summit was in cloud. To the east were Shishpare and, closer, the steep spires of Hachindar Chhish and Aikache Chhok. Tucked over Rakaposhi's right shoulder was Haramosh, and on its eastern flank was the massive symmetrical white shape of Diran. Thousands of feet below I could make out the small dark juniper tree beside our basecamp toilet tent – the only tree in the vicinity. I wondered if Baig and Naseer had any idea where I was. I doubted it. I stirred myself – I had to get down.

Two 30m abseils off V-threads got me close to the base of the ice slope, and I scuttled down the remaining 10m on my front points. Four more abseils off slung rock bollards and I was back at the start of the traverse, my heart thumping. The snow looked worse than ever, and by the time I had reached the far end of the traverse and climbed back up onto the broad rib, I was holding back tears. I mustn't let nerves and fatigue get the better of me now, I thought. There's a long way to go.

But progress down the rib was rapid and I started to cheer up. It seemed like no time before I was back in the cwm wondering why it had taken me so long to climb the rib earlier in the day. I sat down behind a large block of green ice and had a couple of squeezy carbo shots. The sun was getting low in the sky and a beautiful afternoon light made everything glow. A sense of smugness and achievement began to grow. Goodness! I'd made the top. A first ascent, on my own, and with an artificial knee joint! I could go home happy in my success, and without all the angst and worry about what the Kiwi climbing community thought of me or how to tell friends and sponsors that I'd failed. I jumped up and practically skipped along to the top of the gully between the ice cliffs.

Reversing the narrow gully required concentration and the afternoon had turned hot. I'd emptied my water bottle hours ago and was very thirsty, so the nasty sidle back to the slope above camp irritated me. I'd had enough of unconsolidated snow and balling crampons, exposure and the unknown. I spent forty minutes cold-welding a number six stopper into a rotten crack for an abseil anchor, then 30m later repeated the procedure to descend the rock band above the final snow slope. Suddenly I could see the tent, and then Paul stuck his head out through the door, waved and disappeared again.

I felt such overwhelming gratitude towards Paul when we hugged, and nearly burst into tears for the second time. He had held the fort for me, and all the stress I'd bottled up over the previous days came out in one big rush. I was so happy and so quietly overjoyed … but also so desperately tired. After forty minutes Paul left to descend to ABC – two nights in a yellow plastic bag was beyond the call of duty – and I fell sound asleep on my stomach in the tent. I woke an hour later, made another brew, and then, too tired to cook a meal, passed out until seven o'clock the next morning.

On the descent to ABC my legs were like jelly. Two 1000m days in succession, breaking trail all the way, had taken their toll, but regardless I felt dreamy and satisfied. I'd not let the situation get the better of me and I'd battled on to get my summit. The trip had been successful and I could go home content. Paul was waiting at ABC, and we packed up and made our way lethargically back to base camp, stopping often to snack on our remaining food, chat, and enjoy the sunshine and the view.

Over the next couple of days a steady stream of visitors arrived along the trail from Budelas, as the snow was clearing and shepherds were bringing their animals up for summer grazing. When they heard that madam had climbed the mountain but not sir, they seemed nonplussed but shook my hand and gave me their best wishes. I was touched and grateful.

Back in Islamabad a week later, Paul and I spent the intervening time before our flight watching Wimbledon on cable TV in our hotel room. While we'd been in the mountains there'd been further bombings in nearby Peshawar and Rawalpindi, and Nazir Sabir Expeditions was adamant that we keep a low profile. When Baig did chaperone us into the city, locals thanked us for visiting Pakistan, for risking our lives to visit their country, they said. I thought this an exaggeration and wondered what they would think if they knew we'd been here to climb a mountain, spending what amounted to their life savings servicing nothing more than our own recreation and our own egos. Despite my happiness I acknowledged that the only person to benefit from my ascent was me. Perhaps I had just wanted to prove a point, to show that, at fifty years of age and with an artificial knee, I was capable of climbing a Karakoram mountain? How selfish. How could this be justifiable?

Mountaineering is one sport in particular that raises a myriad of ethical and moral dilemmas. Not only are mountaineers generally westerners like myself, with money and time in excess to spend on their own recreation, but in their obsession to reach a summit they have been known to forgo family obligations, careers, their own well-being, and even the lives of other climbers. In the last twenty years this tendency has been further exacerbated with the advent of commercial guided climbing in the Himalaya and Karakoram ranges, whereby wealthy amateurs have the opportunity, for large sums of money, to be taken up the 8000m giants by professional guides. These guided climbers put themselves under huge financial pressure to succeed, and morality has been known to take a back seat.

This was illustrated particularly poignantly in 2006, when thirty-four-year-old British climber David Sharp lay near death on Mt Everest while more than forty other climbers, the majority of whom were part of commercial guided expeditions, marched past him on their way to the summit. The incident raised considerable criticism and continues to divide the mountaineering community today.

David, who had attempted the mountain at least twice beforehand and was climbing alone, was found comatose and out of supplementary oxygen at 8500m on the north ridge. Kiwi Mark Inglis, who in the company of professional guides was attempting to make the first ascent of Everest as a double amputee, was the first to come across him. Inglis' party radioed their expedition manager, Russell Brice, asking if there was anything that could be done for the climber, but Brice urged the party to carry on, saying that as David had been a number of hours without oxygen, he was effectively dead. Subsequently, forty other climbers, all using supplementary oxygen, walked past David, intent on the summit. When they returned several hours later, David was dead.

Initially it was Inglis who unfairly bore the brunt of the ensuing outcry from the public, led by a number of high-profile figures who fiercely criticised the decision to abandon David. Sir Edmund Hillary, first to reach the summit of Everest in 1953, was at the forefront and his opinion was highly publicised:

> On my expedition there was no way that you would have left a man under a rock to die. It simply would not have happened. People have completely lost sight of what is important. There have been a number of occasions when people have been neglected and left to die and I don't regard this as correct philosophy. I think you have to have priorities. If the priority is just to get to the summit and let another man die, you do it. But if you have someone who is in great need and you are still strong and energetic then you have a duty, really, to give all you can to get the man down and getting to the summit becomes very secondary.

Keith Woodford, leader of the 1977 New Zealand Mt Everest Expedition, was more circumspect. He commented that it was interesting to note that some of the most experienced Himalayan climbers, who had themselves undertaken dangerous mountain rescues, were very cautious to make judgements. In his essay 'Mountain Ethics and Everest', Woodford pointed out that no matter how strong a climber is, no one can carry another person at 8500m. Such a rescue would have to use a stretcher – itself no easy task and one that would put the rescuers themselves in danger. He continued:

> To even attempt such a rescue would have meant first getting the [guided] clients back to safety, then putting together a big team of guides and Sherpas, and then setting forth again to reach Sharp. He would have long been dead.
>
> So the only other thing they could have done would have been to wait with the comatose Sharp until he was clearly dead.

In New Zealand, climbers would never think twice about going to the aid of another person if it was within their physical capability, he said. 'But Everest is different.'

Fêted Indian mountaineer/explorer Satya Dam, who has made two ascents of Everest, one without oxygen, also joined the debate at the time:

Climbing Everest is like a game where one of the rules says that the climber has a high probability of dying … We must climb such peaks with this foregone conclusion that when it's our time to die no one will come to our rescue. At that altitude everyone is dying and it is pointless to expect one dying person to save another. So to expect that someone in the death zone would actually give up their summit, life, time to save another who is dying is to expect something extraordinary. But then there are many who would do just that and they are heroes, extraordinary people, who would put everything on hold and purely sacrifice themselves for an unknown fellow climber, and we must hail them and applaud them as such. But to blame someone for not doing it is not correct.

My views are extreme, and came as shock to most of my friends.

Bruce Normand thinks the problem arises from a lack of 'ethical guidance' by the commercial guides towards their clients, whom he calls 'tourons'. He said:

Those that climb Everest today aren't mountaineers, let alone alpinists. These are some form of high-altitude marathon runner. Running marathons is a different type of physical challenge, and one of which you should be proud when you achieve it. It's not your job to set the course [it's the guides'] and it certainly isn't your [the client's] job to pick up the runner next to you when she/he falls over.

This argument is refuted by Kiwi author Aat Vervoorn, who in his book *Mountain Solitudes* strips the debate to its basics: 'At sea, in warfare, in mountain search and rescue, heroism in order to help or save others is treated as commonplace and habitual: it is what is normal and expected … there are those that remain socially alert and morally responsible to the point of death.' In the case of Himalayan climbers who put themselves in extreme situations by choice, he says, the excuse that they have moved beyond what is normal morality is 'particularly odious', especially if it seeks to legitimise ignoring the needs of others because of a self-imposed goal. History is littered with people who have felt their cause worthy of this, but 'this argument is specious at the best of times'. He continues, 'To find [the argument] … made in regard to the frivolous activity of mountaineering is absurd, an attempt at self justification by individuals who cannot face up to the fact of their own mediocrity.'

Malcolm Bass is another mountaineer who gives no quarter to those who ignore others in peril:

> There is something sick about the sport if people find this issue a dilemma. What kind of sport is it if there are loads of people lying around dying anyway? If you are strong enough to go up, then you are strong enough to help. There are enough examples to show that people can be helped at extreme altitude, so the 'nothing we could do argument' is invalid. On the way down there may be an argument for someone who is much extended (i.e. at risk of death themselves) not helping another stricken person if it would cause them both to die.

University of Otago scientist and mountaineer Phil Ainslie thinks it might have been possible to revive David with bottled oxygen, and even get him down to safety. If David was given oxygen for a time when the Inglis party found him, he could have recovered something like 80 per cent of his capacity, Ainslie says. But it would have meant someone giving up their chance of making the summit and sharing their supply with the stricken climber. 'What might have determined David's fate was the intense commercial pressure on Everest climbers, many of whom had paid upward of US$75,000 and were effectively being dragged up by the guides. They generally have only one very expensive shot at the summit.'

What would I have done? I hope beyond hope that I would have assisted the fallen climber, but as someone who has never been to 8000m, I need to be realistic. The climbers who left David to die weren't bad people – what are the odds that among forty-plus mountaineers there wasn't even one ethical one? And as Ed Douglas, mountain journalist and author, pointed out, many of those who walked past David would have assumed he was dead (Ed interviewed quite a number of them). Even so, was each so focused on their all-consuming objective that none could see that saving a human life had to take precedence over conquering Everest?

I guess there are times when good people do bad things, and mountaineers, by definition, have to be unusually focused on the challenge of reaching the summit. Everest climbers have already decided that their goal is worth considerable personal sacrifice and hardship, so it's bound to be difficult to shock them out of a mindset that ranks nothing more important than getting to the top. Maybe they become immune to ethical reasoning, and all too easily find rationalisations for their non-ethical actions, like Satya's 'rules'. Perhaps I'd be no different, had I paid US$75,000 and dedicated three months of my life to climbing the highest mountain on the planet. Possibly the importance of the story here is not that the climbers did the wrong thing – of course they did the wrong thing – but, rather, how difficult it can be to make ethical choices when such powerful considerations are at play. Everyone has a goal or a dream that could make them walk past a dying man. It isn't right, but it's reality. As Canadian climber Barry Blanchard said, 'I don't know what to think about Everest anymore, poor mountain. It seems to be the Colosseum of our times.'

Another issue that is batted backwards and forwards, at times heatedly, amongst mountaineers is that of style of ascent. Today, some of the most audacious climbs are made in the light and fast alpine style, which seeks to leave everything behind but the minimum gear required to reach the summit. The oxygen-free ascent of Everest in 1979 by Reinhold Messner and Peter Habeler is one of the early examples of this approach. But whereas only the fittest, most experienced alpinists once dared pertain to this style, these days it has become the norm in western climbing, simply because it's easier. Climbers accept the risk in order to minimise the weight and, hence the difficulty.

The antithesis of the alpine-style ascent is the siege, or expedition, approach. This was embraced on the early assaults on the high mountains of the Himalaya and Karakoram ranges, and was perfected by climbers from the former Soviet Union, who were trained in this style by the state. Siege style sees large numbers of climbers literally 'attacking' a mountain, fixing ropes for much of a route, erecting permanent staged camps, and often using supplementary oxygen and high-altitude porters. It requires a lot of manpower compared to the alpine approach, in which climbers characteristically operate in pairs or threes. Sir Chris Bonington's expeditions on the Southwest Face of Everest and on Annapurna in the 1970s embody the siege approach, and thanks to the extremely popular books Chris wrote are the type of expeditions with which the general public are most likely to be familiar.

The current debate on style centres on whether the siege approach is still relevant in mountaineering today. The issue was brought to a head in 2004, when a Russian team made a siege ascent of the infamous and previously unclimbed North Face of Jannu (7710m) in Nepal. The route was considered one of the last great mountaineering problems, on which some of the climbing world's best had tried and failed.

The Russian team suffered numerous misfortunes and injuries on the ascent: a burst retina due to overexertion, lacerations and a head injury from a rockfall, broken ribs and pulmonary oedema. By the time the leaders reached 7400m, members were dropping out one by one 'like used cartridges' said climber Alexander Ruchkin. Temperatures were down to -40°C, and the climbers were taking three to four exhausting days to Jumar the 3000m of fixed line up the face. Towards the end of May, 'anyone who could still hold a gun' was sent up the line for the final assault on the summit, and on 26 May Ruchkin and Dmitry Pavlenko reached the top after fifty days on the mountain.

News of the historic ascent spread across the climbing world, accompanied by both fanfare and controversy. Word began to circulate that the Russians had left all their fixed rope and camps on the mountain, effectively littering the slope. The news shocked many climbers.

The Jannu team then won the prestigious Piolet d'Or award, which is presented annually by the French Alpine Club for the best climb of the year. In attendance was American alpinist Steve House, who had also received a nomination. House, widely regarded as one of the best alpinists of our time, is a fast and light purist. He later wrote his opinion of the Jannu team in a French climbing magazine:

> Their climb was an amazing accomplishment. At the same time I was astounded that they used the words 'impossible' and 'extreme' when the comforts of their basecamp were never more than a few rappels down their many fixed ropes [to their portaledge: this is essentially a portable shelf for a tent]. I was appalled that they abandoned their camps and their equipment on the wall. The Russians did climb the North Face of Jannu … but they also mutilated it with their heavy style. The Piolet d'Or pretends to award ascents that represent the 'evolution' of alpinism. I maintain the Russians' ascent … is irrelevant to modern alpinism.

The trouble with a siege style of ascent, as evidenced on Jannu and many previous expeditions, is that it requires vast amounts of equipment that become very hard to remove once the climb is finished. On the flip side, imagine the state of the Russian team at the end of their struggle: they'd spent fifty days on the face, had suffered severe physical and psychological deprivation, and had finally reached the top. Is it any wonder that they wanted to get home as quickly as they could, and that the thought of spending another week or two stripping the face of ropes and camps might have seemed, in their exhausted state, just too much to cope with?

When Steve House and Vince Anderson made an alpine-style ascent of the Rupal Face of Nanga Parbat in Pakistan, for which they won the Piolet d'Or in 2005, they left no ropes or camps because they carried everything with them on their backs. But then they were on the mountain for only a short stay compared to the Russians.

Canadian climber Barry Blanchard feels that any mountain can be climbed given enough technology and manpower. 'I think that the best alpinists are those capable of climbing with a rack, a rope, and a pack,' he says. 'I think that Steve could accomplish what the Russians have done in siege style. Could any of the Russians who sieged Jannu accomplish what Steve has with one rack, one rope, and one pack?'

American climber and humanitarian Doug Chabot counters this, saying:

It's worth debating since debate can bring out thoughtful viewpoints. But the Russian ascent was a supremely difficult achievement and still awaits an alpine-style ascent. If someone steps up to Jannu and fires it off alpine style then Steve's quote would carry some weight with me. Until someone does that, the Russians deserve credit. However, it is completely acceptable to question the Russians on the fact they left so much gear and rope on the wall. That's not so cool.

Satya Dam thinks the debate is a 'waste of time' as there are always going to be proponents of either style. 'Frankly I don't see anything wrong with either,' he said. 'To each his own and as long as we don't deface, don't overburden the mountain, keep it pristine and take off all our muck after the climb … It's a matter of choice, funds available, etc.'

Malcolm Bass thinks it is a worthy debating point, but not one to get too hot under the collar about, as there are more important issues to consider. He says, 'But I think it's a shame if objectives that could be climbed by alpine-style teams get done first by a siege team.'

Maybe Alexander Ruchkin, lead climber on the Jannu climb, should have the last say. He was present at the Piolet d'Or 2010 ceremony and was quoted as saying, 'When we [Russians] have a siege-sized budget we have to succeed so we use that style. And when we have the same money as everyone else we climb the same way, namely lightweight.'

The use of supplementary oxygen on the highest peaks is also an issue that periodically raises its ugly head, again not among the general public but among elite mountaineers. Oxygen was first used on Everest in 1922 by George Finch and Geoffrey Bruce, who climbed up to 7770m at the spectacular speed of 300 vertical metres per hour. Caught in a fierce storm, they escaped death by breathing oxygen from a gerry-rigged set-up during the night. The next day, they climbed to 8080m at 275 vertical metres per hour – nearly three times as fast as non-oxygen-users. Yet the use of oxygen was considered so unsportsmanlike that no one in the alpine world would accept the pair's high ascent rate, confusing the facts with emotional considerations. But when Tenzing and Hillary made the first successful summit of the peak in 1953, they used bottled oxygen, and for the next twenty-five years this was considered standard for any successful summit.

Reinhold Messner was the first climber to break the bottled oxygen tradition, and in 1978, with Peter Habeler, made the first successful climb of Everest without it. Although critics alleged that he sucked on mini bottles of oxygen (a claim the climber denied), Messner silenced them in 1980 when he reached the summit of the mountain solo, without supplemental oxygen, without porters or climbing partners, and on the more difficult northwest route. Renowned mountaineer and explorer Harold 'Bill' Tilman argued in 1948 that climbing with bottled oxygen was not climbing 'by fair means', a phrase that was to become Messner's famous motto. 'By reaching for an oxygen bottle, the climber degrades Everest to a 6000m peak,' he said.

The aftermath of the 11 May 1996 disaster on Everest, when eight people died further intensified the debate on the use of oxygen. Jon Krakauer, in his widely read book on the incident, *Into Thin Air* (1997), wrote that the use of bottled oxygen allowed otherwise weak climbers to attempt the summit, leading to dangerous situations, bottlenecks and more deaths. He proposed banning bottled oxygen except for emergency cases, arguing that this would keep climbers who were only marginally qualified off the mountain.

Well-known American alpinist Mark Twight claims that 'an unsupported ascent of Everest, without oxygen, i.e. climbing the peak under the most natural conditions possible, is unheard of today, while plenty of "adventurepreneurs" have made their way to the summit and suffered under the delusion of having actually climbed there.'

Messner, Krakauer and Twight infer the use of oxygen is a form of cheating. So did Bruce Normand when I put the question to him. 'Supplementary oxygen has no place whatsoever,' he said, 'least of all in "cutting-edge" mountaineering. It's solely required for high-paying "tourons" to summit Everest.'

Satya Dam, on the other hand, feels there's nothing wrong with supplementary oxygen:

> To say that it reduces the climbing in the purest sense is to say that we must eat only raw food else we are diminishing the way nature made it. Will Gadd is being vainglorious [Will claims using oxygen reduces Everest to 7000m], nothing else. Just because he and many like him can do it doesn't mean that we must look down upon those who use supplementary O_2. Climbing an 8000m peak with O_2 is still extremely difficult and physically challenging. With the use of oxygen we only reduce the risks that we run, like wearing a seat belt by a Formula 1 race driver. We can't say that those who put on the belt are less than the ones who won't.'

And when does staying healthy and/or alive become unethical? I guess that is a question each individual needs to ask themselves; it's one I'll never need to confront, as I have no desire to climb an 8000m peak. So what's the bottom line? Some individuals have the physical and mental capacity to reach the summit on ambient air alone, but most don't and at some stage will need to use oxygen if they want to succeed. As Malcolm Bass says,' There's no place for oxygen in cutting-edge mountaineering. But if people not claiming to be cutting edge want to use it, that's fine by me.'

A dilemma closely linked to that surrounding supplementary oxygen is the use of the steroid dexamethosone (abbreviated to 'dex') for climbing at altitude. Steroids have been used on the tallest peaks since 1969 as a temporary remedy for high-altitude cerebral oedema, a life-threatening condition that afflicts around 2 per cent of mountaineers each year – I used dex myself when suffering from altitude sickness on Jankuth (see Chapter 6).

As altitude increases, the amount of oxygen in the air decreases and the brain compensates by diverting more blood to it. Capillaries engorge and begin to leak, causing the brain to swell and squeeze against the skull. As a result, victims become confused and clumsy, and can soon die if preventative action isn't taken. An emergency dose of dex can combat the swelling and alleviate the condition.

Some climbers have gone so far as to apply the same ethical argument to steroids as the one they use against supplementary oxygen, saying that both effectively lower the elevation of the highest peaks and amount to unsportsmanlike-like conduct. Recently, however, others have come to believe that if a one-off dose of dex can improve a sick climber, then steady usage can do wonders for a healthy one.

One-time head of the medical committee for the American Alpine Club Geoff Tabin says that climbers have a long history of taking drugs – Hermann Buhl, for example, took a cocktail of drugs (mainly speed) when he soloed Nanga Parbat in 1953. Tabin says:

> In mountaineering it's easy to justify the means to the end, and steroids make sense when you're close to the summit and want to increase your margin of safety. The danger is when steroid use allows a climber to get into a potentially dangerous situation that they otherwise might not have got into. And how do we celebrate our ascents if climbers who we thought were breaking new ground en route to the summit were just taking drugs?

Doug Chabot thinks that alpine climbs are long enough and sustained enough that drug use to aid acclimatisation will make little difference. 'Using performance-enhancing drugs on a three-hour bike race or 100m dash is another story since specific drugs are known to boost performance with a race time frame of hours and minutes, not days,' he said. 'I have never heard of a climber's success being questioned because of drugs. Oxygen, yes; drugs no.'

Bruce Norman puts forward his contrasting opinion. 'This is cheating. And very dangerous. And has no place on cutting-edge alpinism. To climb hard at any altitude, you definitely need to know your brain is, and will stay, in the right place.'

Others are more accommodating. Pete Athans, who has summitted Everest seven times, says climbers who take steroids are experimenting on themselves in a very dangerous environment. But he counters this by saying, 'It's your health, your life and livelihood. As long as you aren't endangering anyone as a result and you are being honest with the rest of the climbing community, why not?'

I agree with Athans, and also with Sharon Wood, the first North American woman to climb Everest. Sharon says it's hard for her to criticise the new technologies or drugs that make climbing Everest easier: 'Imagine what Sir Ed would think if he saw the equipment I used to summit. Things were considerably easier for me in 1986 than in '53 when he climbed it. In the end I think what you choose to use or not to use while climbing is a personal decision.'

The one issue among all others that I personally struggle with is the juxtaposition between my own ambitions and the livelihoods of the people I come in contact with on my expeditions. These guides, cooks and porters are all intent on helping me get the most out of my recreation, while I spend more money in a few short weeks than they would earn in a lifetime. Employing a tourist company to organise the logistics of an expedition to India or Pakistan is de rigueur these days. Although this relieves the climbers of a lot of hassle, I feel it creates a buffer between them and their staff, whose income the company determines. I'm embarrassed to say that I've never been completely sure what my staff are being paid.

I came across a telling article on the Internet, not about the Nepali, Indian or Pakistani porters with whom I'm familiar, but about those who aid westerners up the slopes of Kilimanjaro, which at 5895m is the highest peak in Africa. Every year, up to 25,000 Westerners attempt the mountain, escorted by their Tanzanian guides and porters, who despite being ill-equipped, untrained and underpaid, act as beasts of burden for the week-long trip. And every year, up to twenty of the Tanzanians will die on the mountain, from altitude sickness, hypothermia or pneumonia brought on by inadequate equipment and the relentless pressure to keep working. The Western travel companies often employ doctors to care for their clients, but not the guides and porters, and the death rate among the latter is more than double that of the tourists.

Of the 150 guides registered with the Kilimanjaro National Park, most are self-employed, existing in a cut-throat free-market economy and vying with one another for jobs. Their pay is minimal – porters earn US$3 a day; guides up to US$10. Allegedly, some companies don't pay their staff any salary at all, leaving them solely reliant on tips for their income. Guides and porters also have to find their own equipment, meaning many are clothed in the flimsiest anoraks and inadequate footwear, with no hats, gloves or sunglasses.

This situation reveals the worst side of mountain tourism. Are those of us who use this type of labour for our own recreation exploiting local people and behaving like the most oppressive kind of colonial from a past era? I asked this question of Ed Douglas, who said, 'From my own research in Tanzania, the conditions local tourist porters endure there are much worse than tourist porters face in Nepal. It's edging close to a colonialist attitude, perhaps because the tourists are so passive about the situation they find.'

Malcolm Bass thinks the situation in the Himalaya and Karakoram ranges 'can become exploitative, but it's probably not imperialistic'. He continues, 'The climbers of the Himalayan nations use porters themselves. Alpinism can't cure the economic inequities of the country – it hasn't in Europe! But porters should be paid wages that are better than average for that type of labour in that country, and take into account the episodic nature of the work, the risk, and insurance for their families.'

Interestingly, Indian climber Satya Dam, who has led many expeditions both within his own country and in Nepal, has the following point of view:

> I am vociferously against such exploitations. In my personal expeditions I have always not only paid much more than usual rates but have given the porters and Sherpas high-quality clothing and equipment for future use. How can it be possible that we can seek so much out of such poor people and then give them pittance and often no recognition at all post our triumph? On Everest I even allowed one Sherpa of my team to go up alone, since the member he was supposed to accompany fell ill, and I didn't want the Sherpa to miss his summit and his summit bonus. It was his first Everest summit. Money is nothing but as leaders and members of these expeditions we must look after those who serve us selflessly and much beyond their call of duty.

Doug Chabot questioned whose standards the debate is referring to. He said porters are paid a decent wage compared to other jobs in their community, and continued:

> The real problems seem to stem from trekking agents skimming off the top and taking a cut to hire them in the first place. I get around this as best I can by paying the porters directly and not having the agent do it. Stories abound of porters not getting paid their full wage because the agent/sirdar keeps a percentage.

The antithesis of Kilimanjaro would be the Khumbu region of Nepal, which has undergone tremendous transformation since the 1970s, when Westerners began travelling there in ever increasing numbers for trekking and mountaineering. Today a series of international organisations work towards ensuring the Sherpas' rights as porters are protected. Westerners are also encouraged to check that the companies from whom they hire their porters are paying standard wages. Those involved in high-altitude work can earn up to US$10,000 per annum, compared to the national average of about US$500. Tourism support has also mushroomed in the region, in the form of accommodation lodges and stores that sell or rent-out trekking paraphernalia. Running a lodge can earn its owner as much as US$15,000 per annum. The growth of tourism hasn't been without its problems – deforestation and rubbish disposal being two of the major ones – but on the other hand the Sherpas of the Khumbu have been able to gain substantial economic wealth and a corresponding higher standard of living.

The last time I visited the Khumbu was in 2004. Comparing it with my first trip in the early 1980s, I was appalled at the huge number of Westerners trawling up and down the tracks and crowding into the lodges – almost as appalled, in fact, as I was by the supermarket queue of punters heading for the slopes of Everest and Ama Dablam. But who am I to begrudge the Sherpas a better standard of living, access to medical aid and schools for their children? The Khumbu may have lost its quaint charm, but the local children now have proper clothes and less disease.

In comparison, Pakistan's tourism industry has suffered a series of massive setbacks over the last decade. The US invasion of Afghanistan in 2002, the devastating Kashmir earthquake in 2005 and the worst monsoon floods in memory in 2010, combined with the country's fragile security and negative international image, have kept tourists and climbers away. As a result, Karimabad, once a thriving mountain tourist destination of hotels, restaurants and shops selling carpets and handcrafts, is empty. Shukrullah Baig, who once earned a good salary as a tourist/expedition guide (he was my guide on my 2007, 2008 and 2009 expeditions), enabling him to build his own home and educate his six children, is now out of work for much of the year, as are many others like him. In 2010, leisure tourism in Pakistan, which includes mountaineers and trekkers, was at its lowest ebb ever, making up just 11 per cent of overall tourist numbers (the vast majority of tourists are expat Pakistanis from Britain visiting family).

As a climber visiting a developing country such as Pakistan, it's difficult to know the best thing to do. The amount of money I spend on an expedition could sustain Baig and his family for a lifetime. The money could go towards satisfying those basic human needs I take for granted – food, education, adequate housing and access to medical help. Instead, I spend it on propping up my ego. On the other hand, my expeditions support a struggling tourism industry and create work for those who need it, including Baig. Perhaps the best I can do is encourage other climbers to visit Pakistan and support an industry that has done nothing to deserve the embargo it currently faces. Maybe it's time to give something back, in a way I have yet to identify, to this country that has so enamoured me. After all, other climbers have managed this.

After his climb of Everest in 1953, Sir Edmund Hillary dedicated himself to the Sherpa people of Nepal, establishing The Himalayan Trust to build them schools and hospitals. Over the years two hospitals, thirteen health clinics and over thirty schools have been built by the Trust. Hillary shared Mortenson's philosophy, insisting that all projects were at the specific request of the Sherpa community to avoid giving them things they did not really want.

British climber David James, who founded Mountain Unity in 2009 to help economic development in the remote Wakhan Corridor of Afghanistan, believes that 'trade, not aid,' is the key to sustainable development. Mountain Unity began marketing the Wakhan Corridor specifically to the international mountaineering community and in 2010 increased the number of climbing expedition visiting the Wakhan by 400 per cent, injecting US$50,000 into the local community. These three organisations had small beginnings but grew because the instigators took the energy they had for mountaineering and put it to another use. Could I do this? Eventually injury and age are going to force me out of mountaineering. Why not!

CHAPTER TEN
The Glory of the Climb

Every day you may make progress. Every step may be fruitful. Yet there will stretch out before you an ever-lengthening, ever-ascending, ever-improving path. You know you will never get to the end of the journey. But this, so far from discouraging, only adds to the joy and glory of the climb.

– Winston Churchill

At 4.35 a.m. on Saturday, 4 September 2010, five days before I was due to leave for my expedition to Vasuki Parbat in India, Christchurch, my home of several decades, was hurtled into wakefulness by a 7.1-magnitude earthquake. On the Richter scale, that's the same strength as the earthquake that flattened Haiti earlier in 2010, killing hundreds of thousands of people. New Zealand is used to earthquakes – the country sits on a mesh of fault lines and the ground quivers and jumps on a regular basis. But this was different, and on a grander scale than anything I had ever experienced.

For starters, a malevolent growl from deep beneath the city's pleasant gardens and graceful old buildings woke me. My cat, Spot, shot off the bed with a yelp. It took a moment to register what had wrested me from sleep, by which time the growl had become an unearthly roar, rising from directly under the floorboards. Then the house began to lurch from north to south. Jolt. Jolt. Roar. I sat up with difficulty, and made a haphazard stab at the light switch with my left hand. Nothing, only darkness. In an instant, the jolts wound into a frenzy as a huge force shook the house from side to side like a maraca. My arms and legs flailed like a ragdoll's. I tried to brace myself against the mattress and made an urgent call to Spot not to worry. Thoughts that I should get under the door jamb or climb under the bed flashed through my mind, only to be flung straight back out again.

For thirty seconds, which was all the time it took, I could only hang on, feeling very scared.

Then the shaking stopped, to be replaced by the clamour of dozens of neighbourhood car alarms. I fumbled out of bed and got dressed. Spot brushed against my leg in the dark and meowed plaintively. Together we sat beneath the door jamb for the next two hours, as the aftershocks came and went.

As daylight faded in, I got up and moved around the house. I tried the lights again – still nothing. And the phone – nothing again. Walking into the living room, I was appalled to see the bookcase topsy-turvy, the contents mixed with pictures off the walls and broken keepsakes off the shelves. The lovely Mexican pot Mum had given thirty years ago lay in pieces beneath an oil painting. The cupboard doors in the kitchen were open, and splintered wine glasses mingled with jam and vinegar on the lino floor. I must conserve water, I thought, and filled the bath tub. I felt invaded, as if a nasty and vindictive burglar had been through the house.

At this point I began to realise just how completely unprepared I was for an emergency of this scale. I tried to find a torch, but I'd shipped both my torches off to India only days beforehand. There was no power and I really needed a cup of tea, but my gas cooker had also been shipped to India. Where was my short-wave transistor radio? I needed to know what was happening. Civil Defence could have ordered a mass evacuation of the city. But, like the torches and cooker, the radio was on its way to India. I decided to drive to my boyfriend Graham's place, but then realised my car was in the garage. The garage had an electric door, and with no power I couldn't get in. I sat and contemplated my situation. Perhaps Graham would come and rescue me?

As the morning went on, the aftershocks continued. My parents called me on my mobile to let me know what they'd learnt from the television of the destruction around the city – homes collapsed, the CBD in disarray and now cordoned off by the army and police, and whole suburbs awash with a muddy residue called liquefaction. I prowled around my property looking for mysterious fountains of mud, and cracks in the ground and brick walls, before concluding I'd got off lightly.

Four days later, power, phone and water had been restored to my home, but much of the city was still without. The hourly aftershocks, including a 6.1 that brought my bookcase crashing to the floor for the second time, were beginning to wear the populace down. The CBD remained in lock-down, many of its most beautiful and historic buildings damaged beyond repair. Already the process of demolition had begun, and people were beginning to realise that Christchurch would never be the same again. In two days I was to leave for India, and in many ways I couldn't wait to get out of the sombre city. But I worried about my priorities – was I essentially abandoning a sinking ship?

I'd returned from my third expedition to Pakistan thrilled to have reached the top of Karim Sar but in a growing moral dilemma as to the worth of my overseas climbing. Was it what I should be doing at this stage of my life? I was over fifty. People looked at me sideways when I said I was still an active climber. Should I take up a more appropriate occupation? And should I be giving something back to someone? After all, mountaineering is a selfish, ego-driven sport that benefits no one but the climber.

I was also very tired. Nine expeditions in the space of eight years, not to mention several back-to-back winters spent ice climbing in Canada, were taking their toll on my body and had stretched me to the limit financially. The gruelling treadmill of grant and funding applications was beginning to pall. I was also becoming increasingly irritated with people telling me how lucky I was to be able to go on my expeditions; they were unaware of the endless hours I spent trying to raise the funds. The grants I won were there for all climbers to apply for, I'd retort, you just had to do the work of applying. I'd won the grants, yes, but only because I put a lot of energy and time into constructing a compelling application, and over the decades had built up a high-quality international résumé.

However, not long after I arrived home from Pakistan, Malcolm Bass contacted me. 'Any plans for next year?' he asked. 'How about another try at Jankuth?'

Of course, I couldn't resist. Jankuth had continued to rankle as unfinished business since our attempt in 2004. It was a lovely unclimbed peak, over 6800m, making it a rare find in an area like the Gangotri. I was also very aware that a peak permit might not be that easy to get – Bruce Normand and I had been turned down in 2007. Who was to say things would be any different now? Malcolm was positive. 'They [the Uttaranchal State Government] will have softened,' he said.

By May 2010, however, only twelve weeks out from our departure for India, we still had no peak permit. The Indian Mountaineering Federation was happy with our plan, but the Uttaranchal State Government wouldn't come through, the reason once again being that Jankuth wasn't on their 'list' of peaks. 'We better come up with an alternative plan then,' Malcolm announced, 'just in case. How about the unclimbed West Face of Vasuki Parbat? Ramsden and Fowler failed on it in 2008.'

Paul Ramsden and Mick Fowler are right up there amongst today's top climbers. In fact, Mick, who is in his mid-fifties, would be the one climber in all the world I most admire. Paul and Mick attempt only very hard, unclimbed routes, and if they fail, it's because the route in question is very hard indeed. 'Yes, Vasuki Parbat West Face is difficult,' Malcolm told me, 'plus the pair had a lot of trouble with the cold.'

In the photo Malcolm sent me, the West Face looked dark and intense, a colossal rock wall with a steep mixed buttress splitting its right-hand side. Because it faced the west it was cold, but it was also intriguing. 'Why not?' I said to Malcolm. So on 11 September 2010, after a marathon thirty-hour flight via Dubai, I met him and the other team members in New Delhi for my tenth expedition of the decade.

Meanwhile, next door, Pakistan was suffering its worst flooding in living memory. Four weeks before my arrival in New Delhi, one-fifth of Pakistan's total land area was estimated to be under water and approximately 20 million people directly affected by the floods – more than the combined total of those caught up in the 2004 tsunami, the 2005 Kashmir earthquake and the recent earthquake in Haiti, according to the BBC. It was deemed to be one of the greatest natural disasters of all time. As news of the situation unravelled, my unease grew. How much more can Pakistan take, I thought, and considered handing over the money I was spending on the expedition to the Red Cross. But of course I didn't, and was once again swept up in the excitement of the travel and climbing ahead.

Why does this happen? Why is it that every year, regardless of the outcome or the lack of satisfaction I achieve from the previous year's expedition, I wipe the slate clean and approach the next with such positive anticipation? Failing twice on Beka Brakai Chhok didn't stop me from heading for Pakistan a third time, and nor did the political situation. I'm continually ready to forget the ill effects altitude has on my body and the discomfort of acclimatising. Whatever warnings specialists give me about the deteriorating state of my knees, and no matter how much pain I'm in, I'm content in the knowledge that a triple dose of codeine will see me through. Whatever financial pressure I'm under, I always find a way to fund the next expedition, even if it means coming home to unpaid rent and months of unpaid bills. No matter how many near misses I have in the mountains, or how frightened, hungry or cold I've been, it doesn't seem to affect my desire to go climbing again. After thirty-five years as a mountaineer, I still have the fire. Does that mean, at fifty-one years of age, there's something wrong with me?

George Lowenstein, Professor of Economics and Psychology at Yale University, says in his paper *'Because it is There: The challenge of mountaineering for utility theory'* that the reasons mountaineers give why they pursue the sport don't fit neatly into 'the materialistic notions of human motivation'. The question 'Why?' preoccupies many climbers, particularly in times of hardship, he said, and the answer constitutes possibly the central theme in climbing literature. A prime example is George Mallory's response to the question of why he wanted to climb Everest: 'Because it's there.'

Mountaineering illustrates the importance of motives that are unconnected to consumption, Lowenstein says. Mountaineering is definitely not about the pleasure from being rich or owning lots of material things. In contrast, serious mountaineering tends to be 'one unrelenting misery from beginning to end' and mountaineering death rates are 'mind boggling'. Approximately one person has died for every four who have successfully climbed Everest, and in 1996 eight lost their lives in a single day. Ten years earlier, twenty-seven men and women reached the top of K2 during the climbing season, but thirteen died, several while descending after summitting.

If mountaineers aren't very good at answering the why question, Lowenstein says that a close reading of mountaineering literature at least reveals clues about their motives. The key seems to be that mountaineers themselves *can't remember* the miseries of a climb, which helps explain why they keep going back for more. Lowenstein gives the instance of Joe Simpson, who in his book *Touching the Void* described a climb in the Alps where conditions were 'harshly uncomfortable, miserable and exhausting', and admitted to feeling fear both before and during the climb. But when he and his partner reached the summit, his perspective changed: 'On the summit my memory edited out the anxiety and the tension and fed me happy recollections of the superb climbing, the spectacular positions we had been in, feeling confident and safe, knowing we were going to succeed.'

The strange thing here was that Joe *recognised his memories were faulty*. He could remember the misery at an abstract level, but this made no difference when it came to going climbing again. I applied this theory to myself and realised it was true. After every expedition, memories of the traumas, the hardships and the disappointments never fail to fade, and are replaced by an almost puppy-like enthusiasm for the next climb. At one level I'm aware the previous climb was hard and that the next will also be hard, but on another I simply blank out this information. Once I'm home, any lasting effects of the deprivations I've experienced on my expeditions soon dissolve, and all I want is to be back at that remote base camp, at the head of that desolate glacier, or camped on that snow ledge high on my chosen mountain, with the unknown ahead of me. After thirty-five years of climbing, experience has done nothing to reduce this ability to forget the bad times.

According to Lowenstein, recognition and prestige are important motives for mountaineers. I can attest to the satisfaction I've gained from the international recognition my first ascents have given me, seeing accounts of my climbs on Polish or Italian websites, and being asked to write about them for the American or Japanese alpine club journals. But like Joe Simpson said, this truth seems 'uncomfortably egotistical'. Simpson explained, 'I wanted to do only hard climbs, great north faces, impressive and daunting rock routes. I wanted a "tick list" of hard routes under my belt. It seemed wrong to want such things, shallow and superficial.'

Lowenstein may be right in claiming that fame and self-esteem bring people to the mountains but surely other forces keep them climbing when conditions get miserable? For me, one force is an almost obsessive need to fulfil my own goals. I *want* to make it to the head of that glacier with a 30kg pack, and I *want* to bag that peak. Is this compulsion particularly refined in mountaineers? Lowenstein thinks that most mountaineers actually view ego as a much more acceptable motive for their endeavours than impressing others. He gives the example of Scott Fischer, who almost died in an accident on K2 and then continued to climb the peak with broken ribs. Most people in his situation probably would have given up and gone home. But Fischer possessed an almost irrational drive to get to the top, which had fatal consequences on Everest a few years later (see page 228).

Lowenstein also said that the intensity of mountaineers' drive to succeed is evident in the torment they experience when they fail. This I can particularly relate to. I find failing on a mountain hard to cope with and usually dread going home afterwards, building up the criticism I feel I'm bound to receive to almost unbearable levels. This was particularly bad after my second failure on Beka Brakai Chhok; so bad, in fact, that I mentioned my misgivings in an article for the *New Zealand Alpine Journal 2008*. I was devastated – to the point of not wanting to return home because of the reaction I thought I'd get from friends, family and sponsors. Friends who read the article reassured me that of course they didn't judge me, and that what was most important was that I got home safely. In their opinion, the only people who might judge are those who don't matter. They were right of course. Judgement would come from those who knew little about me, or about climbing in the Karakoram, or who were jealous of my achievements.

In my view, mountaineering is an occupation that is largely impossible to fake. From watching someone in everyday life, it's impossible to gauge how they will act in the mountains; I've seen people who appear strong and tough in daily life fall to pieces at the first hardship, while others discover previously unrecognised reserves of strength. Some climbers put aside future discomfort when planning a climb, but give up when the hardship is actually experienced. Those climbers who are successful may have a particularly strong drive to complete a task. Essentially, the only reason mountaineering reveals character in climbers is because it's hard. Maybe the desire to test oneself, combined with a poor memory for misery, explains why the toughest or most uncomfortable trips often produce the best memories. Pain and discomfort become, to some degree, the point of the trip.

A lot of older climbing literature emphasises the solidarity of the team and the depth of the relationships forged by hardship as a primary reason for why the alpinists involved went on expeditions. More recent literature often conveys a different story, however, emphasising the true loneliness and isolation of mountaineering, and the feeling of separation alpinists experience, even from their climbing partners. Being roped to another is not necessarily a bonding experience, and can even create enemies, as discussed in Chapter 2. In his book *K2: Triumph and tragedy*, Tim Curran reported that during the 1986 climbing season on K2 intense squabbles broke out in the British expedition before the climbers had even left base camp, and that two members of a small French team lugged an extra tent up the mountain so they wouldn't have to sleep together. When Bruce Normand and I climbed together in India in 2007, an antagonism existed between the two of us, and many times I was on the verge of going home. We seemed to be at loggerheads about everything: I was struggling with injury and limped everywhere; he had just summitted K2 without oxygen and was supremely fit. Our isolation from one another was exacerbated by an empathy gap, which rendered Bruce unable to appreciate my disability or the fact that our first ascent of a 6500m peak, which meant little to him, was important to me. He thought he'd been lumbered with a lemon for a partner.

According to American climber Steve House, part of the reason why mountaineers climb mountains is 'that they can do it – they are good at it'. Joe Simpson said the same: 'There is a perverse delight in putting oneself in a potentially dangerous situation knowing that your experience and skill make you quite safe.' When Marty Beare and I survived our (comparatively small) epic on Mt Unicorn (see Chapter 2), we had the same sense of satisfaction in knowing that, although all sorts of things had gone wrong, our skill level, experience and ability to concentrate on the job at hand had enabled us to keep in control of the situation.

I find that my mastery of the sport is, and always will be, securely hitched to my self-esteem. I'm good at mountaineering, and knowing this and putting my skills into practice buoys my ego to such an extent that I've always been reluctant to make any life decisions that might stymie my plans for the next climb or the next expedition. This has included turning down jobs that, however enticing and well paid, don't allow me time off for expeditions, and committing to relationships when my partner doesn't understand, appreciate or give me the time I need to fulfil my compulsion. It's my drug, and regardless of the hardships I can't do without it. Joe Simpson echoed my sentiments when he said in *Touching the Void*:

> The climber steps out of the living world of anxiety into a world where there is no room, no time for … distractions. All that concerns him is surviving the present. Any thoughts of gas bills and mortgages, loved ones and enemies evaporate under the absolute necessity for concentration on the task at hand. He leads a separate life of uncomplicated black and white decisions – stay warm, feed yourself, be careful, take proper rest, look after yourself and your partner, be aware.

Meeting up with Malcolm in Delhi reminded me of what a good friend he'd become. This was to be our fourth expedition together – we'd already climbed in India (2004), China (2006) and Pakistan (2008), and although there was always a two-year hiatus between our trips (work commitments meant Malcolm couldn't join an expedition every year) we seemed to pick up our friendship at exactly the point we left off. Apart from a little grey on his head, Malcolm never seemed to age. We were to be joined on Vasuki by Paul

Figg, who had been on the 2004 Jankuth expedition and his wife Rachel, who would remain at base camp.

For this expedition our liaison officer was to be Satyabrata Dam, one of India's great mountaineers and a retired submarine commander from the Indian Navy to boot. We were all curious to meet him, and were delighted when this slight, unassuming man with a mischievous sense of humour and gentle ease joined our party. Satya deserves some mention, because by the end of the expedition I was convinced he was one of the most extraordinary people I'd ever met. Hailing from West Bengal, he was possessed of an exceptionally adventurous streak from an early age, and by forty-six (and now retired from the navy on full pension) had climbed the highest peaks of every continent, including Mt Everest (twice, once without oxygen). He had also skied to the North and South poles and across the Greenland ice cap; had walked the length of Africa from Tunisia to South Africa; and had climbed more than 350 peaks around the world. Added to this was his twenty-five-year career as a submariner, during which he'd dived under the North Pole and been lost at sea when he fell off the back of the submarine.

None of us had ever met a submariner before or anyone with such story-telling potential. We asked him what he'd thought about when he was treading water in the dark Indian Ocean, hoping the submarine would return for him. 'I thought it was all over,' he said simply, 'and was sad my life was going to end somewhere other than in the mountains.'

The heavy monsoon flooding in Pakistan had spread to India, and the skies over Delhi were dark with thunderclouds. The local Yamuna River threatened to overspill its banks, and nervous municipal authorities were making plans to evacuate the adjacent communities. For three days Malcolm and I trotted around the vast New Delhi Customs Clearance Complex after our customs agent, who was doing his best to extract our shipped climbing equipment from a morass of Indian bureaucracy. He was a tall, serious young man, with little spoken English and no smile. He walked rapidly from building to building and from room to room with Malcolm and me in tow, as he collected up a bewildering array of signatures, stamps, photocopied sheets and documents. Sometimes he'd leave us to wait in a room jampacked with neatly dressed young men who squatted on the floor, sat shoulder to shoulder at the tables, or crowded around a single computer, all shouting and laughing at the tops of their lungs while they shuffled big piles of paperwork from here and there. It was like an office environment from another planet, and what should have been three days of frustration and ire passed remarkably quickly, so entertaining were the goings-on. Finally, on the third day, our bags suddenly appeared in front of us, and our man in customs gave us a surprising grin, shook our hands and roared off on his motorbike.

Two days later, we arrived in Uttarkashi, the drive taking twice as long as in previous years because of the appalling state of the roads, which had been damaged by the heavy rains. The next morning we set off on the last leg to Gangotri in a downpour, only to be halted 20km up the road by an upturned truck. It had flipped while crossing a wash-out, and looked rather like a beached turtle, its four wheels pointing forlornly skyward. Fortunately, Kem, the stalwart of our outfitter, Ibex Expeditions, anticipated the worst, and arranged for two 4WD vehicles to collect us from the far side of the incumbent truck and take us on to Gangotri. We arrived in the familiar little town on dusk and in the nick of time, as the incessant rain closed the road for the next two weeks. We heard later that a couple of expeditions had been stranded for days in a muddy little hamlet en route.

Our expedition holed up in Gangotri for another three days, as the Forestry Department deemed the track to the snout of the Gangotri Glacier impassable. The rain came in torrents, but we remained relaxed and upbeat, and got to know our cook, Chandra, a charming middle-aged man somewhat reminiscent of Paddington Bear, and his assistant, Shankar, from west Nepal. On the fourth day the clouds parted, the sun came out and our thirty-five Nepalese porters emerged from nowhere. After the usual mêlée of sorting and assigning loads, we were off. We reached base camp four days later.

Base camp was at the relatively high elevation of 5000m, and was situated a couple of kilometres down the valley from the base of Vasuki's West Face. The face was even more impressive than the photos implied – a colossal brooding, uneasy presence. The campsite was under a metre or so of snow. With enthusiasm we climbers set about shovelling a space for our tents, but in the rarefied air the novelty didn't last long. The tents ended up squatting within an arm's length of each other in a ragged trench, the cook tent leaning against a big boulder and the mess tent between it and our clutch of personal tents. All in all it was a very compact set-up. By now the rainy weather had evaporated, night-time temperatures were down to -15°C and the skies were crystal clear and star-lit. Everything looked good for the ascent.

Acclimatisation was its usual trial for me. We staged a series of camps up the standard route on Bhagirathi II, following the forged trail of the 16th Bengal Sappers, who had suddenly been pulled off the mountain when another Indian military expedition suffered deaths in an avalanche on a nearby 7000m peak called Kamet. It was a lazy five days of gentle daily ascents of 300–400m and afternoons spent reading books, scoping the route and drinking tea in the sunshine. Rachel, an artist, painted abstracts of the surrounding scenery, while Satya, an avid photographer, wandered off to take pictures.

Of course, up at 5500m I was starting to suffer my customary headache and nausea, and ended up spending an extra night alone at the top camp to allow myself time to adjust properly. I had also developed a hacking cough I couldn't seem to shift. The following morning I wandered up to 5800m on the flanks of Bhagirathi and sat alone on the side of the mountain, dreaming. I gazed across at Vasuki. The mountain seemed to stare imperiously off to the horizon. We estimated it would take us ten to twelve to climb it and descend. I returned to base camp feeling thoughtful and slightly uneasy.

Our departure for Vasuki was delayed, and then delayed again, as Malcolm had developed a nasty cold and was feeling below par. No one was worried – we had plenty of time, and in any case being at base camp was pleasant: Chandra and Shankar were cooking superb meals, and we were all interested in the artwork Rachel was producing daily. Further up the Rakti-varn Barmak glacier, an Indian politician and his large entourage of followers and porters had become lost during the bad weather, and two Indian Air Force helicopters prowled to and fro looking for them under the blanket of snow. Later, a search party from the Nehru Institute of Mountaineering arrived on foot. They returned five days later having found no trace of the party and stopped at our camp for a cup of tea. By now everyone assumed the trekkers had perished, and the mood was sombre.

'The only reason there's been a search at all is because there's a politician involved,' Satya said. 'They wouldn't normally search for an Indian party; maybe a foreign one, but it's not a certainty.' This was just another example of how climbing in this part of the world bears no comparison to that in New Zealand, I thought. You really are on your own here.

Malcolm revived, and on 7 October the three of us said our goodbyes and headed for our first camp on the Vasuki Glacier, directly beneath the face. In the late evening we sorted gear, packed and repacked conscientiously, aware of the need to pare our loads down to the absolute minimum. I was already feeling the cold, especially at night, and I was nervous about my lightweight sleeping bag. What will it be like on the face, I secretly worried. At least -25°C, if not colder. The specifications on the bag indicated that it was suitable for 5°C down to -10°C – nowhere near warm enough – but carrying my heavy basecamp sleeping bag was out of the question. This was what the alpine style of climbing was all about. I'd just have to suck it up.

We'd each planned our own food rations, and here I knew I could cut back; my experience on Beka Brakai Chhok in 2008 had shown me just how little food I could get away with. I never had much of an appetite at altitude anyway. For the ten days, I settled on seven packets of instant noodles, seven sachets of instant porridge, ten Clif Bars, fourteen GU sachets, some venison salami from New Zealand, and some instant coffee and chocolate drinks. I knew it would be enough. I stuffed the food in the pack on top of the little sleeping bag.

Malcolm had always advocated the pros of leaving behind his Gore-Tex parka and overtrousers on expeditions, and over the years I'd come round to his way of thinking. In New Zealand everyone wears a three-layer Gore-Tex shell system because of the likelihood of rain. In the Himalaya or Karakoram ranges, it snows instead. A PrimaLoft belay jacket with a hood and PrimaLoft softshell pants work fine as the outer layer – you just brush the snow off. In any case, three-layer Gore-Tex is notoriously heavy. Malcolm and I both had state-of-the-art Mountain Hardwear PrimaLoft belay jackets, which we were very proud of.

We'd given a lot of thought as to what shelter to take with us as a three-some, and came to the conclusion that a tiny two-man FirstLight tent and one bivvy bag would suffice. We doubted we'd find a ledge big enough for two small tents, and on the nights we couldn't lie flat, we figured one of us could sit in the bag while the other two wrapped themselves in the tent. We'd take a small Jetboil stove and another lightweight gas head in case, God forbid, we dropped the Jetboil. We packed plenty of gas canisters, our one concession to weight. If we ran out of food, at least we would always be able to melt water. Two 8.1mm double ropes, eight ice screws, six camming devices, and a bunch of wires, pegs and quick-draws made up the rest of the load, along with a 60m lightweight haul line, for when the leader had to abandon his pack.

That night I began to worry, and slept little. The hardship of what was ahead was hitting home. What if I couldn't carry my pack on the steep ground? I hadn't carried a pack since I'd broken my back earlier in the year. What if I couldn't handle the cold? What if I jeopardised Paul and Malcolm's chance of success by being too slow, too old, too crippled? I had one titanium knee joint and was looking at another in the next year or so. And I was still coughing, sometimes so much my ribs hurt. What was I thinking, wanting to tackle one of the hardest remaining climbs in the Himalayas? I worried and shivered until, at 4 a.m., my alarm went off and Malcolm thrust a cup of tea into my hands. 'Eh oop lass,' he said, 'Today's the day.'

The first obstacle the face threw at us was a steep, narrow gully smeared with a lick of water ice. A nasty 150m cone of avalanche debris led up to its base, which was dotted with rocks of all sizes – sure evidence that at some stage during the day the gully would become a shooting gallery for projectiles.

'Better be up it quick,' Malcolm shuddered as we geared up at the base at 6 a.m. 'Any sun will melt what ice there is.' I was designated to lead.

Decked out with the rack, I scuttled up the first pitch, stopping every few metres to recover my breath. The ice was at best 5cm thick, very hard and full of grit; finding ice-screw placements was hard work. I managed an occasional wire placement, but they too were scarce and it was a relief to reach the end of the rope. After much puffing and grunting, Malcolm and Paul, who were carrying the majority of the load, arrived beside me.

'Bollocks,' Malcolm said, 'This is hard work.'

But the next few pitches went without incident, and we began to move with a bit more rhythm. At noon I rounded a corner and could see the gully widening into a narrow basin above. From there we would traverse out right to a small col, where we'd spend our second night. I yelled down to the others that I thought we'd be able to head right in a few more pitches, and moved on up the quickly melting ice. We were now in the sun, stones were starting to whirr past, water was pouring over my hands, and I was sweating with the effort.

That night we had our last comfortable camp. I lay in the bivvy bag next to the tent entrance, occasionally passing Paul lumps of snow to melt for water and cooking. All seemed serene, and as darkness came I looked up at the stars and thought, Maybe this won't be so bad after all. Maybe I am up for this climb?' Even so, I felt isolated from the other two, the weak link, the third man. I wondered if the thought was just a product of my imagination.

The next morning we were packed and ready before dawn, as we had a long, steep climb to the base of the mixed band ahead of us and wanted to take advantage of the frozen snow. Paul led out in front with Malcolm on his tail. I soon dropped behind. I was carrying the rack and trailing the two ropes off my harness, which made my load feel interminably heavy. Well after sunrise, Paul called a halt for a rest, and as I front-pointed towards him I had my first serious thoughts of turning back. The prospect of another ten days of frigid bivouacs, potentially with nowhere to lie down, horrified me. Several of my fingers and toes were already numb, and I was coughing incessantly. If I take the haul line and go now, I can get myself down to the glacier, I thought. I flopped down beside the pair and, to their horror, burst into tears.

Extreme, minimalist alpinism isn't for everyone – in fact, the numbers climbing in this style today are negligible, as the risks are very high. One of the early protagonists of the style was American Mark Twight; he was the spokesperson for a group of North American climbers who called themselves 'the brotherhood', and who included such legends as Barry Blanchard, Scott Backes, Johnny Blitz and Kevin Doyle. They are all in their late forties or early fifties now and, as far as I'm aware, have given away alpine climbing for other pursuits, or in Barry's case, a young family. But during their heyday, this group pioneered a style of brash, minimalist alpinism never seen in the US before.

In 1988, Twight, Blanchard, Doyle and Ward Robinson attempted the 4600m-high Rupal Face of Nanga Parbat alpine style, climbing to within 400m of the summit before a storm caused them to retreat. Exhausted by their fast ascent and plagued with altitude sickness, they had to battle their way down. At 7300m two of the team miscommunicated in the wind and dropped their only two ropes. Then Twight dropped one of the team's two tents. At that point they thought all was lost. The next day, they forced themselves to solo side by side down through the storm and 300m lower found an ancient, faded rucksack. Cutting it open, more out of curiosity than anything else, they discovered it contained two 50m ropes. By pure chance, they were saved.

In 2002, with Backes and Steve House, Twight made a remarkable sixty-hour non-stop ascent of the 2700m Czech Direct, the hardest route on Denali's enormous South Face. The three climbers took two stoves, a rack and two ropes between them, and only lightweight down jackets – no tent and no sleeping bags. The first climbers to complete the route had taken eleven days to do so and used fixed ropes. 'It was terrifying to realise at hour 48 that we were 5000' up Denali, with 4000' left to climb,' Twight said, 'that the stoves were out of gas and our jackets – our only "bivvy gear" – weren't really warm enough.'

Minimalist, alpine-style climbing 'keeps me honest' Twight said in one of the many articles he has written. 'Because I know there is consequence, it keeps me scared. Because I know I can't get away with slacking off, that the thing which happens after mediocrity is the ground. It's a game. It's a test. It is the way I live my life.'

Not all alpine-style protagonists go with the minimalist ethic. Stephen Venables, the first Brit to climb Everest without oxygen, said in his article 'Light and High in the Himalaya', 'I feel that the true credo should be a generally lightweight approach to climb the mountain in the safest and most logical and most enjoyable way. I, for one, like to have enough to eat, and somewhere comfortable to sleep, and aim to return alive. I am happy to compromise to achieve those ends.'

On Vasuki I was discovering just how much I was willing to compromise for a summit.

It hadn't taken much for Malcolm and Paul to talk me into carrying on, and we'd continued up the steepening slope until the late afternoon, when we settled on a bivvy site on the down side of a small rock buttress, sheltered from the ever-present threat of rockfall. Above, the terrain steepened again as the narrowing ice slope petered out into a dark rocky gully running up the left-hand side of the mixed band. As we chopped a ledge, I made a mental note to check my fingers and toes, which had been numb with cold for hours. The sun, which only hit the face briefly each day, had sunk behind the Bhagirathi Massif and it was staggeringly cold.

That night it was my turn to cook and melt water, and I did this lying prone in my sleeping bag. Paul was wedged in beside me; Malcolm was curled in the bivvy bag at our feet. We were all irritable and tense, and melting enough water for our next day's needs seemed to take for ever. That night, I lay awake with the cold, coughing spasmodically and shivering for many hours. The others slept soundly – I wondered enviously how they managed it through the noise of my coughing, let alone the cold! Why have I got such doubts about this climb, and they don't, I wondered. Why aren't they feeling the cold and the weight of their packs? How come their digits aren't perpetually numb? Why am I the only one with this damn cough?' At 3.30 a.m. the alarm sounded on my wrist. I reached for the cooker and began to melt water for breakfast. The stars were blazing white flares above us.

I was leading again, up old grey ice towards the gully. The giant orange and grey head wall reared over our heads – I couldn't recall ever seeing such a massive wall of rock. The gully boded evil, as we knew that at some stage during the day it would release a barrage of rocks down the ice slope. I was climbing well, systematically running out the pitches, building neat two-screw anchors, but inside I was anything but well, anything but systematic. And I was cold, always cold.

At 2 p.m. the ice slope ran out. We were at the base of the gully, which was starting to spit a trickle of small stones. The sun had come onto the lower slopes, and then gone again – it wouldn't reach us. I built an anchor at the base of a small buttress guarding the gully and brought Paul and Malcolm up. It was now or never; I needed to speak. I took a deep breath, and then erupted in a spasm of coughing. 'Guys,' I spluttered. 'I'm going to head down.'

They both looked up in surprise. 'What?'

'I can't do this – it's not for me,' I said, as tears sprang to my eyes. 'I can't stop coughing and I can't handle the cold.'

I started to wrest my pack off, and looked at Malcolm. He was crying. 'How are you going to get down? Don't you want us to come too?' he said.

'No, I'll be fine. I'll just go really slowly and carefully.' I began to hand Paul bits and pieces from my pack. 'I'll take the haul rope and one screw, and a V-thread hook and a couple of wires – that will do.'

I put my pack back on, and joined the two climbing ropes together with an overhand knot. 'Please be careful.' I gave each a hug, and began to abseil down the connected ropes. At least I'd drop 120m before I had to start solo-ing. Tears streamed down my face.

As soon as I began my descent, Paul and Malcolm headed up into the gully. Malcolm wrote later:

> Pat had just left and I'd led the first hard pitch of this gully, when, with horrible accuracy, a large block came spinning down and hit Paul on the belay below me. He slumped onto the ice screw anchors, and it seemed a dreadfully long time before he moved or spoke. He seemed improbably OK, and after collecting himself, he climbed up to my stance which was protected by a roof. We spent the afternoon there, and began again once it got dark, climbing quite hard mixed ground up the gully to a sitting bivvy.

Meanwhile, I began backtracking, as an ever-increasing volley of rocks bounded past me. There was nothing I could do but keep my head low, and keep on front-pointing downward, counting the minutes, my heart beating fast. Around 5 p.m. I reached the safety of the previous night's bivvy site and sat there mesmerised by the rocks as they continued to hurtle down. I was very worried about the climbers; I knew they'd be hard-pressed to find shelter in the gully. I spent a lonely night on the ledge, and the next morning, setting off at 7 a.m., began descending the snow slope. I arrived at the col around noon, just in time for the start of the daily rockfall. I realised it was too late to head into the lower ice gully, and that I'd have to spend another night on the mountain.

That same day, far above me, Paul and Malcolm were fighting it out on the mixed band, when Malcolm took a 10m fall and temporarily knocked himself out. The following evening the pair reached Fowler and Ramsden's high point, and climbed what Malcolm considered to be the crux of the route: 'A steep groove, little edges either side for mono points, two good nuts, and a long, long reach from the top over a band of sugary snow to stick a patch of good ice. Committing to this pull, kicking deeply into the useless snow and reaching up again was my personal climbing highlight of the route.'

In the meantime, I'd had a testing time abseiling the ice gully with the 5.5mm haul line, using V-threads for anchors. The haul line iced up to such an extent I could no longer hold my weight, but I rigged a clever pulley system on my harness to increase the friction. Halfway down, with the ice melting rapidly, I had visions of sitting out another night on the mountain, but I kept on, and with what I thought was quite some daring, very wet down-climbing, reached the glacier around 3 p.m. I felt nothing but relief to be off the mountain and sat at the base of the gully for an hour in a blank stupor of fatigue. Then I wandered down the valley in a world of my own, reaching base camp around 8 p.m. All was dark.

'Ah, hello,' I said to no one in particular. Then I coughed.

'Pat?' Satya exclaimed, as he struggled to get out of his sleeping bag. 'What's going on?'

Before I knew it I was ensconced in the mess tent with Chandra and Satya plying me with cups of tea and biscuits. I gave the team a brief run-down of events, and then excused myself. I would deal with it all in the morning. I just wanted to sleep.

After a lengthy breakfast, Satya, Rachel and I spent the day scoping the face through the binoculars for signs of Paul and Malcolm. There was none, and I was worried. Satya and Rachael, who up until now had been relaxed about the goings-on up on the mountain and more intent on their art and photography, were galvanised into concern. The next morning, I walked

251

back up the glacier to the base of the ice gully and, to my relief, spotted the pair far above, exiting the mixed band. I could hear their calls very faintly on the wind. Twenty-four hours later, we all watched with excitement as they reached the summit ridge. Alarmingly, we then lost them again for a day, during which I made a long trek to the far side of the mountain to check if they were coming down via the East Face route of the original ascensionists. They weren't. But the following morning, to our joy, we saw them at the top of the northwest ridge, descending slowly. Malcolm wrote of this:

> We reached the narrow, sinuous summit ridge late on the eighth day, and followed it north towards the summit until darkness fell. The next day we passed over the summit, and kept on the ridge, losing height very gradually. A spectacular day this, our tools often plunged into the east face whilst our feet were on the west. Late in the day we began our descent of the Northwest ridge before bivvying for a last time at about 6200m. A long, hungry tenth day in deep snow on the Northwest ridge and north face saw us back in base camp for 10.00 p.m. We were utterly done in.

Satya rated Paul and Malcolm's ascent of Vasuki Parbat as one of the best Himalayan climbs of the decade – praise indeed considering the standard of today's alpinists. It is true that the majority of Himalayan climbing over the past two decades has focused on numbers on guided ascents of the 8000m giants (upwards of 200 people summit Everest annually), but a small few have been pushing the envelope on ever more extreme routes, led on by names such as Steve House, Simone Moro and the Japanese 'Giri-Giri Boys'. That Malcolm and Paul should join these elite few was exciting for all of us.

But on Vasuki, Paul had only just avoided being seriously injured, if not killed, by a rockfall, and Malcolm had fallen and knocked himself unconscious. Both climbers suffered cold damage to their hands and feet, but they climbed on. Why?

Eric Monasterio is a Bolivian/New Zealand medical doctor and climber who carried out a four-year study of mountaineers and base jumpers. Obviously, both of these sports are regarded as high risk. In his resulting paper, 'The Risks of Adventure Sports/People', Monasterio said:

> These activities court significant dangers and attract individuals who are prepared to gamble their personal safety and at times their lives in search of a rush of excitement or an unusual accomplishment. The understandable

public perception is that adventure sport participants are an unusual, highly selfish, odd breed of people. Why else would they wilfully choose to court danger and gamble with their lives?

Eric wanted to find out whether people who engage in these activities have 'unusual or unique' personalities and whether there were any biological or genetic reasons to explain this. He wrote:

I found that the personality [of climbers] was quite different to that of average people. Climbers scored higher in the areas of Novelty-Seeking and Self-Directedness and lower on Harm-Avoidance. What this suggests is that climbers generally enjoy exploring unfamiliar places and situations. They are easily bored, try to avoid monotony and so tend to be quick-tempered, excitable and impulsive. They enjoy new experiences and seek out thrills and adventures, even if other people think that they are a waste of time … When confronted with uncertainty and risk climbers tend to be confident and relaxed. Difficult situations are often seen by climbers as a challenge or an opportunity. They are less responsive to danger and this can lead to a foolhardy optimism. Climbers also have good self-esteem and self-reliance and therefore tend to be high achievers.

Eric's study led him to believe that biology and genetics play at least a moderate role in determining who will take up climbing. 'Harm-Avoidance', 'Novelty-Seeking' and 'Sensation-Seeking' behaviours are inherited from our parents and are determined by the levels of dopamine and serotonin chemicals in our brains. Novelty-Seeking and Sensation-Seeking traits are both associated with low levels of dopamine, and the current theory is that these levels can be boosted by taking part in risky activities. High-Harm Avoidance (the propensity to become anxious or scared in the face of risk) is related to high levels of serotonin.

Eric also observed that despite near misses and accidents, the climbers in his study *continued to climb* – a trait he found unique. The average person exposed to trauma would be expected to develop psychological complaints like post-traumatic stress disorder, he said, but climbers seemed to be immune to these reactions. 'People who choose to take up [climbing] appear to have a biological make-up which is different to that of average people in the community and these differences in brain chemistry help to explain why they put themselves in perilous situations.'

When I asked Malcolm why he and Paul had continued with their climb despite their mishaps, he replied:

> I was so determined to climb Vasuki that it would have taken a damn sight more than that fall to have stopped me. I didn't even consider turning back. I remember being very worried that I might have done something to my brain that would hold us back, and telling Paul through my tears how much I wanted to go on. In some ways it felt like we'd already done most of the hard work. I knew from bitter experience how much effort and luck it would take to get back to this position: fit, funded, acclimatised and half way up an unclimbed face with a strong partner in good weather. I really wanted that summit. No one was dead. Paul was up for it and I knew I could lean on him for a day or two if needed (which I didn't). So onwards and upwards!

Malcolm was right – for all the stars to be in alignment, or in his words to be 'fit, funded, acclimatised and half way up an unclimbed face with a strong partner in good weather', was in Himalayan climbing terms nothing short of a miracle. His reasoning for pressing on was acceptable to me, but I knew that to someone with no compulsion towards risky pastimes it would appear preposterous. To even step foot on the mountain would seem incomprehensible.

And there was a deeper layer in Malcolm's reasoning to be explored: what were those underlying reasons for him wanting the summit so badly? Was it the kudos of climbing a difficult new route? The satisfaction of summitting after a series of failures in the Garhwal? The need to prove himself as a climber on the world stage? I probed further and he finally admitted:

> For a long while I'd had a goal of climbing a new multi-day route on a big Alaskan or Himalayan face. I thought we would do it on Beka Brakai Chhok and was very disappointed that we couldn't. I've also felt spanked by the Garhwal, one summit in four trips until Vasuki. Once we'd decided on Vasuki I felt really inspired and quite confident, and became very determined to free myself from the strictures of my own self-imposed goal. Then I would be free to decide whether to do any more Himalayan climbing or not, rather than being driven into it by the goal I'd set myself.

So Malcolm had completed a long-term self-set goal and was now in a situation to take or leave high-altitude climbing in the Greater Ranges. In many ways I envied him – he had found his peace. But after five expeditions together, I knew Malcolm well enough to realise he'd find something else to absorb his focus. If it wasn't Himalayan climbing, it would be something equally demanding – he was that sort of person, energetic, upbeat, driven. I felt sad – maybe this was the end of our climbing partnership. Maybe we'd never climb together again.

I've been home from India for three months now, and although I was morose and down about the outcome of Vasuki at first, the heartbreak of the expedition is beginning to pale along with the dark flush of cold damage to my feet. There's been an ambivalent reaction to my failure amongst climbers in New Zealand; those with any understanding of climbing in the Greater Ranges, of which there are few, know how hard it was for me to turn back and how testing of my skills to retreat alone. Those with no understanding don't matter. I'm actually rather pleased with myself. Ten years ago I would not have reached this state of reconciliation so easily, and my failure would have affected my mood and self-esteem for months to come. I wouldn't have coped with the criticism and become withdrawn and reclusive. Now I'm ambivalent. As Karen McNeill would have said, 'Those people who criticise? They're just jealous, man.'

So am I done with depression? No, it will continue to lurk in the background, but with the help of regular medication and a long overdue smattering of self-esteem, I know I've gained the upper hand. I'm more accepting of my condition and more inclined to ask for help. I'm also very, very tired of the secrecy and cover-up and have huge admiration for those celebrities like ex-All Black John Kirwan who've 'come out' in order to promote an awareness of the illness. These days the 'black dog' no longer drags me to the depths of dysfunction and I'm learning, slowly learning to see things differently. Maybe my successes and my failures in the mountains are *both* achievements. That I'm still climbing after 35 years is an achievement. That I can still climb with a knee replacement is an achievement. Maybe it's achievement enough that I'm still on this earth; that I haven't let depression get the better of me.

I'm already excited about the next climb, which will take place in six months' time. My sister Christine and I are going to Afghanistan, to make an ascent of a beautiful peak called Koh-e-Baba-Tangi (6516m) in the Wakhan Corridor, the long finger of land sandwiched between Pakistan in the south and Tajikistan in the north. Afghanistan has been off limits to climbers for thirty years because of the war with Russia, the Taliban regime and the current Allied occupation, hence Baba-Tangi has only been climbed once, in 1964 by a team of Italians. We'll fly into Dushanbe, the capital of Tajikistan, and travel overland to the Afghan border – that in itself will be an adventure. Then onward towards the mountain by jeep, on horseback and on foot. Once we've climbed Koh-e-Baba-Tangi we shall return the same way. How wonderful, how romantic, how exhilarating is that! And I'm doing it with my sister, to celebrate our glorious fifties. Not for us garden clubs and golf and grandchildren.

But why do I want to go back to the mountains? To the cold and discomfort, the danger and the potential for another failure? Obviously there is something more than the satisfaction and kudos gained from making a summit that's been drawing me to climbing for thirty-five years. True, there have been lapses, when I've strayed towards kayaking and rock climbing, but I've always come back to alpinism as the thing that's determined the way I've led my life. Why?

Importantly, it keeps me in touch with the outside world. Few countries share our enviable lifestyle, and living in New Zealand it's all too easy to ignore the troubles of countries less fortunate than our own. I love Pakistan, and not just for its mountains. I'm fascinated by its politics and history, but most of all I admire the Pakistani people for their enduring fortitude in dealing with a tumultuous political and social agenda and the everyday problems this throws at them. Their lives keep mine in perspective.

I love the whole expedition process – researching the unclimbed peak, raising the funds, flying out of Christchurch with that sense of joyous anticipation, knowing I've got a day in Bangkok or Singapore to relax by the pool before arriving at my destination, sorting last-minute bureaucracy and travelling to the mountains in a jeep with all the gear. I love to look through the window as we drive along, observing people going about lives so very different to my own. The walk into base camp with my climbing mates, our cook, porters, sirdar, liaison officer, goats and chickens is a chance to relax and socialise before the acclimatisation period. And finally there's the summit. It's like a wonderful, if short-lived, vocation.

I love the way the petty problems of my everyday life fade to the background, regardless of whether I'm on a six-week expedition to the Himalayas or a weekend climb at Mt Cook. Work problems, unpaid bills, and family and relationship dramas dissolve the moment I start the walk up the valley towards the mountain. Problems and anxieties resume their rightful place, my mood lifts and my psyche begins to find a peace.

And I have nurtured a skill few people have. Over thirty-five years I've developed the technical ability to climb in the greatest mountain ranges of the world, and this in itself is tremendously satisfying. I've made ascents of previously unclimbed mountains. I can join other elite mountaineers in their exasperation at the public perception of Everest as the pinnacle of alpinism. Everest is for guided 'tourons', as Bruce would say, with pots of money, who flock to the summit in their hundreds every season.

But more than that, my skill has offered me such wonderful experiences. Sometimes I have to pinch myself when I think, was it *me* who reached the summit of the unclimbed peak in India in a gathering storm on dusk, with lightning flashing on the horizon? Was it *me* who made the first female ascent of one of the greatest ice climbs in the world? Was it *me* who drove the famous Karakoram Highway and who drank tea with a nomad in a smoky tent on the Tibetan Plateau? Was it *me* who walked the length of the longest glacier in the Himalayas?

There are negatives, of course, the most painful being the loss of a dear friend on a lonely mountain in the wilds of Alaska. I've given away long-term partners and a marriage, a permanent home and financial security to pursue what I'm just beginning to accept has been my only path. There have been defeats and failures, but anyone who climbs mountains will have failures; I accept this now. It's the journey and the trying that matter; the heart that goes into the attempt rather than the summit. My body is wearing thin but even that isn't all bad. By default, it has added another string to my bow – it has given me the time and patience to write this book. For the past three decades I've been first and foremost a climber. Now I'm not just a climber – I'm also a writer.

Climb the mountains and get their good tidings. Nature's peace will flow into you as sunshine flows into trees. The winds will blow their own freshness into you, and the storms their energy, while cares will drop off like autumn leaves.
– John Muir

Glossary

Abalakov Ice anchor constructed from two drilled interlinking holes threaded with nylon cord.

Abseil To descend the rope using a friction device. To 'rappel.'

Belay (noun) Stance at the end of a pitch of climbing. (verb) To pay out or bring in the rope, providing security for the climber.

Belayer Person who 'belays' the climber.

Bergschrund Large crevasse found at the base of a steep snow slope.

Bivouac/bivvy Planned (or sometimes unplanned) night out without proper climbing equipment.

Bivvy bag Gore-Tex or nylon bag climber sleeps in when bivouacking.

Camming device Rachet-type device placed in a crackline for protection against a fall when climbing rock.

Crampon Ten or twelve-point metal aids clamped to the climber's boots for security on ice-covered slopes.

Crevasse Fissure of ice on a glacier.

Crux The hardest part of the climb.

Crux pitch The penultimate pitch of the climb.

Cwm A steep amphitheatre-shaped hollow at the upper end of a mountain valley. Another name for a cirque.

Helmet Fibreglass or plastic helmet worn to protect the climber from projectiles from above, or a fall.

Hex Hexagonal-shaped alloy aid for placing in cracklines for protection against a fall on a rock pitch.

Ice axe Tool used by climbers when climbing ice and snow. Similar to a walking stick, it has a pick and a shovel at the head, and is used to cut steps in ice or secure the climber to the slope.

Ice screw Stainless steel screw for placing in ice as protection against a fall.

Jumar Rachet-type device for ascending a rope.

Karabiner Alloy oval-shaped device with an opening gate used for clipping to the rope.

Moraine Unconsolidated rock wall at the sides or terminus of a glacier.

Pitch A rope-length of climbing.

Protection Aids used to protect the climber from a fall eg. Ice-screws, wires, hexs, camming devices.

Prussick loop A loop of nylon cord used as a simple means of ascending a rope.

Pterodactyl A revolutionary style of ice axe with a reverse-curve pick, developed in the 1970s.

Quick-draw Two karabiners linked by a short nylon sling.

Rack A collection of protection devices (camming devices, wires, hex's) and quick-draws carried by the climber. To 'rack-up' is to arrange the protection on the climber's harness.

Rap To rappel, or abseil.

Rockclimbing shoes Specialist shoes or slippers with a sticky rubber sole worn when climbing rock.

Rope length The length of the climbing rope – generally 50m or 60m.

Serac Ice pinnacle in a glacier.

Sling A loop of nylon tape used to protect the climber by placing over a spike of rock.

Slot Crevasse.

Snow cave Cave dug into the snow by climbers as a temporary shelter.

Solo To climb alone.

Spectre Metal hook hammered into ice as protection against a fall.

Steel ring anchors Pre-placed permanent anchors at the top of a rock climb.

Swami seat A simple climbing harness made from a length of nylon tape.

V-thread Ice anchor constructed from two drilled interlinking holes threaded with nylon cord.

Warthog Metal spike hammered into ice for protection against a fall.

Wire Small metal wedge used in the same way as a hex.

Chronology

1975	Joined the school tramping club, met Norman Hardie and climbed my first peak, Mt Binser.
1976	Captained the school tramping club.
1976/77	Began climbing at Mt Cook with Dennis from Twizel, after taking part in three instruction courses with Alpine Guides Mt Cook.
1977/78	Worked for the Mount Cook National Park Board and began my goal of 'ticking off' all the 10,000ft peaks. In March 78 Chris Todd and I began our traverse of the Southern Alps.
1978/79	Amongst other ascents, climbed the Right Hand Icefields of Mt Hicks, the East Face of Mt Sefton and the South Face of Mt Cook with 'English John'.
1980	Met Brian Deavoll and for the next four years tramped and climbed extensively in the upper reaches of the Canterbury Highcountry.
1984–86	Brian and I married, and for the next two years visited every country from Singapore to the UK, climbing and trekking for long periods in Nepal and Pakistan. We returned to New Zealand late in 1986.
1986	In November I traversed from Arthurs Pass to Mt Cook with Brian and my brother Bill.
1988	Brian and I separated, and eventually divorced in 1990.
1988–1992	Gave away mountaineering for rock climbing and kayaking.
1993	Returned to mountaineering with my second ascent of the South Face of Douglas Peak with Andy Cockburn. This was

followed soon after with the Strauchan Face of Dilemma with Karen McNeill.

1994–2000	Climbed with Marty Beare in the Mount Cook region, including routes on the South Face of Mt Hicks, Mt Unicorn, Vampire Peak and Mt Tasman.
1998–1999	Andy Cockburn and I travelled abroad for his nine month academic sabbatical during which I rock climbed prolifically. The trip ended (for me) with four months climbing waterfall ice in Canada.
2000	Returned to Canada for another winter season climbing ice. Made the first female team ascent of the South Face of Douglas with my sister Christine.
2002	First trip to Alaska, where I climbed two difficult routes on Mt Huntington and met Malcolm Bass.
2003	Returned to Alaska with Marty Beare for a very successful trip, most notably an ascent of 'Deprivation' on the North Buttress of Mt Hunter. Climbed the Caroline Face of Mt Cook.
2004	The Anglo/Kiwi expedition to Jankuth in the Indian Garwhal region – Marty Beare and Malcolm Bass were also on this trip.
2005	Karen McNeill and I made a successful first ascent of Xiashe in western China.
2006	In April Karen disappeared on Mt Foracker, Alaska. Malcolm Bass and I made the first ascent of Haizi Shan in western China.
2007	Headed to Pakistan in June with Lydia Bradey for an attempt on Beka Brakai Chhok. Returned to India in September to make a first ascent of a 6400m peak at the head of the Gangotri Glacier.
2008	Returned to Beka Brakai Chhok with Malcolm Bass and failed to make the summit for the second time.
2009	Pakistan again – this time to make a solo first ascent of Karim Sar.
2010	Back to the Indian Garwhal with Malcolm Bass and Paul Figg to attempt the West Face of Vasuki Parbat. I turned back from the summit but the others are successful.
2011	Plans afoot to climb Koh-e-Baba-Tangi in the Wakhan Corridor, Afghanistan.

Bibliography

Boardman, P. (1982). *The Shining Mountain*. New York: E. P. Dutton and Co.

Coffey, M. (2003). *Where the Mountain Casts its Shadow: The dark side of extreme adventure*. New York: St Martin's Press.

Curran, J. (1989). *K2: Triumph and tragedy*. Wilmington, MA: Mariner Books.

Curtis, R. (1999). *Outdoor Action Guide to High Altitude: Acclimatization and illnesses*. Princeton, NJ: Princeton University.

Dingle, G. (1972). *Two Against the Alps*. Christchurch: Whitcombe and Tombs.

Du Faur, F. (1915). *The Conquest of Mount Cook and Other Climbs: An account of four seasons mountaineering on the Southern Alps of New Zealand*. London: Allen and Unwin.

Dunham, M. (2005). *Buddha's Warriors: The story of the CIA-backed Tibetan freedom fighters, the Chinese invasion, and the ultimate fall of Tibet*. NY: Penguin.

Fanshawe, A. and Venables, S. (1999). *Himalaya Alpine-style: The most challenging routes on the highest peaks*. Macclesfield: Bâton Wicks.

Gammelgaard, L. (2000). *Climbing High*. London: Pan Books.

Green, C. and Rawlinson, K. (2009). *Ruthless Women have Extra Testosterone, Scientists Say. Independent Women*. [website], www.independent.co.uk/news/science/ruthless-women-have-extra-testosterone-scientists. Accessed 17 April 2010.

Hardie, N. (2006). *On My Own Two Feet: The life of a mountaineer*. Christchurch: Canterbury University Press.

Heichel, W. (2003). Chronik der Erschliebung des Karakorum: Teil I-Western Karakorum. Munchen: Haus des Alpinismus.

Henley, N. (2002). *The Healthy vs the Empty Self: Protective vs paradoxical behaviours.* M/C Journal [website] www.journal.media-culture.org.au. Accessed 17 April 2010.

Jenkins, M. (2006). The Hard Way: Infinite sorrow. [website] Outside magazine.www.outsideonline.com/outside/features/200609/sue-nott-karen-mcneill. Accessed 17 April 2011

Jordan, J. (2007). *Savage Summit.* London: Harper Collins.

Josephson, J. (2010). *Waterfall Ice: Climbs in the Canadian Rockies.* 4th edn. Calgary: Rocky Mountain Books.

Krakauer, J. (1998). *Into the Wild.* London: Pan Books.

Krakauer, J. (1997). *Into Thin Air. A personal account of the Mt Everest disaster.* NY: Anchor Books.

Lowenstein, G. (1996). *Out of Control: Visceral influences on behaviour.* Organisational Behaviour and Human Decision.65: 272–292.

Lowenstein, G. (1999). *Because it is There: The challenge of mountaineering for utility theory.* Kyklos 52: 315–344.

Lupton, D. and Tullock, J. (2002). *Life Would be Pretty Dull Without Risk: Voluntary risk taking and its pleasures.* Health, Risk & Society. 4, Number 2, 1 July 2002, pp. 113-124

Masters, J.(1953). *The Lotus and the Wind.* UK: Michael Joseph.

Monasterio, E. (2006). The Risks of Adventure/Sports People. Alpinist Magazine.[website]. www.alpinist.com/doc/web07f/rb-erik-monasterio-mountaineering-medicine. Accessed April 17,2011.

Mortenson, G. and Relin, D. (2006). *Three Cups of Tea: One Man's Mission to Promote Peace.* USA:Viking.

Nakamura, T. (2003). *East of the Himalayas – to the Alps of Tibet.* Tokyo: Japanese Alpine Club.

Pain, M. and Young, J. (2009). *The Zone: Evidence of a universal phenomenon for athletes across sports.* Melbourne: Monash University.

Roberts, D. (1986). *Moments of Doubt and Other Mountaineering Writings.* 1st US paperback edn. Seattle, WA: The Mountaineers Books.

Rose, D. and Douglas, E. (1999). *Regions of the Heart.* London: Michael Joseph.

Simpson, J. (1998). *Touching the Void.* London: Vintage.

Synnot, M. (2004). The Russian Way. Climbing Magazine. [website] www.climbing.com/exclusive/features/russianway. Accessed 17 April 2011.

Taylor, R. (1991). *The Breach: Kilimanjaro and the conquest of self.* US: Wildeyes Incorporated.

Venables, S. (2002). High and Light in the Himalayas. BMC. [website] www.thebmc.co.uk/Feature. Accessed 17 April 20011

Vervoorn, A. (2000). *Mountain Solitudes: Solo journeys in the Southern Alps of New Zealand*. Nelson: Craig Potton Publishing.

Woodford, K. (2006). Mountain Ethics and Everest. Opinion editorials, Lincoln University [website], (updated 8 October 2009), www.lincoln. ac.nz/News--Events/Opinion-editorials/Mountain-ethics-and-Everest. Accessed 17 April 2011.